RAGGED EDGE

RAGGED EDGE

The brutal true story of the Isle of Man TT –
the world's most dangerous race

STUART BARKER

First published in the UK by John Blake Publishing
an imprint of Bonnier Books UK
4th Floor Victoria House,
Bloomsbury Square,
London WC1B 4DA
England

Owned by Bonnier Books
Sveavägen 56, Stockholm, Sweden

www.facebook.com/johnblakebooks
twitter.com/jblakebooks

First published in hardback in 2023

Hardback ISBN: 978 1 78946 680 5
Trade paperback ISBN: 978 1 78946 694 2

British Library Cataloguing-in-Publication Data:

A catalogue record for this book is available from the British Library.

Design by www.envydesign.co.uk

Printed and bound in Great Britain by Clays Ltd, Elcograf S.p.A.

3 5 7 9 10 8 6 4 2

John Blake Publishing is an imprint of Bonnier Books UK
www.bonnierbooks.co.uk

This book is dedicated, with the greatest of respect, to all those riders who never made it to the 38th Milestone.

Author's Note

I first visited the Isle of Man TT in 1984, at the age of fourteen, and instantly became obsessed with it. Since then, I have returned many, many times, and, as a motorcycle journalist, I was thrilled to later cover the event for MCN and to edit the Official Isle of Man TT Programme for ten years. I have also written several biographies of TT riders, including Steve Hislop, David Jefferies and Joey Dunlop. In 200.7 I wrote a book about the history of the TT to mark the event's 100th anniversary.

Over the years, I became friends with many of the riders – in some cases close friends – and I have lost several of them too and seen first-hand the devastating effect their deaths had on their families and loved ones.

It is not the intention of this book to 'take sides' when it comes to the debate over whether the event should be banned. To me, that's for the riders to decide – they're the ones taking the risks. Instead, my intention is to tell the truth about the TT, and that means covering the darker side of the event too. I feel it's highly disrespectful to all the riders who have lost their lives in the event to simply brush their deaths under the carpet, so I have refused to back away from discussing the dangers. The TT is an extreme event; any honest book about it is bound to be an extreme book.

The TT has given me great pleasure over the years, but also great heartache, and that will hold true for anyone who's followed it closely or been involved in it in any way.

This book is an exploration of the psyches and attitudes of TT racers. Drawing on over 100 exclusive interviews and, using the riders' own words whenever possible, it attempts to discover what drives competitors to participate in such an extreme event, and to reveal how they deal with the (often hideous) injuries and the loss of friends. It seeks to find out what makes TT riders tick.

While the dangers are a big part of the TT, they're not everything; just as many comedies have unfolded as tragedies, and just as many triumphant and emotional moments have been witnessed on the Isle of Man too. This book also attempts to cover all those aspects.

It will, I hope, offer a brutally honest portrayal of one of the most extreme sporting events on the planet, and an insight into the minds of the courageous men and women who have taken on the TT Mountain Course over the last 115 years.

Stuart Barker
Kettering
December 2022

Contents

Authors Note   vii

Chapter 1   *The Start*   1

Chapter 2   *Comedy and Tragedy*   11

Chapter 3   *The Hunger*   29

Chapter 4   *A Mountain to Climb*   41

Chapter 5   *Who Dares, Wins*   55

Chapter 6   *Operation TT*   71

Chapter 7   *Going the Distance*   87

Chapter 8   *Ragged Edge*   99

Chapter 9   *World Championship*   117

Chapter 10   *Risk*   133

Chapter 11   *The Boss*   147

Chapter 12   *The Pits*   155

Chapter 13 **The Man Who Saved the TT**   167

Chapter 14 **A New Beginning**   181

Chapter 15 **Ordinary People**   199

Chapter 16 **Chariots of Fire**   209

Chapter 17 **Heaven Can Wait**   219

Chapter 18 **Red Flag**   237

Chapter 19 **The Modern Era**   251

Chapter 20 **What It Means**   273

Chapter 21 **An Uncertain Future**   281

Achnowledgements   291

CHAPTER 1

The Start

*'One mistake and it's the last mistake you'll
ever make in your life.'*
ROGER MARSHALL

The claxon sounds, harsh and alarming, like an air-raid
siren. It announces there are five minutes to go until
the start of the race. The television helicopter lifts off, the
urgent beating and downwash of its rotor blades adding
to the general cacophony and reminding everyone that
there's no turning back now. It's happening. The medical
helicopter fires up its engine and runs through final checks.

The start line on Glencrutchery Road – a road that every
other week of the year is under a 30mph limit and used
by everyday traffic as it heads into, or bypasses, Douglas,
the capital of the Isle of Man – is thronged with people.
Mechanics, timekeepers, flag marshals, medics, glamorous
promotional girls, race organisers, VIPs, photographers,
television crews, reporters, riders' families, friends, helpers
and loved ones.

Television crews attempt last-minute interviews with the riders. Some competitors prefer to be left alone, others embrace the distraction; none reveal anything poignant. They are already in another world; already deep into the race, thinking about conditions around the course, race strategies, pit stops, rivals, handling problems with their machines, last-minute changes they have made. Their thousand-yard stares give this away. They're really not engaged with the person with the microphone, or the real world, any longer.

Four minutes to go.

The grandstand is packed, every ticket sold out months ago. To ensure accommodation and flights or ferries, fans must book up for the TT a year in advance of it actually happening. Demand far exceeds the Isle of Man's ability to meet it. Every hotel room is booked, every campsite full, and hundreds of locals have either let out rooms under the Isle of Man government's 'Homestay' scheme or have vacated the island altogether and rented out their homes for fat returns.

The riders become increasingly isolated as their mechanics leave the start line with a final word or gesture of encouragement, or a well-meant warning to take it easy. No one will be heeding that advice though. Each has their own routine to deal with nerves, and to bolster their belief that they will be coming back. 'The last words I always said to my mechanic were, "I'll see you later for a pint,"' says triple TT winner Ian Simpson. 'Just to make myself believe that I would be coming back.'

When Glenn Irwin made his debut at the 2022 TT,

he couldn't believe the atmosphere on the start line. Despite being a very successful rider in the British Superbike Championship and having already won six North West 200 road races at that point, he had never experienced the atmosphere of fatalism that exists on the TT grid. 'The grid stuff – I nearly fucking couldn't talk up there,' he said afterwards. 'It's weird. There's a lot of emotion. You're about to do something that, let's face it . . . people don't say the reality. But people shake your hand and they fucking look at you [when they say] good luck . . . they look at you like they don't know if that's the last time.'

The attitude of others caused Irwin to question what he was about to do. 'When you get that before you ride your motorbike, obviously part of your brain is going to go, "What are you doing? Why the fuck are you doing this?" And the other part is going, "Shut up – I want to do it." So, there was a lot of emotion on the grid.'

Superstitions run deep amongst TT competitors and, if they're not observed, panic can quickly set in. 'Before one particular race, I forgot to tell my mechanic I would see him later for a pint,' Ian Simpson says. 'He was leaving the grid and I panicked, and started frantically waving at him to come back. Only when I said, "I'll see you later for a pint," could I settle and concentrate on the race ahead.'

There are countless other examples. John McGuinness – the most successful living TT racer with twenty-three wins to his name – always keeps an old penny tucked into his leathers for luck, after a helper once found a penny on the grid and shoved it down McGuinness' leathers. He won the race. The penny stayed.

McGuinness also says a silent prayer on the start line to all the friends he's lost at the TT, asking them to watch over him.

Despite having no idea why, former podium finisher Keith Amor always insisted on putting his left boot on before his right boot while multiple winner Ryan Farquhar did the opposite – right boot before left.

Amor, like all the other riders, tried his best to ignore Douglas Borough Cemetery, which lies adjacent to the start line and directly opposite the TT grandstand. The cemetery contains a memorial wall with plaques in remembrance of many TT riders who never made it to the finish line. Amor didn't need reminding of the risks he was about to take.

Three minutes to go.

Time slows down, and most riders take a few moments for themselves to sit in silence, trying to find a focus and calmness to allow them to do what they're about to do. 'Being up on the grid is just one big mental pressure,' Amor admits, 'and the tension is unreal. You can feel it amongst everyone.'

'The adrenaline starts kicking in, and I do get nervous,' Conor Cummins has admitted. He, better than most, knows the very real dangers he's about to face. He almost lost his life in a crash at the 2010 TT. 'But I try to control it by staying calm and thinking about what I'm going to try and do in the race.'

The riders are now lined up in single file, arranged in their predetermined starting order, based on experience, sometimes on preference (amongst the front runners, at least) and, further down the field, on the lap times the riders set during the week's practice which precedes the opening race: this race, the TT Superbike race, for 1000cc machines making 230bhp and capable of speeds over 200mph.

Although there's a certain honour and kudos in starting as number 1 on the road (every camera is focused on you, every spectator around the 37.73-mile course awaits in tense anticipation to see you, and all eyes are focused on you on the grid), there can also be a price to pay. As the first man on the road, hidden dangers exist that are not so prominent for the other riders. The first man away is sometimes referred to as 'the road sweeper' for it is he who will scare the wildlife out of the hedges (mother ducks with their ducklings in line astern have been encountered at 180mph); it is he who will first come across any stray dogs or cats that have found their way on to the course; he who will have to clear the dust or damp patches – depending on weather conditions – first. He is the pathfinder, the trailblazer that all the other riders will follow. And there's another reason why there is generally no great competition to be first away: he will have no one to chase; he will have to set the pace according to the conditions, and he will be the target for every rider behind him. He is the hare that the hounds will be chasing.

'Being the road sweeper did concern me a little bit,' James Hillier says of his turn at being first man on the road in 2013. 'It was good, in the sense that there was no hanging about on the grid – I could start the race sooner and get finished sooner. It's quite weird how you spend all year looking forward to that race, but as soon as it approaches you just want it to be over with. It was definitely a benefit starting at number 1 from a publicity point of view, but I'd rather not do it again. I would sooner have a bit of a carrot to chase now – someone to hunt down.'

John McGuinness became known for trying to break his opponents by setting a blistering pace early in the race. He has opted to start number 1 on many occasions. By the time he lines up on the grid for the first race of TT week, he has already taken care of everything he can back home. A married father of two, he confesses, 'When I'm getting ready for the TT, I wash the cars, mow the lawn, put the finances straight; stuff like that, because you never know.'

It is this brutal grasp of reality that proves TT riders are not crazy. They are perfectly aware of the risks; they just choose to accept them, regardless of the potential consequences.

Two minutes to go.

The first rider is now sitting astride his machine under the inflatable archway that straddles the start line. The race starter, standing on a rostrum – in front of, and to the right of, the lead rider – holds his flag, stopwatch at the ready. A start line official stands under the inflatable arch, alongside the lead rider, with his hand on his left shoulder. When he releases his hand, the rider is free to go.

The seconds continue to tick down, every one of them now seeming like an age, not only for the riders, but for their families and loved ones. Some insist on being involved in pit lane to keep themselves distracted. Others watch from the grandstand. Still others listen in on the radio back in the paddock but refuse to watch. In just under 17 minutes, at the end of the first lap, their rider will be howling over the start line at 180mph. And that's not even the fastest part of the course. On the Sulby Straight, riders will be travelling at up to 206mph, between trees and through the village of Sulby itself; pubs, houses and schools looming large, and very solid, on either side of the road.

The grid is now cleared of mechanics and helpers, and the riders sit alone astride their running machines, revving them constantly, keeping the engines warm and ready for what lies ahead. Unlike every other motorcycle race on the planet, there has traditionally been no practice lap at the TT. The lap is simply too long – although from 2022 onwards, a race-morning practice lap has been factored in. Before then, riders had to instantly transition from standstill to full racing speed in an instant. From zero to 200mph, with no time to get their brains and sensory systems up to speed. Any hesitation would cost time, and the TT is a race against the clock.

Although mass starts have, on occasion, been attempted in the past, they have proved to be too dangerous, so TT riders now start alone, at 10-second intervals, and race against the clock. Their times are adjusted according to the order in which they started, and this 'corrected time' dictates the result at the end of the race. Riders can be several miles apart on the course, but with only seconds between them on corrected time.

The Superbike race is run over six laps, which equates to 226.38 miles. It will necessitate two pit stops: one after the second lap, and one after the fourth. Fuel is, obviously, essential, but riders also have the option to change a rear tyre, should they have shredded the one they started on. But that's in the future. Right now, all riders must focus on calming their nerves and making a good start. The first few miles are crucial. Every rider knows they must attempt to set a pace so hot it demoralises the others and breaks their will to respond. It means attacking the course at 100 per cent, right from the off, and there is no room for error.

One minute to go.

A hush descends over the crowd, as the time ticks by in seconds now, not minutes. The spectators are fully aware of the dangers that lie ahead; fully aware that 264 men – and one woman – have been killed on this most formidable course since the first TT was held in 1907. 'It's the most dangerous racetrack in the world,' testifies seven-time TT winner and former lap record holder Mick Grant. His former team-mate in the 1980s, Roger Marshall, makes an even more chilling assessment: 'One mistake and it's the last mistake you'll ever make in your life. When I look back at some of the old pictures in my scrapbook, there's only half of the grid left alive.'

Every rider responds differently, but they all feel this fear before the flag finally drops and they can then transfer their focus and channel that fear into sheer speed. Even the late, great Joey Dunlop – the most successful TT rider in history with twenty-six wins to his name – felt the fear. 'Oh, you have fear, you have,' he admitted. 'But see once you get to Bray Hill? It's gone. Everybody's the same but, once that flag drops, you're in a completely different world – you're on your own.'

Bray Hill is the terrifying five-storey downhill drop just

seconds into the lap. At the bottom, the suspension on the bikes bottom out, causing the belly pans of the bikes to scrape the road, inches from the kerb at the inside of the apex, showering sparks from footrests at 180mph. It's one of the most terrifying and breathtaking sights in motorsport and has been the scene of several fatalities.

Thirty seconds to go.

All eyes are on the man and machine carrying the number 1 plate as he fidgets, checks his gloves for the umpteenth time, looks down at his machine, as if that will reveal anything new. Satisfied, John McGuinness' eyes now focus exclusively on the starter to his right, the chequered flag in his hand. Tick, tock, tick, tock . . .

Fifteen seconds.

The atmosphere is palpably tense. It's electric. It's like no other sporting event on earth. Tennis players at Wimbledon do not risk their lives; footballers do not have to mow their lawns and set their finances straight ahead of a big match. Formula 1 drivers can crash with seeming impunity and walk away. Everyone knows that's not the case here.

Five seconds.

Four.

Three.

Two.

One.

The starter raises the chequered flag and snaps it down with practised ease. The start-line marshal releases his hand from McGuinness' shoulder, and the 23-time TT winner releases the clutch, revs his Honda Fireblade to the max, pulls a slight wheelie as the bike launches and heads off on the flat-out run to the fearsome Bray Hill. There's no more time for nerves; no more time for doubts. The race has started. How it will end, no one yet knows. How many riders will return is also open to question.

The TT has begun.

CHAPTER 2

Comedy and Tragedy

'I had to make up my mind whether to stop and maybe lose the race, or to plunge blind through a wall of fire that stretched right across the road at the Devil's Elbow.
REM FOWLER

It was dangerous, right from the start. 'My most exciting moment was when I had to make up my mind whether to stop and maybe lose the race, or to plunge blind through a wall of fire that stretched right across the road at the Devil's Elbow. It was caused by a bike that had crashed there. Owing to the density of the smoke and flames, I had no idea where the wrecked machine was. I decided to risk it and luckily came through okay. I shall never forget the hot blast of those flames. I think that the 1907 TT was the most hectic I have had in all my riding years.'

So said Rembrandt 'Rem' Fowler after winning the inaugural twin-cylinder TT in 1907. And a wall of flame wasn't Fowler's only problem on that historic day. He had more personal issues too. 'I had an abscess in my neck lanced two days before the race – in photographs the bandages could be seen flapping in the wind!' he said. 'I was in no fit state to ride, for I was in a very run-down and nervous condition. Twenty minutes before the race, however, a friend of mine fetched me a glassful of neat brandy, tempered with a little milk. This had the desired effect, and I set off full of hope and Dutch courage.'

Fortified by brandy and milk, Fowler rode into the annals of motorcycling history on that grey, windy and cold Thursday of 28 May 1907. He and Charlie Collier (who won the single-cylinder race) became the first race winners at the Isle of Man TT. At a time when British roads were covered by a blanket 20mph speed limit, Collier's fastest lap of the original 15.8-mile TT course (known as the St John's Course) was 41.81mph, while Fowler's fastest was 42.91mph.

While everything else surrounding the TT has changed since its inception in 1907, the spirit of the competitors has remained the only constant. Their willingness to take potentially catastrophic risks, and their sheer bloody-minded determination to overcome every possible obstacle in pursuit of victory, has remained unchanged and undimmed since the very first TT. In order to understand the mindsets of modern-day TT gladiators, and to appreciate how the event itself has evolved into what it is now, it is necessary to know something of the history of the event, and of those who have taken part in it.

The British government has never allowed the country's

roads to be closed off for racing purposes. That changed in 2017 when a new law allowed for just this to happen – should there be strong enough interest in staging such an event – but in 1904 the Automobile Club of Great Britain (now known as the RAC) was given short shrift by the British government when it sought permission to stage the first ever Tourist Trophy race for cars. And so, the club turned its attention towards a small island in the middle of the Irish Sea.

The Isle of Man is not part of Great Britain or the United Kingdom; it holds the status of a 'Crown Dependency', meaning it is a self-governing possession of the British crown and is, largely, free to make its own laws. So, when the Automobile Club offered a financial incentive to the Manx government (Tynwald) to close its roads for a car race, a law was hastily passed to allow this to happen, and this proved to be the genesis of the Isle of Man TT races.

While the law was originally passed to cater for car racing, it wasn't long before the two-wheeled community, though still in its infancy, wanted its own race for motorcycles and, in 1907, the first Isle of Man TT was staged on the 15.8-mile St John's Course, which started in the village of the same name, joined the current TT course at Ballacraine and followed it to Kirk Michael, before turning left and following the coast road back to the village of St John's.

It was a haphazard affair, with none of the glamour of today's event. Competitors, officials and spectators milled around the Tynwald Green and the area next to the Tynwald Inn, which formed the first TT paddock. The makeshift scoreboard positioned there was a blackboard borrowed from the local school, and journalist Laurie Cade later recalled that 'It was a queer-looking crowd on the village green. The grandstand, if my memory serves me, consisted of a couple of beer crates on which the officials stood.'

Practice for the first ever TT race was held on the morning of race day, on roads that were still open to everyday traffic. The session threw up several unexpected problems for the competitors. Chief amongst them was that the road surface was plain Macadam (un-tarred) and the dust thrown up by riders made visibility a serious problem, as Rem Fowler discovered. 'One of the main hazards was overtaking other riders,' he recalled almost fifty years later. 'They were obscured in thick clouds of dust, and it was very difficult to judge where they were.'

The race organisers sprayed an acid solution on the roads in a bid to suppress the dust, but this was thrown up by the bikes' rear wheels and sprayed on to following riders. As a result, one of the unexpected hazards of an already dangerous event became acid burns. Riders found the acid was soon burning through their clothing, inadequate as it was, and leaving it in tatters. In an era long before one-piece leather suits and crash helmets, the nearest anyone got to 'protective' riding gear was a long leather jacket, a raincoat or a rubber poncho. Aviation goggles offered at least some protection from the dust clouds and acid.

The top speed of motorcycles in 1907 may only have been around 60mph, but the dangers of racing were just as great as today. Minimal suspension (if any), skinny tyres, almost non-existent brakes, lack of protective clothing or helmets, deeply rutted and dusty roads – which were strewn with nails from horseshoes – and an absolute lack of roadside protection meant the pioneers of TT racing faced an undeniably dangerous challenge.

That first TT race would, to modern eyes, have looked decidedly comical. Apart from the quaint notion of a compulsory 10-minute break for lunch, riders received information about their position in the race directly from friends or helpers who would simply run alongside the competitors as they 'raced' up the steep Creg Willey's Hill. In fact, the original single-cylinder race result proved to be controversial as the winner, Charlie Collier, had the advantage of pedals on his Matchless machine, which helped him power up Creg Willey's Hill; a luxury not enjoyed by Jack Marshall on his Triumph. Such was the outrage caused, pedals were banned the following year. Current riders take Creg Willey's Hill at around 140mph. Running alongside them is no longer an option.

The racing wasn't desperately close in that first TT either. Whereas races are often won by mere seconds now, Rem Fowler won the twin-cylinder class in 1907 by a full half an hour.

But it was a start. After more than four hours of racing, twelve riders from the twenty-five who started made it to the finish line. There had been thrills, spills, controversy and displays of dogged determination from the first men to ever take on the challenge of the TT. But none who took part could have realised the significance of what they had been part of, and none could ever have imagined that riders would still be taking on the same challenge over a century later, on 200mph missiles. The TT had begun.

* * *

The acronym 'TT' stands for Tourist Trophy, and it originated with cars. In 1905, the Manx authorities had staged a race for road-going touring cars and called it the Tourist Trophy. The name was copied for the first bike race in 1907 – since they, too, were production 'touring bikes' – and it has stuck ever since, becoming completely synonymous with motorcycles.

A long-standing TT tradition was instigated in 1908 – the use of marshals around the course. Lessons had been learned from the previous year when sheep had strayed on to the track, and local traffic had caused further problems (although there were estimated to be only forty vehicles on the island's roads at the time), so the Manx authorities decided that volunteer marshals would be given the powers of special constables for the duration of the practice and race period. The same system is still in place today.

Another aspect of the TT that has never changed is the bravery and determination of the riders, not all of whom are famous names. In 1909, Andrew Sproston finished eighteenth out of nineteen finishers. Sproston had crashed into the wall at Ballacraine just after the start and broke his ankle. He rejoined the race and, clearly in considerable pain, stopped to remove his boot at the end of the first lap. He started off again – by pushing off with his right foot only – and held on to complete the 158-mile race in his stocking sole. When he reached the finish line, Sproston had to be lifted off his machine by two policemen and was carried to the local police station where he was treated for acute exhaustion. But he had done what he set out to do – he had finished a TT race. There would be many, many more stories like his to come.

It usually takes a national crisis like a world war or a global pandemic to stop a TT race but, in 1910, an irate local farmer tried it all by himself. Tired of bikes and cars racing round the roads close to his farm, Arthur Mathews demonstrated his disapproval by riding his horse and cart along the start line, just minutes before the race was due to start. Spectators hurled verbal abuse at Mathews before physically assaulting him. The farmer then pulled out a whip and lashed out at one of his assailants who caught the end of it and pulled it free. Mathews then used his horse's reins as a weapon but was overcome as the crowd managed to separate his horse from its cart. When someone in the crowd then fired a cap gun, the already frightened horse bolted and smashed into one of the parked-up race bikes before being caught and subdued. The police tried to intervene, but their efforts were in vain, and it was only when TT official Freddie Straight got involved that a riot was averted. Straight was one of the four men who had dreamed up the idea of running the TT, and he was not about to see his creation being foiled by a local farmer. Showing a great deal of diplomacy, Straight managed to placate the farmer, not with threats, but by honouring him with a committee members' armband, thereby making him an official of the meeting. Mathews was satisfied, the crowd cheered its approval, and the 1910 TT races were ready to roll.

Live coverage of the TT began that same year, after a fashion, as *The Motor Cycle* magazine had arranged for special wire transmissions to be made to many parts of Britain to keep enthusiasts updated with what was happening in the race. From garages in Glasgow to Harrods in London, motorcycle fans eagerly gathered round and awaited news on the latest lap positions.

With motorcycle manufacturers finally adding gears to their machines in 1911, it was felt those machines were now capable of tackling the much longer 'Mountain Course' that had first been used for car races in 1908. This course included an eight-mile uphill climb from Ramsey to the highest point of 1,400 feet at Brandywell. It was 37.5 miles long (about a quarter of a mile shorter than today's course) with the start line located on the level section of road between the bottom of Bray Hill and Quarterbridge corner, about half a mile from the current start line. Riders followed the same route as today's racers with one main exception; the course turned right at Cronk-ny-Mona before turning left on to Ballanard Road, and right again at St Ninian's crossroads, where riders then plunged down Bray Hill and back to the start line. Only the seven-mile section from Douglas to Ballacraine was tarred, and the Mountain section was little more than a deeply rutted cart track. Because the course was so much longer, refuelling depots were set up at Braddan and Ramsey.

Give or take the odd alteration, it is the same course that is still in use today, although the first lap record for the course in 1911 was 50.11mph, whereas current racers are lapping at average speeds of 135mph.

Current racers, fortunately, no longer have to stop to open gates over the Mountain section of the course. In 1911, the first rider in practice had to stop and open three different gates for his fast-approaching colleagues or make arrangements with a local shepherd to do the job for him. The gates were to help control livestock, but wandering sheep and cows still presented a constant hazard to the riders, as did the road surface. Rutted and dusty in dry weather, or rutted and muddy when wet, the only constant were the endless potholes which remained whatever the conditions.

The 1911 TT also saw more than one race for the first time. Whereas there had been single- and twin-cylinder classes right from the first TT, they were classes within a single race but, in 1911, two races were held – the Junior TT (for smaller 300–340cc bikes) and the Senior TT for bigger 500cc bikes. The Senior TT still brings the curtain down on the TT festival and is still the most important road race on the planet.

Sadly, the 1911 TT saw the first fatality in the event's long and troubled history, when Victor Surridge was killed during practice after crashing at Glen Helen, directly in front of his horrified team manager.

As if racing around the TT course wasn't dangerous enough, in 1913 it was made even more so by angry suffragettes. During practice for the event, Manx suffragettes had strewn broken glass all over the Mountain circuit. While the Isle of Man had become the first country in the world to grant the vote to women in 1881, it was only to those who owned real estate to the value of £4 or more, so there were still plenty of embittered women on the island. A team of road sweepers had to be formed to clear up the potentially lethal mess, and many claimed they were picking up shards of glass 'by the bucketload'. The team worked until 4am on the morning of the first race day to reduce the risk to the competitors, who were not told of the debacle.

The 1913 TT also saw the first fatality in a race. While Victor Surridge had been killed on his Rudge in 1911, it had been during practice and not during a race. Frederick Richard Bateman had also been riding a Rudge and had been leading the second part of the Senior when he crashed on the fast descent from Keppel Gate after suffering a puncture. He had just turned twenty-three years old. With speeds rising and two deaths already having occurred at the TT, crash helmets became compulsory for the 1914 event. Sadly, the move was not enough to avoid another tragedy.

The five-lap Junior race was held in atrociously wet and misty conditions in 1914, but that didn't stop the lead riders from having a monumental scrap. It was, however, to end in tragedy. Frank Walker had been leading on the second lap when he crashed out. He remounted and gave it everything he had – and a little bit more – for the remainder of the race. Walker crashed two more times but still got back on his Royal Enfield and, incredibly, was lying in third place as he raced along Ballanard Road towards the chequered flag. The TT organisers had allowed for a run-off area after riders crossed the finish line, but they couldn't have foreseen that excited spectators would mob that area after the first and second men came through. As Walker approached the flag at speed, he realised he was going to crash into spectators. Showing the utmost bravery and concern for the safety of others, Walker veered his bike to try to avoid hitting anyone but crashed straight into a wooden barrier and suffered what would prove to be fatal injuries. He was taken, unconscious, to hospital and hung on to life for five days before finally succumbing to his injuries. Despite crashing three times during the race, Walker finished in third place, then gave his life so that no one else would be injured. In just a few months, his country would be in dire need of men such as him.

As dangerous as motorcycle racing was, it was nothing compared to the danger that now faced an entire generation of young men throughout the world – including many of those who raced at the TT. Just 55 days after the chequered flag dropped on that Senior race, the First World War broke out, and the largely irrelevant pastime of TT racing was brought to a halt. But both directly and indirectly, the breakthroughs in technology achieved by factories and engineers who had tackled the TT for the last eight years would prove invaluable in military terms. The TT, in its own small way, contributed to the Allied victory in the Great War. Sadly, many of its pioneering riders would never set foot on their beloved Mona's Isle again.

When racing finally recommenced in 1920, Dougie Alexander caused a sensation in practice by slashing more than five minutes off the lap record. However, just as the pressmen were falling over themselves to report the sensational story back to the mainland, Alexander admitted to his prank – he had sneaked off the course and taken a detour, which was eight miles shorter. Just for laughs.

But speeds *had* improved, and the 1920 event saw the first calls for a 350cc limit as the bigger 500cc bikes, with their top speeds of 75mph, were thought to be just too fast.

The 1921 TT was the only time a 'dead' rider won a race. Howard Davies, like many TT riders, had endured a hectic war. Initially serving as a dispatch rider, he later joined the Royal Flying Corps. Having already been shot down once, he was downed again in 1917 and spent the remainder of the war in a German POW camp – unbeknown to *Motor Cycling* magazine, which published a report stating that Davies had been killed in action. When he miraculously reappeared at the TT, Davies wryly commented on the report saying that 'The facts are all correct save the central one – I am not dead.' All the same, Davies kept a copy of his obituary in his wallet from that point on and admitted that 'On reading that notice, I was tickled to death at being alive.'

Stanley Woods – a winner of ten TT races between 1923 and 1939 – vividly described the state of the TT course in the early 1920s, saying, 'The Mountain road from Ramsey, as far as Creg-ny-Baa, was sand and gravel (it wouldn't be surfaced until 1925). On the upper reaches it was sand only; rutted, with grass growing on top of the ruts. And there was no fencing. The road was hardly more than ten feet wide. If two cars met, it was a job to pass.'

Woods' debut in 1922 was, quite literally, a baptism of fire. During his refuelling stop, two gallons of petrol suddenly ignited, engulfing the Irish rider in flames.

He was later complimented for the quick thinking which saw him drop to the ground and roll the flames out, but later admitted he had panicked and tripped and was not worthy of the compliments. 'It was purely automatic,' he said. 'I jumped off the bicycle, then I tripped over my own feet and rolled on the ground. Then we picked ourselves up and straightened the handlebars and we went off again.'

The tragic death of Archie Birkin during practice for the 1927 event finally persuaded the authorities to close the course to normal traffic the following year. Since the TT began, practice sessions had taken place on the course while it was open to everyday traffic and, in 1927, Birkin was forced to swerve to avoid colliding with a fish delivery van while exiting Kirk Michael village. He crashed into a wall and was killed. The site of the fatality is still known as Birkin's Bend.

Yet, even when the roads were closed for practice as well as racing, hazards persisted. During the 1927 Junior race, Jimmy Simpson had a close encounter with a dog on the course, again in Kirk Michael. 'Right in the middle of the village there was a woman on one side of the road and a greyhound on the other,' he explained. 'And, just as I approached, the daft creature called the dog across to her. I hit it for six into a brick wall. I didn't fall off, but it slowed me a bit and affected the steering.'

Speeds, as ever, continued to increase and, in 1927, Stanley Woods became the first man to lap the course at an average speed of 70mph and reached a top speed of 93.70mph. Things were getting serious.

That same year, spectators in the grandstand were

treated to the first ever commentary on a TT race, though it proved disastrous; the commentator found the job utterly impossible and abandoned his post halfway through the race.

The TT took its first steps to becoming a truly international event in 1930, when a prize-money fund was set up for the first time. Anyone winning a TT would pocket a healthy £200 (around £10,000 in today's money) and travelling expenses were introduced to assist competitors. This led to a huge increase in the number of foreign riders taking part in the TT, which, in turn, made the race even more famous around the world.

Having been the first man to lap the course at 60mph in 1924, and the first to lap it at 70mph just three years later, Jimmy Simpson achieved another landmark in 1931 by averaging 80mph over a full lap. In just seven years, the outright TT lap record had gone up from 60mph to 80mph, and top speeds were in excess of 100mph. The increase in pace – largely caused by technological improvements – was staggering.

Wal Handley was known as 'the man who couldn't be frightened' due to his antics in the TT but, in 1932, that moniker was sorely put to the test. With HRH Prince George watching the Senior race, Handley had been splitting the Nortons of Stanley Woods and Jimmy Guthrie for three exciting laps when his brakes locked at an 'S' bend, known then as Alma's corner. Handley was thrown spectacularly from his Rudge at 85mph and landed briefly in a bed of nettles before bouncing back into the middle of the road. His bike was lying on the track, just inches away, with its engine still running and fuel pouring out from the tank, soaking both Handley and his bike. With his back badly hurt, Handley was effectively paralysed and could not get himself off the track to safety. While other bikes swerved to get past both him and his wrecked machine, Handley's greatest fear was that the bike would catch fire and engulf him in flames. He was eventually carried to safety and made a full recovery but, sadly, was killed in an aeroplane crash in the early part of the Second World War while serving as a captain in the Air Transport Auxiliary.

Another long-standing TT tradition began in 1935 when travelling marshals were first used. As was so often the case, this attempt to improve safety measures around the TT course was prompted by a tragedy the previous year, when Syd Crabtree had been killed after crashing in heavy mist on the Mountain section of the course. The mist was so dense that no one saw or even heard the accident. In an age before travelling marshals, Crabtree's body lay undiscovered for 40 minutes before a search party came across it. Crabtree's sad demise was responsible for the introduction of travelling marshals the following year. These bike-mounted marshals could search the course for any missing riders and deliver first-aid supplies while racing continued. It's a valuable practice which continues to this day.

As the TT's fame continued to grow, the event got a massive boost in 1935 when Britain's biggest music-hall star played a TT rider in the film *No Limit*. The comedy starred George Formby as chimney sweep George Shuttleworth, who builds his own 'Shuttleworth Snap' for an assault on the TT races. It became one of Formby's most famous films and, for the best part of sixty years, was shown in Manx cinemas during TT week.

And still the speeds increased exponentially. In 1937, Freddie Frith became the first man to lap the TT course at an average speed of 90mph, and Stanley Woods clocked an average speed of 122.49mph over a one-mile section of the Sulby Straight. On motorcycles with such primitive brakes, suspension and tyres – not to mention the even more primitive gear worn by the riders and the state of the course itself – the speeds were becoming truly terrifying, but the 1939 TT hinted at a far more terrifying future. As the riders lined up for the first race of the week, a boy scout proudly walked alongside them, holding aloft a huge flag bearing the Nazi Party's swastika emblem. With Adolf Hitler being determined to prove Germany's superiority in every sphere of life and sport, the BMW factory was state sponsored for the 1939 TT and arrived with three supercharged bikes capable of doing 135mph. One of the three riders, Karl Gall, was killed during practice, while the other two fought it out for top honours in the Senior TT.

Germany's Georg Meier won the race on his BMW from his Scottish team-mate Jock West. Germany had gained its great propaganda victory by beating the previously all-conquering British bikes in the world's greatest motorcycle race. Within three months, an infinitely more serious battle would erupt between the two countries. It would last for six years, claim the lives of countless millions and change the world forever. The trivial pursuit of motorcycle racing would have to be put on hold while Britain fought for its very existence. The dangers of the TT suddenly paled in comparison to the horrors that awaited many of its competitors. Yet the bravery they had displayed whilst racing round the world's most dangerous circuit would stand them in good stead for the battle that lay ahead. After finishing the 1939 Senior race in second place on his BMW, Jock West adapted his skills to flying a Spitfire and took the fight to his former employers.

CHAPTER 3

The Hunger

*'I determined there and then that, if I never did anything
else in my meaningless life, I would try to ride round the
TT circuit like those boys. My mind was totally made up.'*
STEVE HISLOP

Given that they're fully aware of the dangers of the TT,
what continues to drive riders to tackle it in the first
instance? Why are so many people so willing to take so
many risks when they could race on much safer, purpose-
built short circuits?

Steve Hislop would eventually become a TT legend,
winning eleven races, and building up a reputation as one
of the fastest and most accurate men ever to grace the
Mountain Course. He knew during his very first visit to the
meeting as a spectator in 1983 that he simply had to take
part in it. His description of what he witnessed that day
gets closer to capturing the sheer, naked thrill of the TT
than most others. 'We were sitting on the banking just after
the 11th Milestone, enjoying the fresh air and watching

the traffic go by before the big Senior Classic race got under way,' Hislop recalled before his untimely death in a helicopter crash in 2003. 'Like everyone else around the course, we had our little transistor tuned in to Manx Radio to listen to the race commentary, so we knew who was who and what was going on.'

It's a scene familiar to anyone who has ever spectated at the TT, but what he saw next would set Steve Hislop's life on a different course. 'I could hear the bikes setting off over the radio, but it was some time before I could actually hear them on the road for real,' he continued. 'Eventually, I picked up the sound of Norman Brown's Suzuki RG500 engine screaming along the mile-long Cronk-y-Voddy straight towards us, then he blasted into view and shocked the life out of me. Having seen the normal road traffic going past for the last couple of hours, words cannot describe the difference in speed as Brown went past our spectator point. Fuck me, he came through the corner at the end of Cronk-y-Voddy down towards the 11th Milestone, lifted the front of the bike over a rise in the road, braked hard, and back-shifted two gears before changing direction and blasting off towards Handley's. He was going so fast he almost blew me off the bloody banking.'

Hislop's brain struggled to compute what his eyes were seeing. 'Joey Dunlop was hot on his heels on a Honda RS850,' he continues. 'He had it up on the back wheel too and was pushing every bit as hard as Brown. I was like, "For fuck's sake!" I just couldn't believe that anything on earth could go that fast. I was completely blown away with the whole spectacle.'

His mind was made up.

'In those split seconds that it took Brown and Dunlop to hammer past me, my life had changed forever. I determined there and then that if I never did anything else in my meaningless life, I would try to ride round the TT circuit like those boys. My mind was totally made up.'

John McGuinness had a similar epiphany as a young spectator, after making the short trip over to the Isle of Man from his native Morecambe. 'I remember going to the TT with my folks when I was a kid and we watched from Bray Hill and, like anyone who watches a race bike go down Bray Hill for the first time, I nearly jumped out of my skin but, at the same time, I decided there and then that I wanted to do that someday. It took me a while to make up my mind about racing at the TT though. One day I'd decide that I wanted to do it, then I'd think about the dangers and decide against it. Eventually I said to my then team boss, Paul Bird, "Shall we do it then?" and that was that.'

McGuinness eventually made his TT debut in 1996 and it proved to be a baptism of fire, but he was not to be deterred. 'I shared a room with Mick Lofthouse at my first TT and he got killed in practice,' he says. 'You'd think that would put you off for life but, I suppose bike racers are just not right in the head.'

Not every rider in history entered the TT entirely of their own free will. Pat Hennen was the first American rider to win a 500cc Grand Prix, and his debut at the TT in 1977 was met with great excitement: he was the last genuine 500cc Grand Prix world championship contender to take part in the TT. As he sailed to the Isle of Man in 1978, he was just three points behind Kenny Roberts in the 500cc world championship. He was a genuine superstar and, in 1978, in only his second year at the TT, he became the first man to post a sub-20-minute lap of the 37.73-mile course. Moments later, he crashed at over 160mph and suffered severe brain damage that ended his career and affects him to this day.

His brother Chip still believes Pat was coerced into taking part in the event, against his better judgement. 'I'll never forget one of the Suzuki racing officials confronting me about why Pat had raced at the Isle of Man,' he says. 'I explained to him that, when Pat negotiated his contract with Maurice Knight, he told him he wasn't going to do the Isle of Man because it was simply too dangerous. I was present in the room during the negotiations. Maurice was very unhappy about it, since Barry Sheene had also refused to do the race, but Maurice relented. Then four weeks later, after Pat had returned to the US for the Christmas holidays, Maurice phoned Pat and told him that he had reconsidered letting him continue to use Suzuki GB's racing transporter for the 1978 season. He said Pat was going to have to find his own transporter unless he agreed to do the Isle of Man. It was pure and simple blackmail. I told Pat not to worry about finding a transporter, but it really concerned him, because the start of the '78 season was only a short time away. He finally said, "To hell with it," and phoned Maurice and told him he would do the Isle of Man.'

It was a decision Pat Hennen would live to regret.

Although Roger Marshall loved riding at the TT, he also

testifies that there can be external pressures to race there, for various reasons. In his case, it was to try to secure a route into Grand Prix racing. In Marshall's heyday in the 1980s, the TT Formula 1 World Championship was still in existence, and it meant a lot to the factories. Held mostly on dangerous road circuits – including a round at the TT – rather than on purpose-built tracks (although it would eventually incorporate more of these), the series was the forerunner to today's World Superbike Championship. It was just much, much more dangerous, and Marshall found himself pushing the limits on tracks that offered no second chances. 'If you wanted a factory ride you had to race on the scary F1 road circuits,' he says. 'The Japanese thought as much of winning the F1 world title as they did of winning Grands Prix. So, if you wanted to get a factory ride in Grands Prix, you had to go to these scary road circuits and do the business.'

It can work the other way round too. Ron Haslam loved riding the TT and was keen to continue doing so, even after he landed a factory Honda ride in the 500cc Grand Prix world championship. This time, it was the race organisers who screwed up and prevented him from appearing. 'In 1983 I was contracted to HRC (Honda Racing Corporation) to do the Grands Prix, but I still wanted to race at the TT, and HRC was happy to build me a bike,' Haslam says. 'I contacted the organisers and said that all I wanted was my flights and expenses. Whoever I got on the phone asked me where I finished the previous year, and I told him I didn't finish my last race. The expenses at that time were based on where you finished the previous year, so he said they wouldn't pay my expenses. What he didn't seem to know was that a lot of the promotional material for that year's TT was based around me – coins, stamps, advertising and stuff. I wasn't asking for any appearance money, just my costs, but they said no. I gave it a week, but they never phoned back, so I had to tell HRC not to bother building a bike.'

It wasn't until a fortnight before the TT started that the organisers realised they had lost their biggest star. 'Two weeks before the TT, another bloke phoned me up and said he could pay my flights,' Haslam continues. 'But by then it was too late to have a bike built. The organisers thought they had already got me to do the TT for free, because they thought I was contracted to Honda Britain, but I was actually contracted to HRC in Japan. So, then they phoned again and offered me my expenses, plus £30,000 for my back pocket, but I told them "I don't care if you offer me £100,000 – I don't have a bike."'

In an attempt to save face, the man behind the decision turned to the press. 'The next thing I knew was that this guy put it in the papers that Ron Haslam wouldn't be racing at the TT because he wanted too much money!' Haslam says. 'To be fair, the organisers did phone again later and apologised and said, "The man you were dealing with is no longer with us." They realised what had gone on. But that's the reason why I stopped racing at the TT.'

For other riders, racing at the TT is a family thing. Sidecar racer Conrad Harrison always took his son Dean to the TT when he was competing, and the boy soon became obsessed with the idea of racing there himself one day. 'The only reason I started racing was for the chance to do Scarborough (a parkland race in England) and the TT because, as a kid, I always went to those two meetings with my dad,' Dean Harrison says. 'He obviously races sidecars so, everywhere he went, we went along as a family, and those were the two main events for him back in the day: he didn't do a lot of other racing apart from the TT and Scarborough'.

Racing became associated with family holidays in Harrison's mind, and there was a certain inevitability about him one day racing the TT himself. 'I grew up at the TT,' he says. 'I've been every year since 1993, when I was just four years old. That was our two-week holiday every year and, as a kid, I really looked forward to going. When you're six or seven years old, you don't really understand some sides of racing, you just see the fun side of it, but I'd help my dad carry things around the paddock and catch a ride in the sidecar with him up to the pits and stuff like that. I thought it was pretty cool to have a dad who was a TT racer.'

Michael Rutter's late father Tony had also been a TT racer, and a seven-time winner, so Michael, too, felt the draw to follow in his dad's tyre tracks. But he also had practical reasons to counter the more romantic considerations. Michael was already a successful short circuit British Superbike racer when he first decided to tackle the TT in 1994, but he realised he could make the TT work for him. 'Basically, at the time, it was a place where you could earn some money!' he says. 'My dad told me that, if I could do a bit of everything (short circuit racing and road racing), then there would always be someone who would be interested in employing you. So, it was good for me because, when the TT was going well, I could get a ride there, which would then help me for British Superbikes and vice versa. If BSB was going well it would get me a ride for the TT, even if my results at the TT hadn't been so good.'

Ironically, Dan Kneen's primary motivation for doing the TT was the belief that it would be safer than riding around the streets on his road bike. 'It wasn't really in my plans to do the TT because I didn't think I'd be any good at it,' he explained. 'I wanted to have a go at the Manx Grand Prix though (the amateur version of the TT, held later in the year), because I was getting too wild on the roads, trying to get my knee down with my mates everywhere. It was obviously going to end in tears.'

Tragically, it was the racing, and not his road riding, that ended in so many tears for so many of Dan's fans, loved ones, family members and friends: he was killed during practice for the 2018 TT.

Rather than having a long-standing and burning desire to compete at the TT, Peter Hickman merely saw it as a career opportunity. Hickman is now the fastest man in TT history and has nine wins to his credit, but originally entered the event out of practical necessity. 'I was at the point in my career where I was struggling to get a British Superbikes ride, even though I'm easily a top ten rider,' Hickman said of his decision to enter the TT in 2014. 'I felt that doing the roads might help to raise my profile a little bit and help to get me back into British Superbikes. Thankfully, that's exactly what happened.'

Australia's David Johnson, another rider who spent most of his time racing in support classes within the British Superbike championship, felt much the same as Hickman. 'I was getting a bit fed up of being on uncompetitive bikes and was at a bit of a crossroads in my career, so I thought I'd try something different,' he says. 'Paul Phillips (TT Business Development Manager) had spoken to me about trying the TT and so I thought "Why not?"'

For fellow Australian rider, Josh Brookes, the TT was love at first sight. He was a factory Honda rider in the British Superbike Championship when he first visited the TT as a spectator in 2009. 'I was just literally walking up through the paddock with Neil Tuxworth (Honda team boss at the time) and I walked up to the wall and watched the bikes come down Glencrutchery Road,' he says. 'I was just like "Wow! This is impressive." I wasn't surprised by how fast they were going – I've never been surprised by the speed of racing. I know what the bikes are capable of, so the speed didn't really surprise me, it was just the whole atmosphere of the thing, and seeing how professional it was, and how well the bikes were turned out. I couldn't name one single thing that impressed me – it was just the whole environment which I found quite overwhelming, and I instantly thought, "This is something I want to be part of."'

In complete contrast to Brookes, Jenny Tinmouth had harboured a desire to compete at the TT right from her first year of racing in 1999, but it would be a full ten years before she allowed herself to race there. When she did finally enter the event, she became the fastest woman in

TT history, but she was originally cautious in her approach. 'The TT is obviously quite a big risk, but it's one of those things that you've just got to do,' she says. 'For a bike racer, it's the ultimate. I'd wanted to do the TT for a long time, but I wanted to get myself up to a certain standard before I tackled it. I didn't want to make an arse of myself. The 125cc class was dropped from the TT programme in 2004, so I realised I needed to learn to ride a 600cc machine. Once I'd done a season on a 600, I was confident enough to do the TT.'

It's not only the riders who have to want to do the TT; teams and sponsors do too. And while some shy away from the event because of the high risk of adverse publicity should anything go wrong, others list the TT as their main event of the year, and some team bosses can be every bit as passionate about the TT as their riders. 'The TT gets worldwide TV coverage all year round – it's not just on TV during the two weeks of the festival,' explains Neil Tuxworth, who has overseen more TT wins as a team boss than any man in history. 'It's such a well-recognised event that's not part of any championship. It's a one-off event that gets us maximum publicity and longer exposure.'

Philip Neill, manager of the TAS team, acknowledges the TT's commercial appeal, but says there's much more to it than that. Despite losing his rider David Jefferies at the TT in 2003, and then losing Dan Kneen in 2018, Neill remains a diehard fan of the event, regardless of any financial incentive. 'Clearly there is great commercial value in the TT in this day and age, and it's obviously nice to be part of that,' he says. 'There are benefits for the manufacturers, there are benefits for the sponsors and, ultimately, there are benefits for us as teams. The organisers have done a great job of building a great commercial platform for us to work from. However, we are one of the teams that would still be at the TT even without that incentive. We've been there since the days when there weren't those same commercial opportunities, so it's clearly a passion thing for us – it's in our racing DNA. That passion is what takes you to the TT in the first place – no one ever starts any sporting activity based on commercial reasons. We want to be part of the history of the TT.'

It's that rich history that brings the Padgett's team back every year too. 'History,' says team boss Clive Padgett, simply. 'The TT is steeped in history for Padgett's. Right from the 1950s we've been going there. My dad was going racing as a rider and team owner since before I was born, so I've never known anything else. It's the biggest event in the world as far as I'm concerned. As a team, we've won TTs in the 1960s, 1970s, 1980s, 1990s, the 2000s and the 2010s, which is a pretty amazing six-decade run. I'm very conscious of adding to that.'

And then, of course, there's the lure of the challenge itself; a lure acknowledged by Bournemouth Kawasaki team boss Pete Extance. 'One of the big attractions for our team is the pure kudos of the Isle of Man TT,' he says. 'In my mind, it's still the greatest single motorcycle event in the world, on what is undoubtedly the toughest track, and with the toughest conditions that any rider can endure. So, for a team to be able to finish a race at the TT – let alone be challenging for wins and lap records – is something very special for us. There's a greater sense of achievement in doing well at the TT than anywhere else.'

Once the decision has been made, once the hunger is there to do the TT, the next step for riders is to begin learning the course – and their lives will quite literally depend on the work they put in.

CHAPTER 4

A Mountain to Climb

'I think that, when your life depends on it, you have to learn it quickly. There's no better incentive.'
KEITH AMOR

The 33rd Milestone, high up on the TT course, yet just over four miles from the finish line, is a lonely, windswept moorland, as beautiful as it is desolate. The vista is of an epic scale; heather-strewn hills, boggy marshes, dry stone dykes with occasional, lichen-covered wooden stiles, all enveloped by a heavy silence, rarely experienced by the general populace of an increasingly urbanised world. It forms a peaceful, timeless panorama; the distant bleating of sheep and the irritated cries of herring gulls being the only sound other than the wind, which so frequently makes its presence felt at this altitude on a hilltop on an island situated in the middle of the Irish Sea; an island subject to its own micro weather system.

But on a warm summer's day, when the weather is

favourable, the temperature creeps up, the wind drops and a rare stillness descends; it is an idyll, far removed from the stresses, pressures and ceaseless noise of the modern world.

And then the idyll is shattered.

It begins with the urgent, throbbing beat of the rotors on the helicopter carrying the television camera: the harbinger of the leaders in the TT race. The helicopter rises into view from behind a hill, and its speed gives an indication of what's coming. The pilot has to effectively cut corners to have any hope of keeping up with the speed of modern TT racing motorcycles, the aircraft hugely outgunned in terms of top speed.

Then the howl begins. Almost imperceptible at first, and greatly affected by the wind direction, but gradually increasing as the leading motorcycle approaches. The sheep pay no heed and continue to nibble at the rough hilltop grasses. But the silence has been shattered and the noise becomes ever more violent and intrusive as the first man on the road bears down, the helicopter banking desperately to capture his every move.

One mile distant, man and machine burst into view. Just a glance of sunlight off bodywork at first, as the rider rounds the 32nd Milestone and howls down towards Windy Corner, before temporarily disappearing from view, obscured by the rugged hillside that stands between Windy Corner and the 33rd, the following helicopter the only guide as to his position.

When the rider explodes into view a few seconds later, the speed is a shock, yet less than a handful of people are there to witness it. Reaching the 33rd Milestone on foot involves a steep climb of over an hour, over bogs and uneven ground, and few are prepared to make the effort. But the effort is worth it. Many parts of the TT course are now severely overcrowded, and it can be a struggle to find a vantage point with a clear view. But up on the Mountain, the views are unique in the entire world of motorsport. There is, quite simply, nothing else like it on earth.

The rider now approaches at a speed that is difficult for the human brain to compute, as he negotiates the swooping left- and right-handers that precede the 33rd itself. The helicopter flashes overhead, the menacing throbbing of its rotors more familiar to a war zone than a peaceful Manx hillside. As it cuts out the 33rd – in order to be able to keep pace with the rider and motorcycle it is trying to film – the helicopter disappears from view, and all that is left is the relentlessly building sound of the tortured engine of a Superbike at full chat, no mercy being shown by the rider and no quarter being asked or given. All in.

As rider and bike approach, the noise becomes ever more violent with every gear change, the rear wheel sliding sideways in protest as over 200bhp is forced through it.

As rider and bike flash past with a vicious assault on the eardrums, and at an incomprehensible speed, any spectator who witnesses it can only look at their companions in shocked silence. The spectacle literally takes the breath away, and no words other than expletives can convey the shock to the system that the sight of a TT rider at full racing speed evokes. There is no other sight in motorsport that can hope to compare. It is akin to attempting to watch the trajectory of a bullet being fired from the barrel of a gun.

As both helicopter and rider disappear from sight, and the sound of the howling engine note begins to fade, the gentle sounds of the landscape return; the distant sheep bleat, the breeze rustling through the heather, and all is normal again. Until the next competitor shatters the natural world, in a flurry of speed and violence.

There could be no greater contrast to sitting in a distant grandstand, peering through binoculars and a chicken-wire fence at a purpose-built short circuit. To spectate at the Isle of Man TT is a visceral experience like no other, and it is easy to understand why both competitors and spectators alike become hooked for life. Whatever the dangers of the TT, whatever the moral implications of watching men and women risking their lives for the sake of entertainment, the thrill is undeniable.

To be able to ride at such heart-stopping speeds, riders need to know every inch of the TT course, and that's a process that takes time. It does not happen overnight. This is how they do it.

* * *

The Isle of Man TT Mountain Course is the longest, bumpiest, scariest, toughest, fastest and most dangerous racecourse in the world. At 37.73 miles long, it has over 300 corners and kinks; so many, in fact, that scores of them have yet to be given names, more than a century after the first race was held on it in 1911 (between 1907 and 1910, the TT had taken place on the 10.5-mile St John's Course).

It's made up of everyday roads which, for the remaining 50 weeks of the year, are used by everyday traffic. It runs through towns, villages and hamlets, and it's surrounded by walls, trees, houses, pavements, roadside furniture, lamp posts, telegraph posts, iron railings and grass bankings. It encompasses several bridges (the most notorious of which is the humpbacked Ballaugh Bridge, which sees riders literally take off for 20 feet), it crosses slippery steel tram lines and climbs 1,400 feet over the shoulder of Snaefell Mountain, before dropping back down to near sea level again.

There are blind corners, blind crests, fearsome plunges, and often damp parts where overhanging trees block out the sunlight and prevent the roads from drying. Riders also have to be wary of violent crosswinds, especially over the exposed Mountain section. Wildlife has been known to stray on to the course: dogs, cats, ducks – even, on one tragic occasion, a horse. The horse had been startled by a medical helicopter when it landed in a field to attend a fallen rider during the 1986 TT. It jumped on to the track, right into the path of Ireland's Gene McDonnell. Both man and horse were killed instantly.

The course has several hairpin corners, which have to be taken at painfully slow speeds – like Ramsey Hairpin and Governor's Dip – and these slow corners reduce the average lap speeds considerably. But there are fast sections too. Seriously fast sections. On MotoGP or British Superbike circuits, riders might reach full throttle in top gear for about one second per lap, if that: the straights just simply aren't long enough to go any faster for any longer. At the TT, riders can be at full throttle in top gear for miles on end, even on a 230bhp Superbike. The Supersport 600cc machines are held at full throttle for around 75 per cent of the lap, while smaller bikes are held at full chat for even longer. 'I reckon we must have been holding the 125cc bikes on full throttle for about 85 per cent of the lap,' says veteran racer Ian Lougher. 'You only have a Superbike at full throttle for around 13 per cent of the time.'

Only.

The TT course has corners that see riders having to tilt their heads to avoid clattering them off stone walls (Handley's), others where they have to adjust their position on the bike to avoid clipping iron railings (Braddan Bridge), fearsome plunges so steep that, when the riders reach the bottom, the suspension on their bikes 'bottoms out' and the whole underside of the bike scrapes along the road (the bottom of Bray Hill and the bottom of Barregarrow are two such examples). There are jumps that see the riders airborne for over 30 feet (Ballacrye), and crests where the bikes rear up on to their back wheels, shimmying and bucking as the riders fight to get the front wheel back down on to the road and under control again (Rhencullen 2). There are straights which are so fast, and so bumpy, that riders struggle to even see where they're going at over 200mph (Sulby Straight). In short, the course presents almost every kind of hazard possible, and these hazards must be anticipated and dealt with at mind-warping speeds.

It's all part of the unique challenge of the TT. 'The circuit presented an entirely different challenge to the normal circuits,' John Surtees remembered before his death in 2017. As a six-time TT winner, seven-time motorcycle

Grand Prix world champion, and the only man to have won world titles on two wheels and four (he won the Formula 1 World Championship in 1964), Surtees was accustomed to different challenges in motorsport but said the TT course was utterly unique. 'One is from the fact that it is so long. Two, that it is just standard roads. Three, that there are all the other factors which you have to learn about the island; about the changing weather conditions, and what can affect one part of the course and what can affect others. Where you are on the road when this happens and that happens. It's a learning curve: the more you ride on it, the better you become on it.'

Unlike on purpose-built short circuits, there are no run-off areas at the TT (apart from a very occasional slip road) and no gravel traps to slow a rider down, should he out-brake himself or run wide for any reason. Straw bales and Recticel air fences are employed on some corners to offer at least some protection against the stone walls and trees that hem in the course, but the course is far too long to be protected all the way round. It simply wouldn't be feasible. That means that, should riders crash, they are extremely vulnerable, despite wearing the best protective gear that money can buy. 'It's the most dangerous track in the world,' says multiple winner Mick Grant, without any degree of exaggeration.

Top speeds of over 200mph have been recorded on the fastest sections of the course, and the current fastest average lap speed stands at over 135mph (this average speed would be much higher if it were not for the aforementioned hairpin corners). To see motorcycles doing these kinds of speeds on public roads for the first time is a strange experience. It looks surreal. It does not compute. It takes time for the brain to fully register what it is seeing. It appears like some invisible deity has pressed the fast-forward button on the remote control of life. It just doesn't make sense – like seeing a fighter jet pass under a bridge on a motorway. It's faster than anything most people have ever seen in their lives. Which is why they return, year after year, to get more of this highly addictive, and often deadly, drug.

And that's just the spectators.

For the riders, it's a whole different world. Their lives depend on the homework they do in learning the course before they ever race on the Isle of Man. And the detail they have to learn it in is completely alien to the rest of us. Each night before a race, eight-time TT winner Jim Moodie would lie down, close his eyes, and mentally complete a full lap of the course, counting his gear changes all the way. The TT course requires hundreds of gear changes every lap yet, if Moodie found he'd forgotten one, or mentally selected the wrong gear, he would return to the start line in his mind and begin all over again. Most TT riders could do this. Every bump, every kerb or straw bale that sticks out, every dip, every layer of over-banding on the Tarmac, every drain cover, every white line, every jump, every section that tends to hold water after a rain shower . . . they need to know it all. This is the ammunition that keeps them safe. And it's why TT riders can enjoy longer careers than most short circuit racers, because experience is everything, and it only comes with time. Joey Dunlop won the last of his twenty-six TT races at the age of forty-eight, and John McGuinness took part in his 100th TT race at the age of fifty.

It wasn't always necessary to know the course in such detail. In the first TT, riders were lapping the St John's Course at average speeds of just over 40mph and most had to dismount to push their single-geared machines up the steep Creg Willey's Hill. Riders had plenty of time to see where they were going. But as speeds have continued to increase over the decades, learning the course intimately has become ever more important.

For most of the TT's history, there was no other way to learn the course than to drive it, ride it, or walk sections of it. In more recent times, onboard camera laps showing a forward-facing view at racing speeds have proved invaluable, as has the TT video game ('TT Isle of Man: Ride on the Edge'), such is its accuracy. There are also organised trips to the Isle of Man for newcomers during the winter, which include endless laps in cars or minibuses with experienced riders acting as guides.

Ron Haslam had no such luxuries when trying to learn the course in the 1970s. 'I went to the island a week before my first race and borrowed a bike and a car and spent the whole week going round the course,' he says. 'At first, I thought I'd never learn it – I'd had two days at it and was still completely lost. I can remember thinking, "I don't know how I'm going to cope with this."' Somewhat paradoxically, Haslam felt his lack of course knowledge made him safer. 'It wasn't as dangerous as I'd thought. Because I didn't know the course well enough, it made me slow down. When you're not positive on what's coming up next, you automatically close the throttle. It got more frightening when I started to get to know it better – that's the dangerous time. It's so easy to make a wrong judgement when you *think* you know what's coming up, but you're still not 100 per cent sure. That was the dangerous part for me. It wasn't until my third year that I really knew where I was going and knew all the drain covers, the hollows, the jumps – everything. Until then I was riding at about eight-tenths, but after my third year I knew it like a short circuit, and I rode it as hard as the bike would go. I was riding at ten-tenths by then.'

John McGuinness remembers experiencing the same feelings as Haslam when he was learning the course in 1996. 'When you're learning the track and you don't quite know where you're going, you get a horrible feeling of being in no man's land,' he says. 'You're not going quick enough to be on the pace, but you're still going quick enough to be slightly out of your depth.'

Like Haslam, Rob McElnea was another rider who had to figure things out on his own in 1979. 'I've always been quite handy at learning tracks – I suppose I just had a knack for it,' he says. 'I divided the track into sections, and there were some sections you needed to focus a lot more on than others, and those are the sections where you make the time up. You can't really learn the course on open roads because it's so different when you can only use one side of it. So, I learned it mostly during practice sessions. It's a cliché, but you don't ride the TT like a short circuit – you can't, because you simply don't know it that well.'

Guy Martin agrees that driving or riding the course under normal traffic conditions is of limited use. 'Riding the course on a road bike is a waste of time,' he says in his usual forthright manner. 'You're stuck up the arse of a car all the time, and you learn bugger all.'

Joey Dunlop, as ever, had his own way of doing things. When he first entered the TT in 1976, Dunlop had no idea which way the course went. 'It was wet, and I rode a 250, and I never was round it before, even in a car, and I didn't know where to go to,' he explained. 'I remember coming up to Ballacraine and I didn't know whether to turn, left, right or straight ahead.'

In order to learn the course better, Dunlop would complete dozens of laps in a car at night, having realised that headlights in the dark can pick out bumps and crests that are invisible to the naked eye in daylight. Johnny Rea remembers using the same tactic in the 1980s. 'I always did the same at the road races at home and at the TT,' he says. 'I did as many laps as I could at night-time. To start with, you knew the road was going to be quiet and, because you could see the headlights of any oncoming traffic, you could use the proper racing lines. It definitely helped.'

It helped to the point where Joey Dunlop got to know the course so well, he could drive sections of it at night *without* headlights. TAS team owner Hector Neill was unfortunate enough to bear witness to this. 'We were in the pub at the TT one night drinking vodka – Joey liked vodka – and he says, "Hey, Heccie, you want to do a lap?" This was about two or three in the morning. We were coming down into Barregarrow (a fearsomely fast, narrow, downhill section with walls and a house at the apex) absolutely flat out, as fast as the car would go, and Joey switched the headlights off. I nearly fainted. I said, "Joey, what the hell are you doing?" and he told me that he wanted to show me that he knew the course so well he could drive it blindfolded. I would never do it again, I can tell you!'

Things had moved on somewhat by the time Davey Todd made his debut in 2018. An updated version of the TT video game had been released that year, and it offered unprecedented accuracy, making it a vital tool in learning the course for some riders. Todd became so proficient at the game that he posted the second fastest time ever recorded on the global database. 'I watched onboard videos every single night after work for months, and I even got hold of the PlayStation TT game and hammered it until I got the second fastest lap of anyone in the world!' he says. 'I wasn't a gamer, and didn't even have a console, so I stole my brother's and learned how to play it. I was terrible to start with, and crashed an awful lot, but I persevered and learned loads. I felt there was a limitation with onboard laps because, if you made a mistake in your mind – like thinking the next corner is a left but it's actually a right – then the lap just carries on, because the rider obviously knows what he's doing. But if you get it wrong in the game, then you actually crash and learn from it. I played it for hours and hours on end, every night. In the end I was doing 15-minute laps, which would be pretty incredible if I could do it in real life!'

When Glenn Irwin made his debut in 2022, he also took advantage of the game, but pointed out the need for caution: a game doesn't kill you if you get it wrong. 'I started off with the Xbox to learn roughly where I was going,' he says.

'I mean, there are corners you can take on the game flat out, but you can't do it in real life, so you have to be careful, but it's good for learning where the track goes.'

With these relatively new learning tools at their disposal, newcomers are now lapping at unthinkable speeds. Irwin's best lap of the fortnight was 129.84mph – only 5mph short of the outright lap record. It would usually take years for even the most elite riders to reach this kind of pace. It was the fastest lap by a newcomer in the history of the TT.

Twenty-one times a TT winner, Michael Dunlop also acknowledges the benefits of camera laps and computer games in learning the course. 'There are a lot more onboard laps available to watch compared to when I started out, so it's very easy to pick up your phone and watch them,' he says. 'You've also got the PlayStation TT game. When I started out, you had to just come over here and suffer and get on with it, but the TV coverage is phenomenal now, and the quality of the footage and the cameras are state of the art. I don't know if it's any easier to learn the course, but you have more reference material, for sure.'

When Peter Hickman first tackled the TT in 2014, he became the fastest newcomer at that point, with a lap of 129.10mph. It seemed impossible, but he insists it was all down to the homework he had done before even turning a wheel in anger. 'I put a lot of time and effort into learning the course, pure and simple,' he says. 'I did at least seventy laps in a car between January and the end of April in 2013. I made seven trips to the Isle of Man and did at least ten laps during every trip. On top of that, I was watching lots of onboard videos and playing the PlayStation game, so I really did my homework. Most people don't realise that a lap takes at least an hour in a car when the roads are open (as opposed to the 17 minutes it takes bikes at racing speeds), so that's more than 70 hours of driving round and round the course.'

Ahead of his first TT in 2013, Australia's Josh Brookes combined all the above techniques and left no stone unturned in his bid to learn the course. 'I'm trying to learn it in every way possible,' he said at the time. 'I've been round the course on motorbikes and in cars; I've even been round in a bus listening to John McGuinness talking about his experiences. I don't care if I have to go round the course on horseback, as long as I'm learning. I need to imprint every corner on that course in the back of my eyeballs, and I need to know every part of it like I know the street I live on. I don't care what form of transport I go round on, so long as I get to know the course as well as I possibly can by the time that race week comes around.'

There's a good reason for such diligence: the better a rider knows the TT course, the better the chance of posting competitive lap times and scoring good results. But, far more importantly, the better they know it, the more chance they have of preserving life and limb. Keith Amor became the second fastest newcomer to date when he first entered the TT in 2007. He best sums up the motivation that drove him to learn the course so quickly. 'Well, I think that when your life depends on it, you *have* to learn it quickly. There's no better incentive.'

At the TT, a little knowledge can be a very dangerous thing.

CHAPTER 5

Who Dares, Wins

'You have to have risk to get the buzz.'
GUY MARTIN

The Isle of Man TT is a road race, as opposed to a short circuit race, and there are very significant differences between the disciplines of road racing and short circuit racing. Short circuit races are generally held on purpose-built tracks with surfaces as smooth as billiard tables and ample run-off areas, gravel traps and air fencing to make things safer should a rider crash. Road races don't afford such luxuries, and the bumpier road surfaces, proximity of roadside hazards and complete lack of run-off areas mean those events have to be treated very differently. Some riders compete successfully in both disciplines, while others specialise in one or the other. But the differences cannot be overlooked. 'It may not be obvious to the casual observer that there's such a difference between the two disciplines but, believe me, there is,' Steve Hislop insisted.

Hislop won two British Superbike championships as well as eleven TT races, so he was in a perfect position to explain those differences. 'Road racing is about stamina; it's about ignoring the dangers and not being afraid to clip brick walls and brush hedges, and it's about nursing the bike over extremely bumpy and taxing roads,' he said. 'On short circuits, it's a flat-out sprint from the start, over a relatively short distance, and you're bunched up tight with thirty other riders, literally leaning on each other. Also on short circuits, you're leaning the bike over more, decking everything out on the absolute limits of adhesion. Because there's more run-off space, you can afford to ride that bit harder too, because crashing is safer than on the roads. I suppose it's like the difference between a 10,000-metre cross-country run and a 100-metre sprint, and there are not many athletes who excel at both of those disciplines.'

When Mick Grant was racing in the 1970s and 1980s, riders were expected to race both on the roads and on the 'shorts'. Like Hislop, Grant had no problem switching between disciplines, but he also knew the very different approaches they required. 'There are different techniques involved in road racing and short circuit racing,' he confirms. 'I was brought up on short circuits, so I was good at stuffing it up the inside of someone at a hairpin. On the roads, you're riding much faster corners. The fastest corners on most short circuits are taken at about 120mph. At the TT there are loads of corners that you take absolutely flat out in top gear, with the bike on its side. It's a different discipline.'

Conor Cummins has also raced extensively in both

arenas, making his name on short circuits before becoming more of a road racing specialist. For him, the difference lies in being aggressive in one discipline and smooth in the other. 'You've got two different hats, and you put one on for the roads and one on for the short circuits,' he explains. 'Short circuits are real cut-and-thrust stuff, so you've got to be really aggressive, whereas the roads are the opposite; especially at the TT, you've got to be really smooth.'

The late Joey Dunlop won more TT races than any man in history, but he was also a far better short circuit rider – certainly in his earlier years – than most people give him credit for. But he was stunned by the pace of short circuit racers on the mainland when he first ventured out of Northern Ireland to compete in the British championships. 'English racing is a completely different type of racing,' Joey told David Wallace during filming of *The Road Racers* documentary. 'They're all big, broad courses with no trees about them at all. It's very, very hard to adapt to that sort of circuit, where you really have to ride hard and not worry about falling off and hitting a tree or something like that. You would think, when you're riding against them (the short circuit riders), that they're completely mad. I'm just starting to get it into my head now that you can afford to fall off in England – that's why they all go so hard.'

Former British Supersport champion and double TT winner Steve Plater believes that, even within the road racing world, the TT requires a unique skill set. 'You need a completely different approach to the TT compared to any other road circuit, let alone short circuits,' he says. 'You have to be a little bit more relaxed in your approach to it and bed yourself in slowly. There's a big difference between the way you'd ride at the TT and, say, Macau or the North West 200 (two other major road races, held in Macau and Northern Ireland, respectively). The obvious difference is that it's not a mass start. You're racing against the clock, so you haven't got the aggression that you'd have in a mass start race. The TT is so fast now as well, so you really need to focus on the road ahead. The last thing you want at the TT is to have someone in front of you, because you'd start concentrating too much on them instead of where you're going, and if they make a mistake, you'll make the same one.'

The late, great John Surtees also believed the TT required a very particular style. 'The TT needed a different style of riding and you needed to switch on to a slightly different mentality,' he said. 'You had to get the TT rhythm, and the TT rhythm is all about being in the right place on the road at the right time. Whereas you scratch here and you scratch there on a short circuit ('rider speak' for scraping their knees on the track or, in Surtees' day, scraping the exhausts or belly pans of their bikes on the road), what you do at any one point on the TT course controls what you do for the odd mile or so up the road. I didn't have a vast surplus of power, so I had to carry speed through corners, and to do that you had to be very much on the right line. By scratching through corners, you would actually scrub off speed. The Isle of Man, for me, was very much about rhythm and positioning on the road, and when I went to the island I switched into the island mode – but that didn't mean that you didn't ride just as hard.'

In Surtees' time, all riders raced on road courses as well as short circuits, and even the Grand Prix world championships incorporated both kinds of courses, out of necessity – there simply weren't enough purpose-built short circuits in every country to race on.

The motorcycle Grand Prix world championships are the oldest motorsport world championships in existence, even predating Formula 1 by a year. Established in 1949, the British round of the championship was the Senior TT, from that year until 1977, when the event was deemed too dangerous, and the British Grand Prix at Silverstone was set up as a replacement. The Senior TT continued, of course, as did the TT itself, but this loss of world championship status marked a watershed in the kind of riders who raced at the TT from that point on.

The issue was not only that the TT course was deemed too dangerous for the rapidly increasing speeds of motorcycles, but also that it took so long to learn the course, and the event itself took up over two weeks of riders' and teams' time, as opposed to the much shorter time commitment required of a normal Grand Prix meeting. 'A normal Grand Prix lasted three days, whereas the TT was a two-week event, and it cost the riders an awful lot of money to compete there,' Mick Grant explains. 'There was very little prize money, and it was awkward for the GP riders to get to the Isle of Man from the Continent. They had to drive to a port, get a ferry to England, drive again, and then get another ferry to the Isle of Man, which was a lot more difficult than just driving from the Spanish GP to the French GP, for example. Then they had to pay for a hotel for two weeks instead of just three days, as well as all the other expenses. It was good for the organisers, but not the riders. This was in the days before lots of long-haul Grands Prix, and it just didn't make financial sense.'

But the real issue was that riders were being forced to race there (in some cases, against their own better judgement) in order to chase world championship points. When Italian rider Gilberto Parlotti was killed doing just this in 1972, his good friend (and ten-time TT winner) Giacomo Agostini announced he would no longer be returning to the event. The TT had suddenly lost its greatest star. Phil Read and Barry Sheene were also at the forefront of the protests against the TT. While Read was a multiple TT winner, Sheene only contested the event once – to chase world championship points – in 1971 before denouncing the event and refusing to return. He would remain a fierce critic of the TT for the rest of his life, and delighted in offering quotes to the press like 'Why bother to race there when it's so much easier just to shoot yourself and get it all over with?'

Barry Sheene became the most famous bike racer on the planet in the late 1970s and was a household name in Britain thanks to his two 500cc Grand Prix world titles and celebrity lifestyle. Sheene had no fear of road circuits, as his performances at places like Oliver's Mount in Scarborough and Spa Francorchamps in Belgium proved. In fact, he had been leading the 125cc TT in 1971 at one point, before slipping off in the wet conditions at Quarterbridge. 'The Mountain circuit did not frighten me in any way,' he said. 'No circuit frightens me. I just couldn't see the sense of riding around in the pissing rain, completely on your own against a clock. It wasn't racing to my mind.'

By the time the TT lost its world championship status in 1977, most of the top Grand Prix riders had already stopped racing there and, with the notable exception of Pat Hennen in 1977 and 1978, wouldn't ever again.

With hindsight, most people feel that removing the TT from the Grand Prix world championship calendar was a good thing. Nine-time winner Charlie Williams (who won races both before and after the event lost its status) is among them. 'I've always been a staunch TT supporter, but to take world championship status away from the TT was the best thing that could happen,' he says. 'It was unfair to have a world championship race on such a circuit, and it cost the lives of a few riders.'

Former Honda Britain and JPS Norton team boss Barry Symmons agrees. 'I don't really agree with racing on public roads for championship points,' he says. 'Riders should only race on the roads because they want to.'

Symmons' words are echoed by TT winner and 1980s Grand Prix racer Ron Haslam. 'I'm pleased that they took the world championship away from the TT, because it stopped people *having* to race there,' he says. 'Now all the people that go *want* to go, which makes a big difference.'

It's been forty years since Haslam last raced at the TT, and he admits being shocked at the speeds now being achieved. 'The top riders do go ridiculously quick, and I'd say it's a little bit more dangerous now than in my time. In my time it was dangerous, but the bikes are now reaching such speeds that there's not much chance at all if something goes wrong. You have to rely so much on the bike – the engine holding together, the tyres holding together with that much horsepower . . . So, there's a lot of things that are nothing to do with the rider that could cause an accident.'

At the time when the TT lost its world championship status, most thought the move would spell the end for the event, and that it would slide into obscurity before finally being abandoned. But, in fact, the very opposite happened. In a compensatory gesture, the FIM (Fédération Internationale de Motocyclisme) granted the TT three new world championship classes, called TT Formula 1, TT Formula 2 and TT Formula 3.

The one-round 'world championships' were something of a farce: most riders would agree that you should not be able to call yourself a world champion after winning just one race. But the new arrangement at least gave the TT something to hang its hat on – a reason for its continued existence.

The F1 championship was for big production-based Superbikes, and it would grow to include many more rounds throughout the 1980s (originally on road circuits, but eventually incorporating short circuits too) and would prove to be popular. The series can be seen as the forerunner of today's World Superbike Championship but, in 1977, it was just a one-round series and, with decent money on offer for winning it, one of the men who had called for the TT to lose its Grand Prix status, Phil Read, decided to return to race there. He was not made welcome. 'When I arrived, I parked my van outside the hotel on Douglas seafront,'

Read explained before his death in 2022. 'A policeman tapped on the door and said, "Mr Read, I advise you to move your van out of the way, round the back, because there's a bit of a feeling here." I also had a Rolls-Royce at the time and was going round the circuit with a friend. When we stopped for petrol, they refused to serve me. The marshals threatened to go on strike too. I thought, "My God, I didn't think I was so important!"'

Such was the strength of feeling about Read's apparently cynical comeback, he was even pelted with stones during practice sessions. It was an ugly, and dangerous, beginning to the new championship.

As the TT Formula 1 championship grew in the 1980s, riders like Joey Dunlop, Carl Fogarty and Steve Hislop breathed new life into the TT and ensured its survival into the modern era.

The TT has now become a very distinct event from Grand Prix and other short circuit racing, and this has given birth to a new generation of riders who have opted to specialise in pure road racing, with the TT being the focal point of their year. The crucial point is that riders are now (mostly) free to enter the event or to avoid it: there is no longer pressure to race there just for points.

Many riders, like Joey Dunlop, Phillip McCallen, John McGuinness and Michael Dunlop, opted to become road racing specialists, although not always exclusively – they still took in some short circuit races, but never enjoyed the same levels of success as they did on the roads. Riders like these realised they actually preferred racing on real-world roads rather than clinical, featureless short circuits.

One of these specialists was Ryan Farquhar, who made an entire career out of racing almost exclusively on the roads. For him, it was simply a case of chasing a bigger thrill. 'I just love the buzz you get from road racing,' he said before his retirement in 2016. 'It's a different type of riding and it's more jumps and bumps. I would get bored riding round short circuits all the time. Obviously, there's still speed involved, but it's just a different thing. I just get a far bigger buzz out of the jumps and going past lamp posts and things. It's better craic too. In road racing everybody seems to be more down to earth. The teams in British Superbike paddocks are full of guys that are all hairdos and sunglasses, whereas road racing's not really like that.'

Conor Cummins agrees about the thrill factor. 'Road racing is a far bigger thrill, simply because you're on real-life public roads that are used by normal traffic every day of the year. So, to be going through a 30mph zone at 180mph just feels so *bad!* It's like the naughty little kid in you that's not gone away. The first lap I ever did of the TT was unbelievable, even though I was behind a travelling marshal; it was just such a bizarre feeling.'

Geoff Duke was one of the first superstars of motorcycle racing and would ultimately win six TT races and six Grand Prix world championships in the 1950s. He remembered experiencing the same feeling as Cummins back in 1949 when he made his debut on the TT course. 'I've never been able to describe the feeling of elation and absolute wonder of going down Bray Hill for the first time. I could have wept for joy.'

Somewhat paradoxically, Cummins also believes the

dangers of road racing make him a safer rider. 'Road racing makes you a better rider,' he says. 'You're forced to be accurate with your lines, because if you don't get them right, you'll crash into a wall and really hurt yourself. So, it's almost as if it's *scaring* you into being accurate. We're probably all nutters really, doing what we do.'

The rush of racing the TT course is not an easy thing to give up. Of course, not every rider enjoys the luxury of choosing to retire – many are forced out of the sport due to injury or are killed while competing. Charlie Williams was one of the lucky ones who got to choose, but it still wasn't an easy decision to live with. 'When I retired from the TT it left a huge gap in my life and I've never been able to replace the thrill I got from riding there,' he admits. 'I was tempted to make a comeback just to get that rush again, because I got terrible withdrawal symptoms for years after I stopped. It took about four or five years before I could accept the fact that I was just a spectator and not a racer any more.'

Williams cites the case of a less fortunate rider who simply couldn't resist the urge to experience the TT rush one more time. 'I knew a guy called Brian Warburton who was a good runner at the Manx Grand Prix,' he says. 'Since retiring from bike racing, he had tried everything to replace the buzz; he did skydiving and umpteen parachute jumps but said he still couldn't replace the rush of racing at the TT. In the end, he missed it so much that he made a comeback but lost his life in a crash.'

Seven years after giving that interview, and at the age of sixty-four, Charlie Williams finally gave up fighting the urge and returned to the Mountain circuit to race in the 500cc Classic Manx Grand Prix. He finished in ninth place.

Phillip McCallen won eleven TT races in the 1990s before retiring after breaking his back. Even with such a strong incentive not to race, he also struggled with his decision to retire from the TT in 1999. 'As a rider, you know that the adrenaline rush, the buzz of racing at the TT, will never be replaced once you retire,' he admits. 'It's such a high, and such a feeling of satisfaction to stand on the top of the rostrum at the TT, and it's hard to come to terms with not having that feeling. When I first went and watched the races after I'd retired, I'd still think, "I could go faster than that – maybe I should do it again," but eventually you just have to accept that it's over, however hard that may be.'

McCallen has, so far at least, resisted the urge to return, and now seems more content in retirement than some others. 'There was a bit of a sigh of relief, really, when I finally made my mind up,' he says. 'Like other racers, half of me wanted to keep on going and the other half wanted to stop, so your mind's all over the place because you don't know the right thing to do. You realise that the buzz, and the thrill, and the enjoyment, and everything you got out of racing will be gone forever. But after you've stopped racing for a while, you look back and realise how dangerous it all was, and you just don't want to get hurt any more. That's the upside to retirement – I certainly don't miss all the injuries.'

Riders try all sorts of things to replace the buzz of racing. Steve Hislop took up flying helicopters before he retired, knowing that he would need some form of excitement after hanging up his leathers. Speaking in 2002 he said, 'I've always known that I'd need something to replace the adrenaline rush of racing when I retire, so that's why I decided to start flying. Adrenaline is the best drug on earth, and if you could bottle it and sell it, you'd make a fortune. I get as big a kick from flying a helicopter as I do from racing, so I'm chuffed that I've found something to replace the buzz of racing when I retire.'

Sadly, Hislop never got the chance to retire from racing. He was killed in 2003, when the helicopter he was piloting came down near his home town of Hawick in the Scottish Borders. He is cited by many riders and team bosses (F1 TT winner Nick Jefferies and Honda team boss Neil Tuxworth amongst them) as being the greatest TT rider of all time, his precision more akin to the work of a computer than a human being.

Although he never quite managed to win a TT before becoming a TV personality, Guy Martin finished second eight times and won countless other road races. For him, the appeal was purely the danger, and he wasn't afraid to admit it. 'There is no thrill to me in short circuit racing,' he said in 2007. 'I enjoy the British championship because it's so competitive, and because I like riding motorbikes, but there's no buzz like the TT. Where else can you get so close to telegraph poles and walls and kerbs? You have to have risk to get the buzz, and there's no real risk in the British championships. If you come off, you just slide into a gravel trap, and nine times out of ten you walk away.'

While Lee Johnston is fully aware of the dangers and knows how crazy TT riders might appear to be to outsiders, he insists he's not even brave. 'I think it was (fellow rider) Cameron Donald who summed it up best for me,' he says. 'He said that short circuit racing is like climbing with a harness on, whereas road racing is like free climbing. Some people say we're mad, but I'm not mad at all – I'm not even brave. When I was growing up, I had an awful lot of mates who were way madder than me and would do things that I wouldn't do. I think it's just about what you're comfortable doing in your own skin. Me, doing that speed at the TT, feels okay and I feel in control or, at least, as much as you can be in control at those sorts of speeds. I look at other sports like rugby league and think those boys are mental! I couldn't think of anything worse than some 18-stone bloke running at you flat out, wanting to pull your head off just to get hold of a leather ball!'

It has long been said that TT racers ride well within their abilities and that they never push at more than 85 or 90 per cent. There may have been an element of truth in this at one point but, in recent years, as the competition has become ever fiercer, TT racers insist they're now riding at 100 per cent. 'Every road race I go to now, I ride it just the same as I would ride a short circuit,' Guy Martin said when he was still racing. 'The days of riding at 80 per cent on the roads are long gone. To win a road race now, you have to give 110 per cent. If you want to win, that's the way you have to do it.'

Triple TT winner Dean Harrison agrees. 'Everyone's riding as fast as they possibly can now,' he says. 'People think we only ride at 99 per cent but, believe me, if we did, then somebody would ride at 100 per cent and win all the time!'

While every rider acknowledges the great difference between short circuit racing and road racing, there is disagreement as to which discipline is the most demanding. 'Road racing is a lot more hard work, and a lot more stressful than short circuit racing,' Cameron Donald argues. He won two TT races in 2008 but also won short circuit championships in his native Australia. 'Just mentally, the strain of racing on the roads, to me, is harder. Riding at your limit on either kind of circuit is extremely difficult, but just the extra demands of the dangers involved and the sheer speeds – the roads are so much faster – it's a different ball game.'

Dean Harrison takes the opposite viewpoint. 'When you're riding a roads course, it's not as intense as a short circuit race,' he insists. 'In British Superbikes, you're going absolutely mental for eighteen laps – you're aggressive and attacking it, and on the point of crashing in every single corner. The TT is more chilled because you're out there on your own and there's no one to use as a reference point.'

Peter Hickman, the current fastest man at the TT, agrees with Harrison. 'Yeah, and you're not fighting with other riders like you do on a short circuit, so it's just more relaxing. Like a very, very fast Sunday run! I always take a couple of steps back at the TT and just chill out a bit. You're still riding at 100 per cent but it's a different 100 per cent compared to short circuits.'

While Hickman finds it easy to adapt to the roads after racing in the British Superbike Championship, he admits it's far harder to get back up to BSB pace after racing on the roads. 'Switching from short circuits to road racing is very easy but switching back the other way is hard,' he says. 'It takes me a full practice session at BSB to get back up to speed on the short circuits. You're braking a lot later and cornering a lot harder, and just more on the edge and a lot closer to crashing all the time. It's a much faster way of riding than you do on the roads. The speeds are higher at the TT, but the actual way you take each turn is a lot faster in BSB.'

So, as distinct as road racing is from short circuit racing, it seems that racing around the TT course is a discipline all of its own and requires a style all of its own. Smoothness is important, track knowledge is crucial and keeping momentum also plays a significant part. But, on a track as dangerous as the TT course, results often still come down to who's prepared to take more risk; who's prepared to put their neck on the line; who's prepared to cross over the ragged edge into unknown territory.

Who dares, wins.

CHAPTER 6

Operation TT

'The two biggest challenges are the logistics of the event and the preparation of the bikes.'
PETE EXTANCE

The logistics involved in staging the TT are staggering. Removing bus stops, manufacturing winner's caps, polishing and repairing trophies, turning off traffic lights, cutting back trees, sourcing picnic tables, arranging aerial photography of temporary grandstand sites, and making sure enough printer paper has been ordered for the timekeepers. These are just a few of the seemingly endless tasks that need to be carried out before racing motorcycles can start hurtling down Bray Hill at 180mph.

As one TT meeting ends, preparations for the following year's event begin immediately, but the work intensifies exponentially in the final few weeks before the starter's flag finally drops. Few people realise the level of logistics involved behind the scenes, all in a bid to make this most dangerous of events as safe as possible, and to ensure its smooth running.

Preparing the 37.73-mile Mountain Course is one example. To make it safer for riders, some 970 units of Recticel foam barriers need to be installed, as do 1,500 small straw bales, 90 large straw bales, 160 tyre columns and 280 pole protectors. Some 1,130 barriers need to be erected to close off side roads that lead on to the course, and 184 'Road Closed' signs must also be put up, along with 64 direction board signs, 37 mile-marker boards and 12 countdown boards to warn of particularly sharp corners. And the signs can't just be left there once in place – they must be managed and maintained throughout race fortnight.*

The road surface itself has to be inspected, and repairs made where necessary, and the section of track at Governor's Dip must be swept and thoroughly cleaned ahead of practice week as it's only used for the TT, not for everyday road traffic. All livestock fencing around the course must be inspected and repaired where necessary. Road bollards, street signs, and even some bus stops, must be removed prior to any racing or practising taking place, and fences must be erected at popular viewing spots like Creg-ny-Baa.

All traffic lights on the course must be switched off and, of course, road-closure orders must be agreed, obtained and executed. Sponsorship boards have to be set up around the course, and scaffolding towers must be built for TV cameras, marshals and race starters. All hedges and verges surrounding the course must be cut before practice begins, 130 stretches of kerb need to be painted black and white (these stretches can be up to two miles long), and 45 white gutter lines and wall markings need to be repainted each year. All white lines on the course must be painted anew, public address systems need to be set up at 16 different locations around the course, 97 portable toilets need to be put in place, and 6 temporary bridges erected to allow people to cross the course between races. A letter detailing relevant changes and alterations must be sent out to every household on the Isle of Man that will be affected by the racing and the associated road closure orders.

Some 374 advertising banners need to be put in place around the TT course, including six on bridges which cross the track. That equates to 1,939 metres – or two miles – of banners. Without this advertising revenue, the TT simply couldn't happen. It takes five staff members ten days to put the banners in place, and they have to work mostly in the evenings when traffic is lighter. It takes another five or six days to take them all down again. Staff also have to be on call 24 hours a day to replace any banners that have been stolen or have accidentally fallen out of place.

TT 'Fan Zones' are a relatively new addition but were necessitated when more and more areas by the side of the course were deemed to be too dangerous for spectators and became restricted areas. Permission must be gained from landowners to set up these TT Fan Zones, and aerial photographs supplied to show landowners the exact position of any temporary grandstands. Safe car parking areas must be established and monitored and ACU (Auto Cycle Union) approval must be obtained for the locations of traffic management signs. Public address systems need to be hired for each Fan Zone location, Wi-Fi areas must be set up (all of which require back-up generators) and public liability insurance must be arranged and paid for. Catering and merchandise-retailing permits need to be allocated and Fan Zone tickets must be designed, printed and distributed. Clean-up crews need to be hired to ensure all Fan Zone areas are kept tidy and safe.

With a course that runs for almost 38 miles, communications systems are vital, and to that end, over 400 state-of-the-art TETRA radio sets must be distributed to ensure everyone involved in the races – marshals, race officials, medical crews, course car crews and timekeepers – can stay in touch. All handsets, batteries, headsets and chargers must be checked and charged where necessary, and TETRA booster sites must be installed in locations where weak signal is a problem. The TT telephone directory must be updated and published anew every year, so everyone involved has everyone else's number. Landline phones are installed at key locations around the course, and these lines all have to be laid and tested. Someone also has to ensure that all the mobile phones handed out to staff have sufficient credit and that the TT grandstand has reliable internet connectivity.

The list of jobs to be completed in the TT grandstand and paddock area is obscenely long – way too long to list here, even in short form. But it includes obtaining road closure orders, erecting fencing, designing and laying out the four main paddock areas, the parc fermé area, and all the trade and retail areas. Then there's the smaller details like obtaining photocopiers, stationery (even the colour of the paper used must be decided upon), and vending machines for the race control office and press room. Picnic tables need to be brought in so fans can sit down while enjoying a burger and a beer, and snacks and soft drinks have to be ordered in so busy race officials can also eat on the job.

Then there are things like the maintenance of the lift in the race tower and the issuing of parking passes. Skips, wheelie bins, recycling bins and waste management systems have to be arranged, laundry and shower services must be provided for competitors and teams, plumbing and electrical support must be on hand, and competitor information packs made up and distributed. Flags of all competing nationalities must be obtained and erected at the TT grandstand, and cushions for grandstand seats cleaned and positioned. The timekeepers' hut needs to be set up, as does the fence on the competitors' return road to the paddock. Various warning lights and pit-lane gates must be installed, a fuel storage permit needs to be obtained, and all regulation fuel fillers cleaned, serviced, installed and then drained after each race. Signage has to be designed and set up on the rostrum, and fire-fighting equipment is also ordered in for safety purposes. The start-line speed-trap display must be installed and checked, as does each light which comes on when a rider reaches Cronk-ny-Mona towards the end of the lap (a long-standing TT tradition which alerts teams to the imminent arrival of their rider). There are 263 separate job details for the grandstand area alone, each of which must be carried out to ensure the smooth running of the TT.

Timing is everything in a race against the clock, and the nine TT timekeepers and five IT personnel need more than just a stopwatch to keep on top of the job. To that end, electronic transponders are fitted to every bike, and the corresponding software needs to be installed in the timekeepers' hut and in the press office. Then there's the usual ordering of enough paper, printer ink and other consumables to last the fortnight. The timekeepers need up to forty laptops and ten printers to do their jobs properly. To aid communication between all parties, thirty-two two-way radio sets are provided.

It's not just the grandstand and the TT course itself that require attention. With 40,000 fans and 10,000 motorcycles arriving on the Isle of Man for race week, almost every aspect of life on the island is impacted by the TT. The Victorian horse tram system, which operates on Douglas Promenade, must be stopped at peak traffic times, bus routes need to be altered when the TT Mountain Course is closed, and temporary one-way systems and speed restrictions need to be implemented. This all requires extra signage, traffic lights and traffic orders, as well as public information messages in the local press (as well as on the radio, online and on flyers which are distributed by hand) to warn of disruptions. The location of all police officers and vehicles needs to be reviewed each year, and roads policing orders obtained for another thirteen related events (such as live bands and stunt shows) as well as for the TT races themselves. There must also be serious incident plans in place to provide cover for a major emergency situation.

The TT simply could not happen without the army of

volunteer marshals who give up so much of their time each year to ensure the races go ahead in as safe a manner as possible. A minimum of 530 marshals must be in place before any practice session or race can take place, and many, many more need to be available to take shifts. They all need to be recruited and trained, then signed on and provided with marshals' packs, programmes and warrant cards. Some 1,170 litres of bottled water are handed out to marshals for each race, and flags need to be provided at all 110 marshalling locations around the course, as do shovels, brushes and large stocks of coconut dust to soak up oil spills. For the TT Zero race (for battery-powered bikes), some 350 pairs of electrical insulating gloves need to be distributed amongst the marshals, to prevent them from receiving shocks when handling these machines. There are 47 marshals' storage boxes placed around the course as well as 36 scaffolds, 15 permanent shelters, 36 temporary shelters and 97 portable toilets.

There are twenty-four technical officials and five administrative staff on duty during every practice session and race to ensure every racing motorcycle is safe and fit for purpose. During a typical TT meeting, these officials will carry out over 2,000 machine checks, with each official putting in at least 100 hours of service over TT fortnight.

Around twenty vehicles are needed to ensure the smooth running of the TT – both cars and bikes – and all need to be taxed and insured. The drivers and riders of these vehicles need to be issued with fuel cards and have their licences checked for validity. Eight bikes are needed for the travelling marshals and six official course cars are required (they do more than 100 laps between them over TT fortnight) as well as six other vehicles for various logistical functions. Parking discs need to be obtained for all vehicles and those vehicles all need to be appropriately painted and marked up with logos. Engineers also need to fit speed-monitoring equipment, radios and flashing lights to all vehicles, and a contract must be agreed with a local company to provide a recovery service.

The TT organisers also need to liaise with the Red Cross, the St John Ambulance service, the Department of Health and the Civil Aviation Authority to ensure they have enough doctors and paramedics to cover the course, and have all flight permissions and restricted-airspace orders for the AirMed cover. Typically, there will be around twenty doctors and thirty-five paramedics positioned around the course, as well as a further forty Emergency Medical Technicians or First Aiders from the Hogg Motorsport Association, St John Ambulance and Red Cross. Eight land ambulances and two rescue helicopter ambulances need to be on standby before any bikes are allowed out on to the course. The Rob Vine Fund (set up in Vine's honour after he lost his life at the 1985 TT) provides £200,000 worth of medical equipment and has to raise an additional £20,000 each year just to keep it up to date. The medical staff attend an average of forty incidents per year.

The race organisers need to debate, and settle on, technical regulations for the event, and draw up the schedules for practice and race week, making sure they also have contingency plans for bad weather and other delays.

Event insurance must be arranged, and permission to run the event must also be obtained. Entry forms must be drawn up for competitors and all race licences must be verified. Help with travel and accommodation must be afforded to riders, and familiarisation trips need to be arranged for newcomers. New riders must be constantly recruited for future years too.

Contract and royalty deals need to be drawn up for retailers of official TT clothing, and the event must be promoted at the Motorcycle Live! show at the NEC in Birmingham, the Stafford Classic Show and other events on the British mainland throughout the year.

The famous TT silverware must all be prepared before the garlanding ceremonies can take place. That means any repairs must be carried out, all trophies must be polished, new or replacement trophies must be designed, ordered and made – and the more valuable pieces must be accompanied by a security guard at all times. Silver and bronze replicas and finishers' medals must be made and engraved ahead of the races, and caps, sashes and laurel wreaths must be specially made for the top three finishers in each race. Champagne must also be bought in, and a suitable dignitary recruited to present all the spoils. In recent years, this honour has fallen to some of the greatest names in motorcycling, including Giacomo Agostini and Valentino Rossi. A venue has to be chosen for the two prize-presentation evenings (usually the Villa Marina in Douglas) and suitably prepared to host an evening with thousands of guests and riders. The evening must be planned and rehearsed so it all goes off without a hitch. Prize money must also be decided upon, raised, correctly allocated and presented to the riders. And special awards and trophies – like the 'Spirit of the TT' Award – must also be awarded to the chosen recipients.

Only once all these tasks – and innumerably more besides – have been accomplished can the TT begin. Organising the TT is as much a race against time as the races themselves.

* * *

Race teams at the TT face huge logistical challenges too. Most other racing takes place over a weekend, with practice on the Friday and Saturday, and racing on the Sunday. Three days, at most. The TT requires a much greater commitment from teams, who can often be on the Isle of Man for almost three weeks. 'The logistics aren't easy, due to the location, but I'd say the time frame involved in the TT puts the most strain on us because we're there for the best part of 18 days,' says TAS team manager Philip Neill. 'We've all discussed shortening the event, but there are obviously very clear arguments as to why it needs to be held over such a long period. In terms of the racing, the big challenge is building a bike that's going to be fast enough and agile enough to be able to do the lap times, but also robust enough to take the unique rigours of the TT Mountain Course.'

Former Honda Britain team boss Neil Tuxworth agrees that the time factor is a serious issue. 'There are a lot of challenges at the TT, but I'd say it's just the sheer amount of time that it takes,' he says. 'To have a sporting event that goes on for two weeks, in this day and age, is really unusual. I mean, MotoGP lasts about four or five days (this includes the time it takes for teams to set up and, later, dismantle their garages), as does World Superbikes and British Superbikes. I feel the event's too long for staff and teams and riders. I've always believed it would be possible to cut it down to around ten days, which would make a big difference. It's not just two weeks – it's more like 17 days for the teams.'

Team owner Clive Padgett speaks of a much longer timescale. When asked what the biggest challenge of the TT is for him, he answers, 'The 364 days leading up to it after the Senior TT has finished! I'm not kidding. It's not something you can just think about the week before – I'm constantly thinking about it, so it's an evolving project, year on year. You're thinking about how to make the bikes faster and more reliable, how we can improve the lap times, how we can get more exposure for our sponsors, how we can make things more comfortable for the team – even what sailings we book the riders on, so they arrive fresh instead of travelling through the night.'

Like several TT teams, Pete Extance's Bournemouth Kawasaki squad also competes in the British Superbike Championship. But, as he explains, the bikes must be prepared very differently for the two disciplines. 'The two biggest challenges are the logistics of the event and the preparation of the bikes,' he says. 'Because we also compete in the British Superbike Championship, it's hard to fit in two weeks on the Isle of Man. From a technical point of view, given the dangers of the TT, we need to make sure the bikes are absolutely 100 per cent perfect, and that's very tough on our technicians. The bikes are checked and checked and checked again; a lot more parts are lock-wired than would be the case in BSB, and we only use brand new parts to make sure everything is in perfect condition. For example, we don't even use our BSB wheels, we take new ones.'

Building a bike that can cope with the extreme rigours of the TT is a challenge. With the exception of the sidecars and the battery-powered TT Zero bikes, all TT race bikes start life as ordinary production, road-going machines that anyone can buy. A Superbike typically costs around £20,000 in road-going trim, but top teams will spend the same amount again by replacing components with superior aftermarket parts. Better suspension units, better exhaust systems, lightweight carbon-fibre racing bodywork, lighter wheels, better braking systems . . . the list is a long one. And, because the TT provides such a unique challenge, due to the bumpy nature of the course and the sustained high speeds, building a bike that is fast enough to win races, but also robust enough to last race distances, is an art in itself.

It's an art that TAS boss Philip Neill knows a lot about. 'Building a TT bike has traditionally been about backing everything off to ensure reliability, but I think that may be starting to change now,' he says. 'I think that with the bikes we were building up to 2005, and maybe even later, there was an emphasis on keeping them as simple as possible. It wasn't even a case of backing them off, it was more a case of not even starting out with a full-blown Superbike. I still wouldn't go as far as to say that you need a full British Superbike-spec or World Superbike-spec machine for the TT, but a lot of those specifications and electronic aids are becoming more relevant and they're appearing more and more on TT bikes now.'

In 2006, the TAS team decided to run a full British Superbike-spec Suzuki GSX-R1000 at the TT, but it proved to be too fragile and broke down. 'The bike broke down because the clutch turned out to be too weak for the type of starts required on the high gearing that you need to run at the TT,' Neill explains. 'We moved on to new bikes the following year and probably went a step further in simplifying them than we perhaps should have done. But now we're edging back towards full-blown Superbike spec again. It's been a case of trial and error, but there are definitely specification upgrades available from the BSB world that I believe can improve performance round the Isle of Man. But the main difference in the bikes is the engines. We build a slightly different spec engine for the TT that has different power characteristics and heavier and more robust internals to increase reliability.'

Electronic rider aids now play a massive part in MotoGP (the motorcycling equivalent of Formula 1) but that level of technology has not yet reached the TT paddock, and may never do, given the very different nature of road racing and MotoGP – not to mention the astronomical costs involved. Even so, electronics are slowly finding their way on to TT machines. 'I can't see it going as far as MotoGP, because those systems are so complex, and the sheer cost would be a restriction,' Neill says. 'Not only the cost of the equipment, but also the amount of people that are required to operate it. But we're definitely going in that direction. Electronics allow you to make finer increments of change, and the more complex the electronics, the finer those increments are. But the downside is that it gives you more to change and more potential to make the wrong moves as well.'

So many aspects of the TT course influence how the bikes have to be set up. Its excessive bumpiness is one of them. 'We remove all the electronic sensors that aren't necessary because if one sensor fails – like a front wheel speed sensor – it can stop the motorbike completely; it just goes into shutdown mode,' Neill says. 'You have to refine things, so there are fewer things to go wrong over the bumps of the TT course.'

The sheer length of the TT course also presents unique challenges when it comes to setting up a motorcycle. Suspension settings that work perfectly well over the bumpier parts of the course will not work so well over smoother sections like the Mountain, so set-up is always a compromise at the TT. 'It's hugely difficult,' Neill admits. 'That's part of the reason why we're trying to, as safely as possible, introduce more complex electronics on the bikes. More than anything, they'll give us the ability to fine-tune the bike and to identify exactly where the rider is on the track when he's having a problem.'

While a rider can easily remember exactly how his bike is behaving at any given corner on a short circuit, that's not always possible on a course that's almost over 37 miles long, and this also makes set-up more of a challenge. 'If you try and speak to a rider after a 37-mile lap and ask if the engine was revving too highly at a certain point, or what gear he was in at a certain corner, and what percentage of throttle he was holding, it's asking the impossible to remember all that over such a long lap,' Neill explains. 'That's the most difficult thing about the TT. As teams, we all have this ongoing discussion of whether we have enough practice time, but you know what? You've got too much practice time if the bike is spot on from the beginning, and you've never got enough if you can't find the right setting on the bike!'

From a rider's perspective, there are certain things that he or she needs from a bike at the TT before they can even think about posting really fast lap times. 'Firstly, you need reliability,' Josh Brookes says. 'More generally, you need stability and user-friendly power. It's one thing to have power, but you need to be able to use it in a controlled way. The riding style at the TT has to be very linear – you don't brake as hard as you do on short circuits, and you don't get on the gas as hard either. You want a nice, smooth spread of power throughout the rev range at the TT, rather than an aggressive power delivery.'

The overriding problem in setting up a TT bike is that the course is so long that the very nature of it changes greatly over its 37.73 miles; from very tight, twisty and bumpy sections to very fast, smooth, open sections. Building a bike that excels at both is simply not possible, so compromise is always key. 'Just after Ginger Hall it's very bumpy, and very difficult for the rider to change direction on a big Superbike,' Philip Neill says. 'I remember in 2002, David Jefferies would actually bend the retaining bolts for the footrests during every session, because he was putting so much force through them to get the bike to change direction. On that section of the course, you actually want less horsepower, because the Superbike is just so difficult to manhandle. But after the Gooseneck, right over the Mountain to Brandish, you're looking for as much horsepower as you can get, because it's like an ultra-fast short circuit.'

In other words, building a perfect TT bike is not, and never will be, possible. It will always be a compromise. But to have the best chance of taking a win at the TT, Philip Neill lists the three most important elements without hesitation. 'Reliability, stability and am I allowed to say the rider? In all honesty, and in that order of importance, that's what it takes to win a TT.'

* All statistics in this chapter were provided ahead of the 2014 TT.

CHAPTER 7

Going the Distance

'You can't train to conquer the TT course – you just have to go up that road balls out!'
Michael Dunlop

'When you hit the bottom of Bray Hill at 180mph, it's not going to make any difference if you've been down the gym,' John McGuinness says. 'The TT is a mind game, and you've got to be strong in the head.'

In MotoGP, World Superbikes and British Superbikes, every rider trains and eats like an Olympian athlete. They are all extremely lean and ultra-fit, they all follow the strictest diets and train almost every day of the year. They need to be in perfect shape, not only to avoid fatigue in long races – often in subtropical countries with hideous heat and humidity, where riders have been known to vomit in their helmets mid-race – but to recover faster from the inevitable injuries they're going to suffer. Their body fat ratios are in single figures (elite male athletes typically have body fat percentages between 6 and 13 per cent; by way of comparison, Moto3 rider Carlos Tatay runs at 5 per cent body fat).

Weight is crucial in top-flight racing, and motorcycle manufacturers go to extreme lengths to make their motorcycles as light as the rules allow; they use hugely expensive and exotic components like titanium and carbon fibre to reduce weight, and even experiment with different paints to assess which is lightest to use on the bodywork of their machines – a saving of mere grams. Having spent untold millions to design and keep their machines as light as possible, MotoGP manufacturers are not going to then undo all their efforts by signing an overweight rider.

This obsession with fitness and diet does not yet prevail at the TT, where the overall weight of machine and rider is not so critical. While some riders do train hard and follow strict diets, more often than not TT racers couldn't care less. 'I just eat what I eat – nip out for a Chinese or whatever,' McGuinness says. 'Your body needs some shit going through it at times – it can't always be having good stuff or it will have no defence against anything. You need to get a bit of crap food and fat into you!'

The inside of a gym is still an alien environment to many TT riders, including Michael Dunlop. 'I don't train – I hate the gym,' he happily admits. 'I do a bit of boxing and motocross, but I wasn't built for the gym. I don't do anything different for the TT, no matter what the rest of the boys think. Okay, I am a big lad, but it stands me in good stead at the TT because I feel comfortable after six laps. To tell you the truth, I feel better at the end of a race. The thing is, you might be able to train your body, but you can't train your brain for the TT – you can't train it to conquer the TT course. You just have to let the good times roll and go up that road balls out. Just ride it.'

Michael Dunlop's attitude towards fitness sounds very much like his uncle Joey's. Joey Dunlop is still the most successful TT racer of all time, but his lax attitude when it came to training was renowned. Former managing director of Aprilia UK, Steve Reynolds, remembers how demoralising this could be for riders who trained hard but still couldn't beat Dunlop. 'I was helping our rider, Ian Newton, at the Ulster Grand Prix one year, and he finished fourth, while Joey blitzed everybody at the head of the field,' he says. 'Most of the riders by then were teetotal and obsessed with the gym, but after the race we saw Joey walking through the paddock with a can of beer in his hand, a fag on the go, and his belly hanging out of his leathers. Ian looked at me and said, "For fuck's sake – why am I even bothering?"'

Although he doesn't train in the formal sense, John McGuinness says being 'bike fit' is far more important at the TT than being athletically fit. By 'bike fit', riders mean they've spent lots of time riding dirt bikes or other motorcycles and exercising the specific muscle groups that are used while riding. It's something that can't be precisely replicated in a gym. 'It's fair to say I'm not the fittest bloke in the world,' he admits. 'If we all had to run round the block, I'd probably come in last, but if it comes down to a last lap race then I'm ready for it. I sometimes think training's more about making yourself look good, it's not about riding a bike. I'm very active as far as being on a bike goes. I'm always out on my motocross or trials bikes, my minibike, my speedway bike or my enduro bike – 200km on an enduro bike is pretty tough going. There's no substitute for being on a bike: the connection between your brain, your right wrist, your arse and the back tyre is where it's at. It's everything.'

McGuinness has another defence for not going to the gym: he believes a happy rider is a fast rider and going to the gym doesn't make him happy. 'It's a weird one,' he says. 'People like Jim Moodie trained so hard, but then Ian Simpson did nothing and he still won races. Steve Hislop wasn't much of a one for training and look what he achieved. When I go to the gym, I feel unhappy – it pisses me off. I know it's something that maybe I should do but, when you're a happy bunny, you ride fast, and going to the gym doesn't make me happy. I'm happier messing around with my kids or playing on my enduro bike.'

A six-lap race of the TT course is about as punishing as a motorcycle race can get. It's 226 miles at speeds of up to 206mph, muscling the bike over bumps and jumps, physically forcing it to change direction through the faster corners, standing on the footrests through the bumpier sections and, all the while maintaining 100 per cent focus and concentration. A six-lap race takes around one and three-quarter hours to complete; that's almost three times as long as a MotoGP race, and yet some of the most successful riders in recent TT history have been overweight and/or out of shape; McGuinness, Michael Dunlop and David Jefferies amongst them. It seems they rely on pure adrenaline and brute force to get them through. 'I'm okay after a race; never too knackered,' McGuinness says. 'When you have a result you're buzzing, and the adrenaline's pumping anyway, so you're not thinking about how tired you are. It does take it out of you, for sure, especially if your bike's not handling properly. A good team, and good bikes, makes your life a lot easier at the TT.'

McGuinness insists his approach is not an attempt to out-psyche his rivals; a way of stating that he doesn't even need to train in order to beat them. 'I mean, I don't walk around with my chest puffed out saying, "I don't need to train,", he continues. 'I'm not trying to be a smart arse, and I'm not particularly proud of the fact that I don't do much. But some people feel the need to train and can get obsessive about it, and I'm just not like that. I'm happy with who I am. I'm probably one of the freshest after a six-lap race, and I haven't really got an answer as to why that is. Maybe I'm just lazy and don't move around on the bike a lot – I've never been an aggressive rider, sliding it around and all that stuff. Maybe some riders just have to work a bit harder than me on the bike.'

Double TT winner Gary Johnson does take his training seriously but concedes that those riders who are slightly overweight are not necessarily at a disadvantage. 'It isn't such a bad thing to be carrying a little extra weight at the TT, because you need those fat reserves to draw on during the race,' he says. 'But you can't just be a fat git all year and then drop your weight for the TT, because your body won't be used to it – you have to bring your weight down slowly.'

For his own part, Johnson puts the work in all year

round. 'With my physical training, I will gradually step it up through January, February and March, and then by April and May I'm out on a pushbike nearly all the time, as well as running and swimming and going down the gym,' he says. 'I do target specific muscle groups in my training in the run-up to the TT, like my legs and my knees, because they take such a battering around the Mountain Course. You're still just riding a motorbike at the TT, but it's for two hours instead of half an hour, as it would be in British Superstock races. I don't want any more muscle though – that's more weight – I just want more strength.'

Having enough strength to fight a 230bhp Superbike around the TT course is important, as the late William Dunlop found out when he first moved up to the big bike class. 'It's not so much about being stronger, more about just being bigger – everything came easier to me at the TT as soon as I built up my size,' he said before his tragic death at the Skerries road race in 2018. 'A lot of the really fast guys at the TT – from David Jefferies to John McGuinness and my brother Michael – are all big lads. I always hear people saying, "Oh, McGuinness is too big," or "Michael's not fit enough," but the facts speak for themselves. Look at the race wins they've got!'

One of the most important reasons for bike racers to be extremely fit is so they can recover from injury faster. But even though he acknowledges this, John McGuinness still can't be persuaded to change his regime. 'The one massive benefit for those who train hard is that, if they have an accident and get injured, then they're going to repair a lot faster than me,' he admits. 'That's the only thing that

I worry about. But they can get obsessive about training and diet – it's like a culture now; people tweeting every time they've been down the gym, as if they're trying to justify their jobs. It's the results that do the talking, not how much training you do. I mean, I wish I had a six-pack and all, but it's what's inside that counts and I'm a well-balanced human being. I've got a great wife, a good relationship with my kids, good mates around me, and it just all works for me.'

Former TT privateer Paul 'Moz' Owen agrees with McGuinness. 'I've always thought the TT is more about your mental attitude rather than physical fitness,' he says. 'I used to work as a lifeguard, and had access to the pool and the gym, so I went to the TT that year totally ripped. I was super-fit, with the six-pack and all, and I was eating so healthy, but come the races I burned myself out because I had no reserves to burn up. You see some lads going for mega-long cycle runs and burning themselves out during practice week, and I just think they'd be better saving their energy for race week, you know?'

William Dunlop also believed in the benefits of not overdoing the training. 'Sometimes, the more training you do, the more damage you do to yourself,' he said. 'And I think I got to a stage where I maybe trained too much and ended up in a worse state than I was before!'

The TT is such a uniquely punishing event that even serious training can't replicate racing around the Mountain Course. 'No matter how much you train, you still get aches and pains during the first night of practice at the TT,' Gary Johnson says. 'I completely blow my knees out every year

– the muscles in my knees get absolutely shot to shit, and
there's no way I can train for that. I need to learn to ride
differently, as I'm overworking some small muscles in my
knees when I'm riding because I'm standing on the pegs for
so long on the bumpy sections of the course. I've not always
had the best-handling bikes, so I've not been able to just
sit on the seat and twist the throttle. I'm usually climbing
out of the seat and getting my body over the front of the
bike, so my knees are like little additional suspension units.
The likes of Michael Dunlop and John McGuinness – who
aren't perhaps as fit as some of the other riders out there –
let their bikes do the work. But if your bike isn't working
properly, then you've got to force it to do what you want
it to do.'

Conor Cummins is another rider who takes his training
seriously and spends the off season building his fitness for
the next TT. 'I really hammer it through the winter – really
make a good go of my training then, when there's no racing
on,' he says. 'Endurance training is really important for the
TT. You need really high endurance levels. I was running a
lot before my big accident in 2010, but I do a lot more cycling
now that I've had to alter my training regime to account
for my injuries. I've had a training programme tailor-made
for me, and it seems to be working well. I cycle two or
three times a week – about 200 miles in total. Swimming's
fantastic too. I did quite a lot of that during my rehab, just
to help me get my injured knee working again. I go to the
gym twice a week, at least, but have been stepping that up
a bit as my injuries get better. I'm convinced that people
like John McGuinness and Michael Dunlop – who say they

don't do any training – must do something. McGuinness is always out on his enduro bike; he's not daft.'

If it's tough even for the bigger men to muscle a Superbike around the TT course, then spare a thought for the women. Jenny Tinmouth is the fastest woman in TT history, with a lap of just under 120mph to her credit, but she's at a huge disadvantage due to her slight build and lack of weight. Her body, though, takes exactly the same kind of battering as the boys. 'I find that the training I do for the short circuits is good for the TT too,' she said before retiring from the sport. 'If anything, I think I find the TT slightly easier than British Superbike races, because you're not quite on the limit – it's more about mental concentration, that's the hardest part. I train whenever I can fit it in, but it's hard when you're working full-time. If I was a full-time professional racer then I'd train all the time but, as it is, I just have to fit it in whatever I can after work, and on weekends when I'm not racing.'

Racing regularly in various classes within the British Superbike Championship helped keep Tinmouth bike fit and meant she didn't find the TT as physically punishing as some riders do. 'I don't get any undue aches and pains after the first night of TT practice because on the short circuits it's so hard – you're on the limit everywhere,' she continues. 'You're braking as hard as possible and the G-forces you're pulling on your arms is incredible. You can't brake as hard as that at the TT because of the nature of the road surface. On the Ginger Hall to Ramsey section, you're standing up on the footrests all the time to give yourself added suspension because it's so bumpy, and a lot of riders really feel that in their legs. But again, you're standing on the pegs in BSB races so much because you're constantly hauling the bike from one side to the other, so I'm used to that. I do get a lot of blisters on my hands at the TT though; that's one thing I do notice.'

In other disciplines of motorcycle racing, good nutrition is considered just as important as hard training. Again, not all TT riders subscribe to this notion. 'My idea of dieting is not going large at McDonald's!' Michael Dunlop says. 'I like stuff like pasta anyway, but I don't bother with energy drinks or any of that stuff. I do have a routine before the start of a TT though – I always take the dog for a walk (Dunlop-speak for going for a pee), and I always drop the kids off at the pool (another euphemism), but apart from that there is no special preparation.'

Once he has performed his pre-race ablutions, Dunlop is good to go, nutrition or no nutrition. His late brother William had a similar cavalier attitude towards diet. 'I just eat whatever I fancy!' he said. 'I'm a McDonald's man at heart. I'll take an energy gel or an energy drink before I go out, but I don't tend to eat much before a race. I'm not a big eater in the morning anyway, so if it's a morning race at the TT I won't have much at all – I'm usually just out of me bed and on to the bike.'

For some TT racers, nerves suppress all appetite: their stomachs are already full of knots at the thought of what lies ahead. 'I tend to drink protein shakes before a race, as it's quite difficult to eat a lot of solid food during race week because you're so nervous,' Gary Johnson confesses. 'You just physically don't feel like eating.'

Older campaigners like Paul Owen grew accustomed to the nerves. Speaking in 2011 when he was still racing at the TT, he said, 'I'm well over being too nervous to eat – those days are long gone, I've been doing this for so long now.'

Conor Cummins feels riders need to get over their nerves to ensure they take on the right foods during race week. 'I usually have a bit of a blow-out with food at the end of the year and enjoy a few drinks here and there,' he says. 'But then that's it – I start getting my mind and body in tune again for the coming season. I've got a good nutritionist who I see regularly, and she's set me out a good programme, so during TT week I just eat normal, healthy food. If it's a morning race I'll have porridge with honey on it, or cereals – all good energy food. Some riders say they can't eat much during race week, but I think you've got to get over that because it will affect your performance. You don't want to be burning out on the second lap – you need to be able to go the distance.'

Gary Johnson also takes his nutrition seriously. 'I stick to a protein-based diet and up my carbohydrate intake for the TT, so I eat lots of rice, pasta, chicken and vegetables,' he says. 'Correct fluid intake is important at the TT too, for fitness and mental strength. Energy gels are a bit of a godsend at times, but the better diet you have, the fewer supplements you require. But I have about three of those gels on the start line before a TT race so I'm carb'd up to the eyeballs!'

In the end, it's each to their own. But the fact remains that the most successful living TT rider, John McGuinness, has achieved all his success without ever subscribing to the modern training approach. 'All this loading up on carbs and listening to pumping music before the start of a race? I don't do any of that. I mean, what are those boys listening to on the grid? Are they trying to learn French or what? I wouldn't want anything blasting in my earhole before the start of a race.'

At the TT, old school still rules.

CHAPTER 8

Ragged Edge

'People have said to me you must be crazy to race round the Isle of Man, but if you were crazy, you wouldn't survive it.'
MICK GRANT

He famously never won a race, but it wasn't for the lack of trying on Guy Martin's part. 'I ride the TT now as hard as the bike will go,' he said before turning his back on the event in 2017. 'There's none of this riding at 80 per cent lark – it's as hard as she'll go. To win now, you've got to be using every inch of the Tarmac, and you've got to be prepared to put your neck on the line – definitely.'

Once riders have learned the TT course to a level where they feel confident enough to actually attack it at full-on racing speeds, the rest comes down to how hard they're prepared to push; how much they're prepared to risk to achieve victory, as they push both themselves and their machines right to the ragged edge – and sometimes beyond.

'I wouldn't say I have bigger balls than anyone else at

the TT,' John McGuinness says when asked how many of his twenty-three wins are down to him taking more risks than others. 'I do see the odd rider at the TT taking big risks though – you see people looking like they're doing 135mph laps, when actually they're just doing 128mph. But it's hard for me to start pointing fingers and pulling them to one side in the paddock, even though I sometimes want to do that. I'd just end up looking like a bit of a tool!'

Veteran racer Ian Lougher started noticing a change in the way riders attacked the TT course as far back as 2007, and it has only become more extreme since then. 'It's great for the TT having all these young, fast guys coming through, but maybe they're pushing a little too hard,' he said at the time. 'I think at the TT you can push up to a point, but then you need to step back that little bit. Some of these guys are pushing to that point and then pushing a bit more. I always keep a little in reserve at the TT; even when I'm really trying there's always a cushion. These days I've probably had to up my game to about 96–97 per cent whereas before 95 per cent was enough to be competitive.'

Unlike every other motorcycle race meeting – which usually has two days of practice – the TT has a full week of practice to allow riders to set up different bikes and to get their brains accustomed to the astonishing speeds they will be travelling at. Most riders enter more than one race at the TT, so they can find themselves setting up a Superbike, a Superstock bike (a lower-specification version of a Superbike), a Supersport bike (600cc) and even a middleweight Supertwin machine. Taking part in five or six races during TT week is not unusual, so riders need more time to prepare the bikes and themselves.

'At the start of practice week, you're just trying to find a set-up and checking out the course,' Conor Cummins explains. 'The road's always slightly different to the year before, with new bits of over-banding and so on. Set-up is always a compromise at the TT; you could spend the whole week just trying to get one bike as you like it. So, it usually won't be until the end of practice week that I start to find a real rhythm and feel comfortable enough to post fast times.'

Racing alone, against the clock, is another element of the TT that makes it unique. 'The TT is totally different to any other racing event,' says double winner turned TV pundit Steve Plater. 'You're racing against the clock for one thing, but mostly you're racing against yourself. It would be far too dangerous to race elbow to elbow at the TT. You don't even want to come across anybody else on the TT course, not because they're unsafe or I'm unsafe, but because it's very easy to get distracted if there's a bike in front of you or behind you. Even the spectators can be a distraction at times, so it's really important to be out on your own at the TT as much as possible. It makes for a much safer environment.'

Plater is clearly speaking in relative terms.

Another factor to be considered is that the course is in a permanent state of flux. 'You can't ever get too comfortable with it because, every year, something different will come along, whether that's the road surface changing, or there's new Tarmac down, or it's got bumpier,' Michael Dunlop says of the continual learning process that the TT involves. 'So, you always have to be aware that you have to take on changes every year. Learning the course just naturally comes with time.'

TT riders never stop learning. It's why speeds increase, year on year, if weather conditions permit. 'It's important to keep a momentum going at the TT,' Cummins said in 2010. 'You've got to keep learning and improving each year from where you left off the year before. Last year I found a load of time which enabled me to get boosted up the running order. I found some better lines and I was just using my head more; just thinking more and not rushing things.'

There comes a point, however, when caution gets thrown to the wind. When asked how hard he would be prepared to ride if he was just five seconds down on the race leader with less than half a lap to go, Cummins' response is chilling. 'I'd ride absolutely balls out to get a win,' he says. 'There's no question about that. I'd ride as hard as I could possibly go.'

That's how much it means. Top racers don't race for money or for the fun of it, they race to win. And they would do almost anything to achieve that.

Phillip McCallen won eleven TT races in the 1990s and was prepared to ride the course harder than most to secure a win. Speaking of his pursuit of the race leader in the 1995 Junior race, McCallen's enthusiastic narrative reveals just how hard TT riders are prepared to push when their backs are against the wall. 'The bike wouldn't rev on the first lap because of dirt in the carburettors,' he says of that race.

'It got better with each lap, and I was still in the hunt, so when it cleared on the fourth lap and revved out to 13,500rpm it felt like I had another cylinder.'

McCallen's reputation as a wild – and sometimes frightening – rider was well earned. 'From that point on I rode that bike so hard – 200 per cent. I was drifting and sliding out of every single corner – doing two-wheeled slides right out to the kerbs. I had it flat on its side in fifth and sixth gear in places, but I still felt I was in control – just because there was a kerb or a hedge there, it didn't put me off. When you "feel" a bike that well, when the tyres are working and the suspension's working, there's just a super harmony between the rider and the machine and you can feel every single thing that's going on. You can take the bike to the edge without going over it. But mistakes can still happen, and when I changed down for the Waterworks, I hit neutral and couldn't get the bike stopped. I tried to bounce it off the kerb to try and stay on, but it didn't happen and I crashed.'

That wasn't the only time McCallen rode out of his skin at the TT. Two years later, he took his Honda RS250 right to the ragged edge and beyond in the Lightweight 250 race. 'I got a sign at Glen Helen that I was 20 seconds down, and I just flipped and rode like someone possessed – so hard it was unbelievable,' he admits. 'I was a silly boy and tried to make all that time up in one section instead of over a full lap. Going through Rhencullen, the bike was right on its side – I was just holding it flat out everywhere. Then I got a sign saying I'd pulled nine seconds back in just a few miles. I really shouldn't have been riding that hard, but I was so mad with myself inside because I was more desperate than anything to win that 250 race.'

Desperation is not a good mindset for a TT rider: it usually leads to disaster, as McCallen discovered to his peril. 'Coming into the first right-hander at Quarry Bends I'd usually knock it back a gear, but I decided to hold it flat out in top, then brake really hard and knock it down two gears for the following left. I held the throttle against the stop and tipped the bike in, flat on its side. Whether it was the camber change on the road or not, I don't know, but I just lost the front. Everything went dead quiet – so quiet that I actually heard the crowd gasp as I slid down the road. When I got up the pain was unbelievable – it was the first time I'd had a proper beating at 150mph. I had friction burns everywhere and gravel all through my legs. I got into a hot bath and my wife scrubbed the gravel out of my legs with a scrubbing brush. I had another race in two days' time, so I just had to get better.'

It sounds crazy, but Mick Grant insists it isn't. 'People have said to me, "You must be crazy to race round the Isle of Man," but if you were crazy, you wouldn't survive it. When I was at my best round there, if I did six laps and was more than two feet offline at any point during those six laps, I'd remember it. That's how accurate you have to be at the very top level.'

That kind of accuracy is not easy to achieve at racing speeds and, with over 300 corners to negotiate, a perfect lap of the TT course is never going to happen, as Conor Cummins explains. 'You're never going to do a perfect lap of the TT,' he says. 'You're constantly thinking, "I could have got on the throttle a bit earlier there," or "I could have turned in a bit sooner there," or maybe you could have held a better line somewhere, so it's never going to be perfect. I couldn't even hazard a guess how many times that happens per lap, so the only answer is to focus as hard as you can for the entire duration of the race. Think two, or even three, corners ahead, and think, "Right, I'm going to be inch-perfect here, no messing about." The TT is the sort of place that, if you're an inch offline somewhere, it can affect you for miles. A lap is all linked together, so if you mess up Ballagarey, that's your run right through Crosby and down past the Highlander all messed up, because you didn't get the speed to help launch on to that fast section.'

But while it's clearly important to concentrate, riders must also be careful not to overthink the dangers of what they're doing, as that would be a danger in and of itself. 'There are quite a few scary corners at the TT,' Cummins admits, with marked understatement. 'The bottom of Barregarrow is quite a ballsy corner, and the bottom of Bray Hill. Conker Fields is another one. It's so fast and you're forced from one side of the road to the other, changing direction and aiming for a "K" painted on a tree (the 'K' stands for 'kerb' and is painted on the tree to warn riders of a potentially dangerous, prominent kerb, but they use it as a visual reference as it allows them to stay on the correct racing line). You've got to have big balls for that. I don't hold my breath or anything as I go through it, I just think as I'm approaching it, "Right, I've got to get this spot on." But you have to be careful; if you think too much about any particular section it's easy to mess it up.'

The TT course isn't for everyone. In 1989 John Reynolds tried his hand at the event for the first, and last, time. Reynolds would go on to become a triple British Superbike champion and was known as one of the toughest and most dogged racers to ever throw a leg over a motorcycle, but he discovered the TT wasn't for him when Steve Hislop came past at mind-blowing speed during practice. 'I entered Barregarrow, which is a very fast downhill section where the bike's suspension bottoms out and, as far as I was concerned, I was going flat out, until Stevie came past me like I was standing still. Sparks flew off his bike as the suspension bottomed out, and he shot off into the distance towards Kirk Michael, with the bike shaking its head all over the place. I thought there and then that if that's what you have to do to win a TT, then it's not for me.'

Reynolds never returned.

Most riders insist that watching the TT is far scarier than riding it. When Ian Hutchinson was without a Superstock ride in 2014, he took the opportunity to watch the race at the frighteningly fast bottom of Barregarrow section – and immediately wished he hadn't. 'When the first bike came past me, I thought, "Fuck me!" It looked so bad I immediately thought, "I don't think I can do that again." But the next year I went out and won the Superstock race! It's probably not a good idea for a TT racer to watch a race. It looks so much worse from the side of the track than it feels when you're on the bike. Every time I go through Barregarrow now, I picture what it looks like from the outside.'

While sitting out the 2018 TT due to injury, John

McGuinness was also shocked when he watched the action from trackside. 'It's getting ridiculous!' he says, only half joking. 'Most years I'm on the bike, but it was amazing to see the commitment from the top men from trackside. I watched at Union Mills, Bray Hill, Gorse Lea and Cronk-y-Voddy, and the riders clearly have nothing left in reserve now. All these people saying TT riders only ride at 90 per cent is bullshit – it's full-bore the whole way round the lap. It's far worse watching than racing. When you're watching, it just doesn't look physically possible, even though I've done it and been in the hot seat so many times. I watched with the marshals at Gorse Lea, and it was just kerb-to-apex, using absolutely every bit of the road, with the bikes completely flat out and laying massive black lines of rubber down. Some of the stuff I saw just blew me away.'

Like all top TT racers, Ron Haslam also struggled to back off his pace if a win was even a remote possibility. When their visors snap shut, riders become racers, and the will to win overrides almost every other instinct – even the instinct for self-preservation. 'You had to go to the TT with a certain attitude,' Haslam says. 'I used to go to enjoy myself and, if I could win a race, then that was a bonus. I never used to think, "I'm going to the Isle of Man to win." But it's very hard to back off once you get close to the leaders' times, because every racer has a natural desire to win, so sometimes you can't help yourself. If you can discipline yourself not to take too many risks, then you can really enjoy racing on the island. But in the later years with Honda, I went to win. It wasn't Honda putting pressure on me – it's just that I went to win. I put pressure on myself. Because I'd won it before, I expected to do it again, and that took some of the fun out of it because it got serious.'

Like Conor Cummins and every other competitor, Dean Harrison believes that no rider can be inch-perfect for almost 38 miles at racing speeds. 'I don't think there's such a thing as a perfect lap of the TT course – you can only try to get as close as possible,' he says. 'I can't actually remember a lap when I crossed the line and thought, "Yeah, that was a blinder of a lap." But it's hard to tell. Sometimes, when you think you've gone slow, you've actually gone fast, and other times when you've gone out and tried your bollocks off, you go slow!'

This is another paradox of the TT: the harder you try, the slower you go. The really fast laps come when riders feel they're not riding particularly hard. Ian Simpson was the first man to lap the course at an average speed of 120mph on a Supersport 600 machine. 'It feels easy when you're at your best, the bike's handling is good and the tyres are working well,' he says. 'That was a nice hot day, and I was sliding the bike all over the place but felt totally in control. It's when you're struggling that it feels too fast – when there's something wrong with the bike you can feel like you're going really fast, when you're actually not.'

At the Centennial TT in 2007, John McGuinness made history by becoming the first man to lap the course at an average speed of 130mph. 'It felt like a pretty fast lap,' he says. 'I was hitting all my apexes and stuff. On a Superbike, at that time, it was probably as close to a perfect lap as you could get. It certainly wasn't a million miles away.

I didn't make any mistakes, but I could probably have nicked a couple of tenths here and there on the brakes. I think I got held up slightly coming into the pits, and that maybe cost me a couple of seconds. It wasn't a flying lap, as I had to slow down to come into the pits. If it had been a flying lap, I would probably have done a 130mph-plus lap.'

Holding the outright lap record at the TT is a real badge of honour and breaking new barriers in terms of average speeds adds to the kudos. Bob McIntyre was the first man to lap at 100mph in 1957, John Williams lapped at 110mph in 1976, Steve Hislop raised the bar to 120mph in 1989 and, eighteen years later, McGuinness pushed through the 130mph barrier. His achievement was not lost on the knowledgeable TT fans who eagerly lined the course that day. 'I knew that something special had happened when I came in for my first pit stop at the end of lap two, because I'd never heard a cheer like it,' McGuinness says. 'I couldn't really hear the commentary; all I could hear was the massive cheer that followed. The team didn't tell me I had done a 130mph lap; they were too busy changing the rear wheel, telling me my position in the race, and cleaning my screen and stuff. Lap times are not important information in the pits. It wouldn't have made any difference to my race if they'd said I'd done a 135mph lap. All that matters is the information as to where you are in the race, how far you are ahead, and who's behind you. It's so manic in the pits that there's no time for unnecessary information.'

McGuinness rejoined the race, still ignorant of his achievement, though suspecting something out of the ordinary had happened. 'When I set off again and got to Quarterbridge, there was another massive cheer, and it was the same at Braddan Bridge. I could hear it even over the noise of the engine – it was really nice to hear. Then I got a pit board at Ballacraine, just saying "130", and that was the first confirmation I had. It was a distraction for a split second, because I thought, "Oh, that's pretty interesting. That's good, that is," but I was thinking more about getting the win; that was more important. Once you've secured the win you can start thinking about the implications of setting a 130mph lap.'

The implications were that, in 100 years of TT racing, John McGuinness had lapped the famous 37.73-mile course faster than any man before him and had become the first to break through the significant 130mph barrier. His place in the record books was assured. 'I'm extremely proud of being the first person to do 130,' he says. 'It's absolutely awesome when you think of the history of the TT, and the famous names that have upped the outright lap record by 10mph in the past; Steve Hislop, John Williams, Bob McIntyre. Mind you, all I got for doing it was a pat on the back, which was a bit disappointing really. I would have thought I'd have got a nice little envelope under the table from the Isle of Man government for all the publicity!'

Holding the outright lap record clearly meant a lot to McGuinness, so, when Australia's Cameron Donald set an even faster lap of 131.45mph in 2009 (although it occurred during practice week and official lap records must happen in a race), McGuinness was not happy. 'I thought, "Fuck,

that was a strong lap," and, yes, it did rattle me a little bit,'
he admits. 'I'd held the outright lap record at the TT since
2004 and, all of a sudden, Jeez, it was gone, and I wanted
it back. Not for nasty reasons – Cameron's a good guy, so
I didn't think, "The bastard!" I just wanted it back for my
own pride. Don't get me wrong, I wanted it back.'

He did get it back, with a lap of 131.57mph in the 2009
Senior TT before breaking down and retiring from the race.

Yet, while being the outright lap record holder is a
badge of honour that commands a lot of respect in any
racing paddock, riders would still far rather have a win,
as McGuinness testifies. 'Fastest laps are great, but no one
remembers them,' he says. 'And they're always going to get
broken, whereas wins are in the record books forever. And
there's no financial benefit to doing fastest laps either.'

While that may be true for the person who first laps at
127mph or 128mph, major milestone laps like being the
first man to break the 130mph barrier are remembered,
and will always stand, no matter how much faster other
riders go in the future. Almost every TT fan knows who
set the first 100mph lap of the course, but not the first
102mph lap.

The difference between a 125mph lap and a 130mph
lap isn't noticeable to the naked eye and, usually, it's not
particularly noticeable to the riders either. After he himself
broke through the 130mph barrier for the first time, Conor
Cummins said, 'I wasn't trying to do a 130mph lap, it
just came to me, because I was in a good rhythm. It just
happened. A 130mph lap doesn't really feel any different
to a 125mph lap – maybe a little smoother, but that's all.

You certainly don't feel like you're physically travelling any faster.'

It's very often the case that the fastest laps feel relatively slow, simply because to go extremely fast, a machine has to be very well set up, and the rider has to be in a smooth, flowing rhythm, and both factors give the impression that the lap is steady, rather than blindingly fast. 'You need to set a pace at the TT that you're comfortable with, because the harder you try, the more dangerous and slow you become,' Steve Plater says. 'A good example of that was John McGuinness in the 2008 Senior. After Cameron Donald broke down, he slackened off, and said he rode like an old granny for the last lap, just to bring the bike home. He was gobsmacked when he learned it was the fastest lap of the entire fortnight!'

Former outright lap record holder, Bruce Anstey, has experienced a similar feeling. 'The TT course is a funny place because, if you try too hard, then you end up going slower,' he says. 'It's all about getting into a nice, smooth rhythm – that's when you end up going faster. The key to going fast round there is to relax and get things flowing. There's no lap timer on the dashboard of the bike, so you don't actually know what your exact lap time is, but you can feel when you're doing a decent lap. You don't get any indication from signalling boards either, you just know because you've had a good run through every section and not been held up anywhere by slower riders. Slower riders can cost you quite a bit of time – it could be anything from half a second to four seconds, just depending on where you come across them.'

While riders themselves are constantly improving and learning from others, the steady increase in lap speeds at the TT is also down to improvements in technology. 'The difference between a 127mph lap and a 130mph lap is mostly down to the bikes improving in recent years,' McGuinness admits. 'When I was doing 127mph laps, the bikes had about 180bhp, and now they've got over 200bhp, so they're accelerating that bit harder, and probably going down the straights that bit faster. The tyres are better, parts of the circuit are better, but maybe we're riding them harder too because the competition's so much stronger now.'

The bikes are getting insanely fast; so fast, in fact, that they're seemingly changing the very nature of the course. 'The bikes are so fast now that places that used to be straights – like the Mountain Mile – are not straights any more,' Cummins says. 'Every little kink turns into a corner at the speeds we're doing, so you have to be 100 per cent focused all the time now; you don't get a breather along the straights any more.'

Incredibly, some of the top riders are now sliding both wheels on certain sections of the TT course. This is commonplace in MotoGP, where there's plenty of room for error, but it's a riding style that's now creeping in at the TT. In 2018, photographer Louis Porter captured an image of Peter Hickman sliding both wheels of his BMW S1000RR on the exit to Kate's Cottage, while heading straight for a grass banking. 'You're doing it a lot, but it depends on the kind of corner,' Hickman explains. 'We're doing it at Conker Trees, which is a lot faster and a lot more dangerous than Kate's Cottage. But there was so much rubber down because of the great weather we'd had, so there was more grip than usual, and it was more predictable, so it allowed us to ride like that.'

While riders are constantly trying to find ways of posting faster lap times, there is no firm agreement on the best places to do that. Ron Haslam favoured the slower sections of the course. 'If you need to make up time, you push harder at the places where it's safe to get it wrong – like at Parliament Square in Ramsey – because if you try to make up time on the brakes and overdo it, you can just run straight on.'

Rob McElnea took the very opposite approach. 'I'd make up time on the fast, open sections, and take things a bit steadier through the trickier parts.'

For Michael Dunlop's bullish style, attacking is the best way to improve lap speeds. 'You just ride a bit harder!' he says. 'You learn stuff all the time because you're always riding harder and harder, and getting faster and faster, and picking up bits and pieces. You're always pushing and always coming across different braking markers, different apexes, different lines, trying to make that next step. It's hard to pinpoint just one thing that makes you faster, it's just lots of little bits coming together.'

The ever-increasing speeds at the TT begs the question of whether there really is a limit to how fast human brains can process information. In the first TT in 1907, the winner was lapping at around 40mph, whereas the current fastest men are lapping at around 135mph. How much faster can it possibly get? 'There's a limit to everything, but I don't know where it is at the TT, as far as lap times go,' Dean Harrison says. 'You have good years and bad years, fast years and slow years, and it's all to do with track conditions that constantly change – the track surface changes, the weather changes. I certainly feel that my brain could process faster speeds, no problem.'

As technology improves, riders improve and competition increases, the end result will be even higher speeds and faster laps. The TT is only going to get faster and faster, and the ragged edge will become ever more ragged, as riders do whatever it takes to win the world's greatest road race.

CHAPTER 9

World Championship

'We knew that we might die – but we just had to race.'
GIACOMO AGOSTINI

After a shaky start in 1947, the TT regained some post-war momentum the following year and, by 1949, it took on a whole new level of importance. The Fédération Internationale de Motocyclisme – the governing body of international motorcycle racing – had finally decided to create a Grand Prix world championship, and the Isle of Man TT was to be the very first round. From 1949 until 1976, the TT would count as the British round of the world championship. For twenty-seven years, it was effectively the British Grand Prix and, during these years, it was seen as the most important motorcycle race meeting on the planet, bar none. These were the glory years for the TT.

Although the classes have now changed, the world championship continues to this day, now under the moniker of MotoGP. From 1949 until 2002, the premier Grand

Prix championship was the 500cc class (now replaced by MotoGP's 1000cc four-stroke prototypes) and the first 500cc world champion was Les Graham. Astonishingly, he remains the only premier-class world champion to have been killed while racing a motorcycle, having lost his life in the 1953 Senior TT.

Geoff Duke rode through the debris. 'I realised that someone had crashed there, and it was obviously serious, but I didn't know it was Les, and I didn't know he had been killed until after the race. It may seem harsh but, when you're racing, you're busy thinking about what you're doing yourself. You only have time to be sad after the race. I suppose, rather stupidly, we all just think, "It'll never happen to me."'

Graham was one of four riders to die at the TT that year, but his tragic death did not deter his son from taking up racing. Stuart Graham won the 50cc TT in 1967 in honour of his late father.

The issue of women racing on the Isle of Man had been a thorny topic for many years and, in the male-chauvinistic 1950s, there were few, other than women themselves, who supported the idea. Female racers had tried to gain entries to the 1947 TT only to be refused and Laurie Cade (writing of the matter in his 1957 book *TT Thrills*) summed up the typical male viewpoint of the time when he said, 'One or two girl riders, who had done well in trials and other competitions, sought the right to race. Wisely they were turned down by the Auto Cycle Union. TT racing is definitely a he-man's game, and I tremble to think what would have been said of the promoters had they permitted the fair sex to ride and one of them had met with disaster.'

In 1954, a woman did compete in the TT, and it may have been down to a simple typo in the race regulations which eventually allowed Switzerland's Inge Stoll-Laforge to become the TT's first ever female competitor, as passenger to Jacques Drion in the sidecar race. The regulations for solo entrants at the TT stipulated that they had to be 'Male persons between eighteen and fifty-five years of age' but the rules for sidecar passengers only stated that they had to be 'persons' over eighteen years of age. Whether this wording was intended to allow for female passengers, or whether it was simply an oversight, may never be known, but the result was that Inge Stoll-Laforge – who was already an experienced passenger in Continental races – became the first woman to compete in a TT. She finished in a highly creditable fifth place, but sadly lost her life in a race in Czechoslovakia three years later.

A major milestone was reached in 1957 as the TT celebrated its fiftieth anniversary, when Bob McIntyre became the first man to lap the course at an average speed of 100mph. He repeated the feat three times in the race but had some challenging moments too. Pictures of him post-race show a gash on his forehead, the cause of which could have been disastrous. 'A stone hit me, thrown up by the wheels of another rider I was about to lap,' McIntyre explained after the race. 'It was probably no bigger than a pea, but at 100mph it felt like a brick. It caught me between my goggles and my crash helmet and cut my left temple. I felt dazed and sick, it brought tears to my eyes, and I felt blood running. But fortunately, the rush of cold air coagulated the blood above my goggles.'

Two years later, John Surtees would discover yet another hazard of TT racing: the weather. Even in June, the Isle of Man can have an unpredictable climate, as Surtees found to his cost. At the end of the 1959 Senior race, he was frozen so stiff that he had to be lifted off his bike. His mechanics feverishly rubbed at his hands in an attempt to restore circulation. 'The 1959 Senior TT was probably the worst conditions I ever rode in,' Surtees said. 'You didn't only have the rain, but also sleet, which was as big as marbles. It actually damaged the fairing on the bike – took the paint off. I wasn't able to use my fingers; I could only keep them clasped together and pull them in, en masse, to operate the clutch and brake levers. All I had on was my normal race leathers. There were no one-piece under-suits like today – I just wore my vest and pants underneath! I never thought about giving up though. I just struggled on and hoped the others weren't doing any better and were finding it just as difficult.'

Surtees, though barely able to operate the controls of his MV Agusta, clung on grimly and won the race. His efforts impressed everyone, and none more so than the members of a team making its debut at the TT that year – Honda. So impressed were the Japanese team members, they presented Surtees with a Samurai helmet to honour his courage. Proud as they are of their warrior heritage, the Japanese do not bestow such honours lightly but, in their eyes, as in the eyes of so many others that day, John Surtees had proved himself a true fighter, and the very epitome of a TT racer.

Two years later, the Honda team would win its first TT with a young rider called Mike Hailwood. The firm would, in fact, win two TT races in 1961 (Lightweight 125 and Lightweight 250) and it hasn't stopped since. Honda now has more TT wins (191) than any other manufacturer and continues to add to its tally.

Mike Hailwood also won the 1961 Senior race on a Norton, making him the first rider ever to record a treble. At a time when there were only four races on the schedule (there are now eight, including both sidecar races), it was a true measure of greatness.

The first woman to ever ride in a solo TT race lined up on the grid for the inaugural 50cc race in 1962. Beryl Swain had taken advantage of the FIM's new rules, which finally allowed women to compete, but there were still many against the idea and, even after she managed to finish twenty-second out of twenty-five finishers, the governing body reversed its decision and women were once again banned from riding at the TT.

Few motorcycle racers have had tougher upbringings than London-born Rhodesian Jim Redman, who won his first TT in 1963. He survived the Blitz only to be devastated when his father committed suicide by laying his head on a railway track and waiting for a train. Just weeks afterwards, when Jim was still only seventeen, his mother died from a cerebral haemorrhage (although Jim claims it was from the shock of discovering the full details of her husband's suicide in the newspaper), leaving Jim as the breadwinner for his three siblings. When the army then demanded Redman carry out National Service – which would have meant his younger brother and sister being sent to an orphanage – Redman refused and emigrated to Rhodesia, where he worked his heart out to make enough money to be able to send for his brother and sisters to join him. When Redman transferred this kind of resolve and determination to the sport of motorcycle racing, it was little wonder he became a six-time world champion.

But Redman's racing career almost ended before it had properly begun. When his great friend and Honda team-mate, Tom Phillis, was killed in the 1962 TT, Redman seriously considered quitting the sport but, after much thought and encouragement from friends, he decided to continue and, in 1963, everything came together and the 'Bulawayo Bandit' not only won two TTs, but the 250cc and 350cc world championships as well.

Redman hated the TT course, but was obsessed with winning a race on it, so had to overcome his fear to achieve his ambition. 'I don't like the course,' he openly admitted in his 1966 autobiography *Wheels of Fortune*. 'There are too many wicked-looking walls and too few escape routes if you come adrift. You know that usually your first mistake there is your last. All the time you are racing there you are running a treacherous gauntlet of solid houses, garden walls and rock faces. Too many good racers have been killed there to ignore its threat.'

Redman's description of racing around the course reveals just how physically hard it is. 'On some parts of the TT course, at speeds of around 140mph, the road feels like a corrugated roof,' he wrote. 'The bike bounces and bucks wildly, making your wrists ache, and you yearn for a rest. It's like a concrete Grand National. A marathon, danger-filled race that you think is never going to end. You ache. Every bone, every muscle and sinew is buffeted every inch of the way. But you forget the nagging pains. You dismiss the cramp, the crick in the neck, and the needle-sharp rain on cheeks that are slapped out of shape by the wind. You have to forget all this. You are too busy keeping one eye on the rev counter and one on the wriggling ribbon of road.'

As the son of a multi-millionaire and boasting film-star good looks and an easy Italian charm, Giacomo Agostini could have lived a playboy lifestyle on his family's money. Instead, he chose to race motorcycles, against his father's wishes (his father offered to buy him a sports car if he *didn't* race bikes), and he proved to be a natural. In 1965, he made his debut at the TT and was hooked instantly. 'My first time, I am very surprised, because it's completely different than any other circuit,' Agostini says. 'I think the Isle of Man excited everyone who raced there. It's a very difficult circuit and very emotional to ride there. Of course, it's one of the most dangerous circuits in the world because it has everything; it's a normal road and it's very fast and you don't have any space when you crash – you've got trees, houses, everything.'

Agostini finished on the rostrum in the Junior TT that first year, but his inexperience saw him crashing out of the Senior at Sarah's Cottage in very wet conditions. Mike Hailwood made the same mistake at the same corner on the following lap but refused to give up. After kicking, pulling and beating his bike straight, Hailwood pushed his battered MV Agusta down Creg Willey's Hill to get it started (against oncoming race bikes), then turned round and set off in determined mood. The bike's screen was smashed to pieces, its exhaust was flattened, the handlebars bent and Hailwood's nose was streaming blood. Yet he rode like a demon back to the pits where he spent over a minute straightening the bars before rejoining the race. Such was his advantage before falling, Mike was still in the lead when he commenced battle, and he went on to win his third consecutive Senior race in what was one of his finest ever performances. And every second of it was captured by Manx Radio, who broadcast the TT races live for the first time in 1965.

While there is now an automatic seven-day ban on riders who have suffered a concussion, that was not the case in 1966, and Bill Ivy's account of racing his Yamaha 125 round the TT course while still suffering from concussion is frightening. 'I was getting headaches and could hardly see, but things improved,' he explained. 'When I started in the race I still must have been concussed, otherwise I'd never have gone so fast. It was sheer luck that I didn't crash! I clouted the straw bales coming out of Schoolhouse Bend at Ramsey. Then I got on the loose surface at the Gooseneck and clanged against an advertisement hoarding on the bank. The second lap was a series of slides, the third was enjoyable – things were back in focus again. No slides, no trouble, and just as fast. Lovely.'

Ivy, concussed as he was, won the race.

By the time he retired from racing at the end of 1977, Giacomo Agostini had won fifteen world championships.

To date, no motorcycle racer in history has won more. Yet he still remembers the 1967 Senior TT as the most important race in his glittering career. At that time, the Senior TT still counted as the British round of the 500cc Grand Prix world championship. Mike Hailwood had already won the title three years in a row and was the defending champion, while Giacomo Agostini had yet to win the first of his eventual eight 500cc world titles.

The 1967 Senior was a face-off between the two greatest riders in the world, on the world's most demanding racecourse, and it is still considered one of the greatest TT races of all time. Reporting for *Motor Cycle News* at the time, Robin Miller wrote that 'The tension was indescribable. It was as if everybody knew something special was about to happen. Plus, there was the knowledge that two men were putting their lives on the line.'

The race was a classic, with both men taking turns leading and both men breaking the lap record to average 108mph. The epic battle suddenly ended on the last lap when Agostini's chain broke as he made his way down off the Mountain, down towards the finish line. He had a lead of 2.5 seconds at the time his chain snapped and was utterly shattered by his loss. 'I remember crying from the Mountain to the finish line,' he would later say. 'I cried because, to win in the Isle of Man, to beat Mike Hailwood, is not easy. I was very disappointed.'

After the race, both men revealed just how hard they had ridden in pursuit of victory. 'What a race that was!' Hailwood said. 'I wouldn't want to go through another like that – I was scared all the way. Ago's MV obviously handled that much better than the Honda, and I was fighting it on every lap. I knew Ago would give it his all, and I knew I had to make sure he didn't get away and, if possible, stay in front. But even though I expected it to be pretty bad, I didn't expect it to be a nightmare. There's not enough money in the world to make me go through that again. If Ago hadn't broken down, I doubt that I would have beaten him. He was brilliant.'

Agostini had ridden with equal fervour. 'When we arrived (at the finish), the shoulders on our black leathers had turned white – we'd scraped along the chalk walls,' he said. 'I knew Mike would not surrender anything. He would not know how to give up. It was always the same and, to beat him, ever, if only once, is a memory you could live on for the rest of your life.'

The pair never would get to race against each other at the TT again. Hailwood retired from bike racing the following year and, by the time he made a comeback in 1978, Agostini had himself retired. Between them, Ago and Hailwood would win twenty-four Grand Prix world championships and 198 Grand Prix races. They remain two of the greatest riders the world has ever seen, yet they were always the best of friends, as Ago still fondly remembers. 'I remember Mike at the end of the race, when we went to the prize-giving, he said to me, "You are the winner," and he took me for dinner, and we had a big party.'

In Hailwood's absence, Agostini utterly dominated the TT between 1968 and 1972, winning the Junior and Senior every year, with the exception of 1971, when his bike broke down in the Junior. Such was his dominance,

Ago won the 1969 Senior by a full seven minutes. Today's winning margins are counted in seconds, but Agostini had the enormous advantage of having the only factory machine on the grid: every other rider knew they were racing for second place. Honda had withdrawn from racing, as had Yamaha, and with Agostini's dominance making every race a foregone conclusion, interest in the event was waning, and the future of the TT looked bleak as it entered a new decade.

The situation wasn't helped in 1970 when the TT suffered the blackest fortnight in its long history. Six riders were killed during practice and race week.

This was the state of the event when a certain Barry Sheene made his debut. Not yet the massive star he was to become, Sheene was nonetheless a well-known name, and was fighting Angel Nieto for the 1971 125cc world championship. Sheene, like many others before him, decided to do the TT in order to gain world championship points, as he knew Nieto refused to race there. Sheene hated it from the start, and never changed his mind.

He hated having to learn such a long course, he hated racing against the clock instead of other riders, and he hated the damp Manx climate. Yet, despite all this, he could clearly have done well at the TT if he had stuck with it. He posted the third fastest time in practice on his four-year-old, ex-Stuart Graham, factory Suzuki RT67, and was leading the Lightweight 125 TT race at one point on the opening lap until he hit thick fog and eased off the throttle. When his overworked clutch bit too hard just after the start of the second lap, Sheene was tossed from his bike at the slow, first-gear Quarterbridge Corner and his race was run – much to Barry's relief as he'd been hating every minute of it.

But that wasn't quite the end of Sheene's TT career: he still had an outing in the Production 250 event, also on a Suzuki. Again, he had posted respectable times in practice but, after suffering a massive tank-slapper during the race (when a bump causes the bike's handlebars to start swinging violently from side to side, threatening to pitch the rider off), parts of his machine started working themselves loose and Barry pulled in after just one lap. He never raced on the island again. 'My regret with Barry was that he didn't continue with the TT,' says Sheene's former rival and friend, Mick Grant. 'Certainly, the way he rode on pure road circuits like Scarborough and Imatra, there was no way that he couldn't have done the TT. I mean, bloomin' hell, Scarborough requires all the road racing skills you'd ever need, and he could do it. He certainly wasn't slow round there.'

Like Barry Sheene the previous year, Italy's Gilberto Parlotti had only gone to the TT in 1972 hoping to gain crucial 125cc world championship points. He was leading the title chase on his Morbidelli after four rounds and needed every point available to have any hope of winning the title. Parlotti's decision to enter the TT would prove a fateful one, in many ways.

Despite never having been to the Isle of Man before, Parlotti had every intention of winning the TT at his first attempt and was leading the race in atrocious conditions when he crashed on the Verandah, high up on the Mountain, on the second of the scheduled three laps, and was fatally injured. Eventual race winner Chas Mortimer remembers the race as though it were yesterday, and recalls how hard Parlotti was riding. 'The conditions were as bad as I'd ever known them in the Isle of Man. Very, very poor indeed. Visibility must have been about 20 yards on the Mountain. But I remember believing I was going to win that race right from the start, then I got my first signal, and it was minus seven or eight, so I thought, "Well, I'll try a bit harder." I knew it could only be Parlotti. By the time he crashed, he had pulled out a 30- or 35-second lead, and I was trying as hard as I could. I nearly fell off at Sarah's Cottage. I lost the back end big style and really thought I was down. I was trying so hard and yet Parlotti was still pulling away – and that was his first TT.'

Giacomo Agostini had been close friends with Parlotti and was distraught to learn of his death. He had taken the young Italian round the course in a car the night before the race as a final tutorial. Since the 125cc race had been run on the Friday morning before the Senior, Agostini was already preparing for his big race when he learned of the tragedy. News of Parlotti's death was enough to convince Ago that his TT days were over. 'When you are younger you don't think about the dangers,' he says. 'But after many years I see my friends killed too often on the Isle of Man and I decided, with some other riders, that we must stop. Of course, I wasn't happy to stop, because racing on the Isle of Man was the best in the world. But if you think about the safety we must say, "No, we don't race any more." Some English people were not happy with my decision but, for our sport, I think it was important because it was very negative publicity – for motorcycle factories and for people who like to buy motorbikes – if they see very bad accidents. It's not a good promotion for motorcycling.'

Agostini was the TT's biggest star and the biggest name in world motorcycling. As such, his word carried a lot of weight, as Chas Mortimer explains. 'You've got to remember that Ago was very, very powerful in those days, and he started the movement about the TT being finished. Barry Sheene jumped on the bandwagon, and so did Phil Read, but Parlotti's crash was definitely the death knell of the TT as we knew it. I wouldn't say there was a feeling in the paddock that week that the TT was finished as a world championship round, but the press started to blow things up after the TT and things started snowballing. The head of the FIM at the time was very anti-TT anyway, and his mob had enough power to finish the job.'

It took a special kind of courage to do what Giacomo Agostini did just moments after learning of the death of his friend. For the sake of MV Agusta, the TT organisers and the fans, he forced himself to strap on his helmet and to tackle the treacherous Mountain Course – that had just killed his friend – one last time. 'I knew there was nothing I could do to get out of it,' he later said. 'The organisation was under way, we knew it was dangerous, we knew that we might die – but we just had to race.'

After winning the race by six minutes, Agostini turned his back on the Isle of Man TT. His employers, MV Agusta, also vowed never to return. They were not alone in feeling that the TT was now just too dangerous for world championship racing; Phil Read and Rodney Gould also decided to boycott the following year's event, and Barry Sheene continued to voice his disapproval. The writing was on the wall for the Tourist Trophy races.

Tom Herron won the last Senior TT that counted as a round of the Grand Prix world championships in 1976 and brought the curtain down on an era that stretched back to 1949 and the very birth of the world championships. But a friend of Herron's made his debut at that same TT, and that friend would usher in a new era for the world's greatest road race. His name was Joey Dunlop.

CHAPTER 10

Risk

'If you get it wrong, it's gonna kill you.'
GUY MARTIN

'Those who risk nothing, do nothing, become nothing'

So reads the inscription on the headstone of the late David Jefferies, from the poem 'Risk' by an unknown author. Jefferies was the TT's fastest man and biggest star when he was killed during practice for the 2003 event. He is still sorely missed.

There can be no denying the very real dangers of the Isle of Man TT. The riders know it, their families know it, the teams know it and the organisers know it, but it's one of the least discussed subjects about the event. It's the elephant in the room. Yet, to attempt to sweep the dangers under the carpet and to deny the tragedies that have occurred there is to disrespect those who have lost their lives at the TT. And there have been many.

It's difficult to put an exact figure on just how many people have died on the TT Mountain Course, because some may have succumbed to their injuries weeks, or even months, after the event, so those riders aren't always included in the toll of fatalities. There is the added factor of the Manx Grand Prix – essentially the amateur TT, held on the same course at the end of August. Riders killed in this event are not always included in the statistics either. The most cited tally now claims that 265 riders have perished on the course, either in the TT or the Manx GP since the first TT race was held in 1907. It's a sobering statistic. But then, some 200 people have died on Mount Everest since 1922, and more than sixty have died on the north face of the Eiger alone, yet there are no calls for mountaineering to be banned, as there are for the TT to be banned.

The 37.73-mile TT course is lined with memorials and plaques commemorating riders who have lost their lives on it. The first to do so was Victor Surridge, who was killed during practice for the event in 1911. He crashed at Glen Helen, right in front of his onlooking team manager. Two years later, Frederick Richard Bateman was killed while leading the Senior TT. He had just turned twenty-three years old.

Sadly, the death toll has increased steadily ever since and, in the blackest years (like 1989 and 2022), five riders have been killed over the two-week TT period.

It's statistics like these that cause people to think TT riders must be crazy, but they are far from it: they have simply weighed up the odds, decided they are acceptable, and have learned to compartmentalise their fear; to put it aside for long enough to get the job done, much as Battle of Britain fighter pilots learned to do in the summer of 1940. They are also very matter-of-fact about the dangers. 'I know a motorbike will get you in the end,' John McGuinness says. 'It might not be this year or next, but it will happen eventually. I've been with guys who are no longer with us, like Lee Pullan, David Jefferies, Mick Lofthouse. If you don't think about the bad things that could happen, then you've got something wrong with you.'

The sheer rush of racing at the TT is what keeps riders returning, year after year, despite the dangers, and despite the very real fear that the riders admit to feeling. For them, it's a chance worth taking, because the rewards are so great. Tommy Robb broke his neck in the 1960 TT but wasn't put off and returned to win the 125cc Lightweight race in 1973. He is still a great advocate of the event, and of all the challenges it offers. 'Having ridden round the TT, having broken my neck at the TT and lain in hospital for a while, and come back to race on it many years again, it is something which I think will always be there,' he says. 'And I personally feel sorry for those great riders in the world who have never ridden in the TT. The frights, the scares, the adrenaline flow, is something you cannot match anywhere else in the world.'

Mick Grant is also prepared to admit how much racing at the TT scared him – although his fear didn't prevent him from winning seven races and setting an outright lap record. 'The TT frightened me, there's no question about that,' he says. 'I was always anxious because I knew that, even if you didn't make a mistake yourself, you could always have a mechanical problem. But at the same time, what a buzz! To go round there and come out of certain corners – like the 32nd Milestone – absolutely perfectly and see an extra 200 or 300rpm on your rev counter, was just something special. Some of those big, fast corners, you'd just find yourself taking a deep breath, and as you came out of the corner it was like winning the Pools. It was just like, "Yes! I did it!" On the boat on the way to the Isle of Man, I would always tell myself to just be careful and, in a way, I was glad when it was finished, but at the end of the day I enjoyed every minute of it.'

Risk/reward. Risk/reward.

James Hillier knows all about the equation. As a father, he also has other people to consider, which only makes things more difficult. 'Obviously, road racing is dangerous but, the way I see it, I take some risks for a couple of weeks a year, and the return it gives me is huge,' he says. 'Not financially, but personally – and you can't put a price on that. A lot of people think that TT riders lead a glamorous lifestyle, but that's not the case. We don't do it for the money, we do it because we love it. It's tricky to explain how I cope with the dangers. I don't want to grow old and regret things that I didn't do. What do you do in life? Do you sit around wishing you'd done stuff, or do you get out there and do it?'

While Hillier's approach to the TT is clearly a considered one, some riders have a much more gung-ho attitude, chief amongst them being Guy Martin. 'If you get it wrong, it's gonna kill you,' he said when he was still racing at the TT.

'I'm not a fatalist or anything, but that's what I like about it. If it was safe, I wouldn't do it. It's that simple.'

Hazards at the TT come in many different shapes and forms. Riders even have to contend with local wildlife and livestock on occasion. More than once, the great Joey Dunlop had close calls with dogs that had escaped on to the course but, in 1956, John Surtees had a slightly larger beast to contend with. 'I think the bike came off worse than I did in my crash with the cow in 1956,' he said. 'The cow got up and went off – how it suffered afterwards I'm not quite sure. But I understand it had been taken away from its calf rather too quickly, and this meant that it jumped over one or two hedges and suchlike, and it ended up on the road at Creg Willey's Hill. I jammed everything on, and luckily the bike wasn't totally un-faired – it had a bit of a nose fairing (bodywork) on it – and I hit it, and it went down, and it shovelled up some chippings and things, and I lost my race bike. I got away unhurt. Hurt feelings – and concern for the cow as well!'

But while Surtees walked away from his encounter unhurt, Irish rider Gene McDonnell was not so lucky. McDonnell was a promising young Irish rider who looked to have a big future at the TT. That future never happened. His death in the 1986 Junior TT was one of the most horrific ever witnessed on a course that had already seen more than its fair share of tragedies.

When Brian Reid crashed at Ballaugh Bridge, the medical helicopter was dispatched to pick him up. As it approached, the helicopter spooked a horse in a nearby field causing it to bolt, leap several fences and hedges, and eventually find itself trotting down the TT course. That section of the course, on the approach to Ballaugh Bridge, is one of the fastest, and riders would have been clocking speeds of up to 160mph as they rounded the blind right kink on the run up to the bridge. Gene McDonnell had no chance. He collided with the horse and his bike smashed into cars in the forecourt of a nearby garage, exploding into flames. McDonnell, just twenty-four, was killed instantly, and the whole island was numbed as news filtered through.

A rider's first line of defence against such fatalities is a simple one: they think it won't happen to them. They have to think like that. Ryan Farquhar's career was cut short due to injuries sustained in a crash at the North West 200 in 2016 but he, at least, survived. He has been building successful race bikes ever since but summed up his attitude while still racing at the TT. 'Every day when I'm working on the bikes, I think about races that I've done and riders that I've raced against: riders like Richard Britton, Darran Lindsay, Owen McNally, Joey Dunlop, Martin Finnegan . . . Riders that I've had good races with, and got to know, and they're not there now. It is sad but they were like me – they knew the risks but thought it was never going to happen to them. I believe it'll not happen to me, but I might be next, you never know.'

Although most riders somehow manage to race on, even after witnessing tragedies, on occasion it proves to be the final straw for a rider, and the bubble of invincibility finally bursts. 'I saw Simon Beck's fatal crash in 1999 and that hit me pretty hard, because I knew him well,' Phillip McCallen says. 'I felt sick inside. When I got back to the paddock, I just thought, "I don't need this." With the injuries I was carrying I couldn't ride properly, and I felt I was letting people down, so I just decided to quit.'

McCallen walked away, and now runs a successful bike dealership in Lisburn, Northern Ireland.

Rob McElnea was very calculated in his approach to the dangers of the TT. He only rode there for four years (and picked up three wins) before calculating the odds were against him. 'I loved doing the TT, but the law of averages stack up if you keep doing it,' he says. 'I decided in January 1984 – without telling anyone else – that I wouldn't be doing the TT any more after that one. I told my team and my wife on the Friday night after winning the Classic that it would be my last TT.'

McElnea held good to his word, but the irony of what happened on the day after his last TT race was not lost on him. 'We flew to France for the Grand Prix and the next morning I broke my bloody leg at Paul Ricard!'

A crash that resulted in a broken leg at Paul Ricard, however, might well have had a very different outcome at the TT.

Other riders race on, no matter how much tragedy they've witnessed. In 2010, privateer rider Paul 'Moz' Owen was presented with the 'Spirit of the TT' award for his actions in the second Supersport race that year. He was following his great friend, Paul Dobbs, through Ballagarey Corner (a seriously fast right-hander) when Dobbs lost control of his machine and crashed, suffering fatal injuries. In a completely selfless act, Owen stopped his bike and ran to help, though there was nothing he could do to save his friend. 'The thought of quitting goes through your mind every time someone gets killed,' he says. 'You think, "I've had enough, I can't do this any more. It could have been me, and I've got a wife and a kid sitting at home."'

But he didn't quit.

'I went and saw Dobbsy's wife, then went and sat in the back of my van and cried my eyes out. The boys came to see me and said, "What do you want to do? Shall we pack the stuff away?" and I said, "No. We've got a Superbike there, and you've been struggling all week trying to get it ready. And if I don't get straight back on a bike now, then I never will." I knew Dobbsy wouldn't have wanted me to stop.'

A very modest Welshman, Owen was at first going to politely turn down the 'Spirit of the TT' trophy. 'My first instinct was to refuse the reward,' he says. 'I did what I did because Dobbsy was a mate, and it just came natural to me to do it. I told them I hadn't done it to win a trophy – I didn't want a trophy. I said they should give it to someone else. But then I spoke to Bridget Dobbs, and she said I should accept it, so I did. But it just felt wrong at first. I've got it at home now. I had a little plaque put on it with Dobbsy's name and the date, so it's a memorial to him.'

John McGuinness is another rider who opted to race on, despite witnessing the death of his closest friend. He was first on the scene following David Jefferies' crash at Crosby Corner during practice week in 2003. 'I think I set off with Martin Finnegan, and we did a lap, and everything was just normal,' he says in recounting the tragedy. 'Normal practice, and flat out up towards Ballagarey, around Ballagarey, down the hill towards Crosby, and I then I saw a stationary yellow flag. I thought it a bit odd, and then I saw a waved yellow flag, but not like mega-waved (a yellow flag warns of a lack of adhesion on the course, letting riders know to take it steady). Out of the corner of my eye, I saw a lass, and she had turned her coat inside out. It had a red lining (a race or practice session can only be stopped with a red flag), and I could see the fear on her face, so I just eased it right off and came up to the corner at Crosby. I could see the black line where someone had lost control of their bike and gone into the wall. I've never seen anything like it. It must have lifted a ton of stone and mortar out of the wall and pulled all that on to the road.'

McGuinness was, as yet, unaware that the crashed rider was his best friend. 'I didn't know who it was. I just slowed down and it was really bizarre. There was a visor on the road, and a seat unit which was totally untouched. It was unbelievable. The seat was like brand new, with a big number "1" on it, and I knew then that it was David, and that there was no way he could have survived that. I just stopped in the road. My Ducati was still running, and I was like, "Fuckin' hell." I was shocked.'

The debris from the crash had all but blocked the course. 'There was no way through,' McGuinness continues. 'You couldn't get through because the bike had hit a telegraph pole and brought the telegraph pole down. All the wires were stretched across the road. So, I was stopped. I was still shocked, and I put my bike against the wall and switched it off. I could then hear other riders approaching. A few had stopped, but Jim Moodie obviously wasn't going to. That was horrific. I thought Jim was going to be decapitated.

I was standing there, and he came round the corner and frightened me to death; bouncing over rocks and stones and all these bits of bodywork, and he went through it all and snapped the cables with his neck and chest.'

Only then did McGuinness see his fallen friend. 'You hear all these stories about how David's boot fell off and all this shit, but it really is a load of shite. Dave was, like, as if someone had laid him on the road perfectly still; his legs and arms neatly alongside him. He was gone, but there was no way he was suffering. He was just finished. It was peaceful really, you know? It was weird.'

As is often the case in extreme moments when the senses are elevated, McGuinness remembers the disaster scene in intimate detail. 'The noises and smells through it all . . . it was really strange,' he says. 'You know if you knock a wall down, you have that smell? That dusty smell, and fibreglass and oil smells? Weird. It was the most horrible experience I've ever had in my life.'

Despite coming so close to being decapitated in the incident, Jim Moodie opted to race on, largely out of a sense of duty to others. 'There's no way I wanted to race that week, but I'm a professional rider, and pulling out would have meant letting a lot of people down – my mechanics, my sponsors, Triumph Motorcycles,' he says. 'They would all have understood me pulling out under the circumstances, but I'm professional and I've got obligations to people, so I raced. Over the years you learn to deal with these things – it's not easy, but you learn to deal with it.'

In an astonishing gesture, it was David Jefferies' bereaved mother who persuaded McGuinness not to pack up and go home. 'I considered quitting after David was killed,' McGuinness says. 'I spoke to his mum, Pauline, and said, "I think that's me finished. I'm done," and she said, "No, you can't do that, you've got to ride." She was the strongest person in the paddock. You've got obligations with sponsors and teams, but at the end of the day your head's not on a chopping block at the TT – you don't have to race. You only do it because you want to do it.'

McGuinness has never forgotten his old friend. 'Every time I go past there (Crosby Corner) I always have a little word with myself, and I'm the same where Mick Lofthouse was killed. I say a lot of strange things to myself. Every time before a race I pray to all the lads who have gone.'

Just two years later, McGuinness had to go through it all again, this time when another close friend, Gus Scott, was killed exiting the village of Kirk Michael during the Senior TT. In what was his debut year at the event, Scott was doing everything right, building up his speed gradually, learning the course and taking no chances. When he sped round the blind, 160mph, left-hand kink exiting the village, a female race marshal was crossing the track to attend to a rider who had broken down. No warning flag had been displayed to indicate her presence on the course. Both she and Scott were killed instantly.

McGuinness then rode through the crash site. 'I saw a blue bike, with a bit of pink, by the side of the road, but thought, "Nah, it can't be Gus," so I carried on,' he remembers. 'After the race, you get whisked to the podium, and you're being interviewed and stuff, and I felt on top of the world after winning three races that week – it was amazing. It was my first Senior win, and I'd always wanted to lift that big trophy, so it was brilliant. Then I went into the press room and was told about Gus, and then my win seemed totally insignificant.'

McGuinness seems at a loss to explain how he and his fellow riders learn to cope with such tragedies. 'I don't know how we do it really – how we somehow manage to switch off to all the deaths. We're kind of brought up that way as Brits – the old stiff upper lip thing. I remember a foreign rider got killed one year, and his mate went straight home and said he'd never come back, and you can't really blame him for that. But here I am – ready for more. I can't explain it.'

Ian Lougher couldn't explain it either when he was still competing at the TT. Despite having taken part in well over 100 TT races, the Welshman is still no wiser as to how he coped with such sustained losses. 'It used to really upset me when someone was killed,' he says. 'So much so that I could never do anything in the rest of the races that week. My heart just wasn't in it. I don't know how I deal with it really. All I can tell myself is that the riders knew what the consequences of racing there could be, and I do too, and if you can't accept them, then don't do it. It's hardest on the families, and the mechanics, and everyone involved with the rider. The TT is dangerous, and you have to respect it, but I suppose you've also got to shut the dangers out or you'd never race there.'

The female perspective on facing the dangers of the TT course is every bit as brutal as the males'. Jenny Tinmouth only raced at the TT in 2009 and 2010 but became the fastest woman in TT history when she did so. Speaking of the dangers in 2010, she said, 'It's the old thing where you realise you could die doing almost anything – as everyone says, you could be killed walking out in front of a bus. You could die at any point, for any reason. As Jamie Whitham wrote in his autobiography, he did all that racing for all those years, and then he got cancer and realised it might be cancer that killed him after all. So, you're fully aware of the dangers, but you accept that we all have to die of something, and you just get on with it – you race at the TT, or you don't.'

As ever, it's the trade-off between risk and reward that Tinmouth and all other TT racers must consider. And for every last one of them, the thrill outweighs the danger. 'It's true that you don't really realise you're alive unless you're doing extreme stuff and putting yourself in danger – that's when you feel most alive,' Tinmouth admits. 'Do I worry about dying? No, not really. I think bike racers just have a different mentality to most people when it comes to that.'

That's not to say that fear doesn't come knocking in the wee small hours, forcing riders to question their own judgement. 'It's strange, but there are some nights when I lie in bed and think, "Bloody hell – I don't really want to do the TT," but when I wake up in the morning I can't wait to get there!' Tinmouth explained. 'Sometimes it's not good to think about things too much. Like when you were a kid and you thought you were invincible – you would try anything because you didn't think about the consequences. It's a similar thing with the TT; it's just best not to think about it too much.'

TT racers don't come more aggressive and bullish than Michael Dunlop. Despite having lost his uncle Joey, his father Robert and his brother William to the sport, his attitude remains undaunted. 'Nobody asks any of us to race at the TT – we don't have to do it,' he says. 'And people don't have to watch it either if they don't like it. This job has its ups and downs, that's for sure, but nobody's holding a gun to my forehead to make me do it. It's not like being conscripted to go to war! People get their buzz out of golf, snooker, whatever. I get mine out of racing between hedges. That's the way I was brought into life, and that's the way I'll go out of it.'

CHAPTER 11

The Boss

'God knows how the riders must feel – on race morning
I'm totally buzzing!
G ARY T HOMPSON

'After the TT is over it's almost as if you've had an out-of-body-experience and it didn't really happen. It's surreal, and it's a real downer. I've been on such a high for two weeks – using a high level of concentration and decision making – and when you come to the end of it, it's a real downer. Going back to normality is horrible and it takes me about two weeks to adjust.'

Gary Thompson clearly thrives on the pressure of having the toughest job at the TT. Whenever a racing motorcycle is out on the TT course, only one man is in charge. Although he is helped by an army of colleagues, the clerk of the course has ultimate power and is literally responsible for making life-or-death decisions. He's the only man with the power to stop a race. He's the boss. And, since 2012, that boss has been Gary Thompson.

A former military man, who served in The Falklands and the first Gulf War, Thompson has also been awarded the BEM (British Empire Medal) for his outstanding organisational skills and an MBE (Most Excellent Order of the British Empire) for his services in Bosnia. 'The BEM was awarded in 1987 when I was part of a planning team for a thing called Exercise Reforger – which stands for "return of forces to Germany",' Thompson explains. 'We brought 102,000 troops across from America, staged them through Holland and Germany, exercised them in an area of Germany, and then staged them back again. It was a two-year planning cycle for a six-week exercise. I received the MBE for operational services in Bosnia in 1996.'

Thompson believes the skills he learned in the military have been readily transferable to running an event like the TT. 'There are stressful periods and certain pressures you face when you're clerk of the course and, although they're not really comparable with those you face in the army, I personally find that my time in the army has helped me to deal with the pressures of running a world-class event like the TT,' he says. 'So, in that sense it's fair to say that I actually do run the TT with military precision! I'm just in the process of drafting the practice and race day schedules and it is very much like a military operation. I'm planning events right down to the minute – that's how accurate the timing has to be to ensure it all runs smoothly.'

But it's not just Thompson's military credentials that make him ideally suited to the highest-pressure job at the TT; he also has a strong background in bike racing, having first spectated at the TT in 1978 and been general secretary of the ACU (Auto Cycle Union) since 2003. He has also been involved with the TT since then, first as race secretary then as clerk of the course.

Although the TT does not begin until late May, Thompson's work begins in the autumn of the previous year. 'Come October, we start working on the following year's TT, with things like detailed risk assessments of all the prohibited and restricted areas, the red flag points, the roadside furniture and all the marshalling points,' he says. 'Then Paul Phillips (TT business development manager) and I will start to work up the supplementary regulations, and then I'll get on to the practice and race day schedules. From about the end of January it starts to gather pace, and that pace continues to increase and gets more intense the closer we get to the event.'

Thompson has made a lot of positive changes since he took over the role of clerk of the course, and not just on behalf of the competitors; he also tries to make things less disruptive for the islanders. 'It's down to me what time the races start and to adjust the racing schedule, as and when that's required,' he explains. 'The organisers used to close the roads at a set time in the morning, no matter what the weather was doing, and I could never understand that. If the weather is too bad for racing, then you might as well leave the roads open so people can get on with things. So, I try to make a decision about racing as early as possible so we can keep the roads open. This helps reduce disruption to local residents, it means the riders don't have to hang around in their leathers getting all nervous and wound up, and it also prevents the marshals from being trapped up on the Mountain getting soaked through for no good reason.'

Thompson's eagle's nest is the race control office, located high up in the main grandstand facing the start/ finish line. 'We have about sixteen people in race control and I'm the head of that team,' he says. 'In the annexe to race control we have representatives from the fire service and the ambulance service, and the guy who co-ordinates all the helicopter activity. In race control itself we have a police presence – usually two or three officers whom I work with on opening up access points on the course, closing the roads, opening access roads, etc.'

Only the clerk of the course has the authority to stop a TT race, by issuing the order for red flags to be displayed all around the course. It's a huge responsibility, and Thompson's resolve was put to the test in his very first year in the job, when he decided to stop the 2012 Senior race due to adverse weather conditions. 'It was a big decision to make – the Senior had never been cancelled in the 105-year history of the TT – but it was an easy decision to make at the same time,' Thompson says. 'We went out in two course inspection cars. There was me, John McGuinness and Conor Cummins in one, and Milky Quayle, Phillip McCallen and Ian Lougher in another (all current, or former, riders). All the way round the course there were wet patches, particularly under the trees, but it was particularly bad up on the Mountain because the mist hadn't allowed the road to dry, so it was wet to the point where there were puddles on the racing line and that meant the decision was made for me – we just couldn't go racing

Above: One minute to go. The tension on the TT startline is almost unbearable. © *Don Morley*

Below: The Mountain section of the course offers spectaular viewing. Tom Thorp and Brian Setchell entertain the hordes in the 1961 Senior. © *Don Morley*

Above: Mike Hailwood crashed, kicked his bike straight, and remounted to win the 1965 Senior – broken screen and all. © *Don Morley*

Middle: Rem Fowler, winner of the first twin-cylinder TT in 1907, rounds the notorious Devil's Elbow. © *Bill Snelling*

Below left: The TT course was just a dirt track in the early years. © *Bill Snelling*

Below right: The man who saved the TT. Mike Hailwood's miraculous comeback win in 1978 reignited interest in the event. © *Don Morley*

Argentina's Rafael Paschaolin overcooks it at Creg-ny-Baa. © Glynne Lewis

Rob Harrison ploughs right into the straw bales instead of jumping over
Ballaugh Bridge after out-braking himself. © Don Morley

Above: Somewhere in this fireball is Guy Martin, who broke several ribs, bruised his lungs and fractured two vertebrae, as well as twisting both ankles. 2010.

© Sean Sayers

Right: Aftermath. Fans pay their repsects at the site where David Jefferies lost his life in 2003. © Don Morley

Left: Happier times. The late Dan Kneen with his girlfriend Leanne Harper.

© Ean Proctor

Above: Mike Casey rudely interrupts a family of ducks at Ballacraine. © *Don Morley*

Below left: Current riders will be approaching 200mph by the end of this straight. This unique picture was taken from a temporary bridge which no longer exists. © *Don Morley*

Below right: The camera helicopter can't keep up with TT racers and has to take shortcuts. John McGuinness outruns it at Creg-ny-Baaa. © *Glynne Lewis*

Left: Fans can get quite close to the action at the TT. Michael Dunlop entertains them on the run to The Gooseneck.

© Dave Purves

Right: It's not easy keeping the third wheel down on a Sidecar. Lee Cain does his best as driver John Holden negotiates Braddan Bridge.

© Dave Purves

Left: John McGuinness' neck shows the strain at 170mph. © Glynne Lewis

Above: This remarkable photo of Ian Hutchinson showcases the toll the TT can take on its riders. Hutchy endured thirty operations on his leg and his ankle is now fused.

© Marc Aspland

Right: Broken but unbowed. Mike Booth's spirit and courage epitomises that of all TT racers.

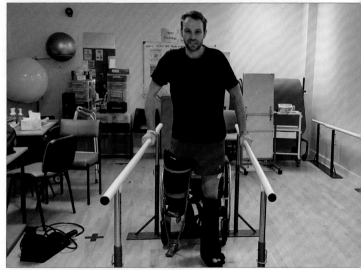

Left: The remains of Kunimitsu Takahashi's Honda 125 after he crashed into a stone wall at Union Mills in 1962.

© Don Morley

Above: Peter Hickman drifitng both wheels round Kate's Cottage, short circuit style.

© Louis Porter

Below: Conor Cummins impresses the marshals at Rhencullen. © Dave Purves

in those conditions. I was as disappointed as anyone. I was gutted, but rider safety has to be paramount. It was a testing debut for me though. I mean, first year as clerk of the course and you have to cancel the Senior TT? It's not bad going, is it?'

Working more closely with the riders (as he did before deciding to stop the Senior race) is another innovation Thompson has brought to the role, and one that has earned him a lot of respect. 'I'm very conscious of the fact that it's the riders who are actually out there doing the business,' he says. 'They're the ones risking their necks to provide entertainment for everyone else. I might know how to run a race meeting, but I would never make a decision without consulting the riders first.'

Thompson says his greatest enemy during TT fortnight is the unpredictable Manx weather. Set, as it is, in the middle of the Irish Sea, the Isle of Man's climate is a law unto itself, and, given the sheer length of the TT course, conditions can be radically varied on different parts of it. In 2012, the weather really put Thompson's organisational skills to the test and showed just how much pressure he faces in his unenviable role. 'The Wednesday of race week was probably harder than having to cancel the Senior,' Thompson admits. 'Again, the weather was atrocious, and the Wednesday is always the busiest race day of the week. In order not to keep everyone hanging around, I delayed the first race until around 2pm. The course inspection car then went round and reported that, in around an hour's time, conditions would be fit for racing. Then I received word that there had been a downpour at Quarterbridge, which caused another delay. We had to have the roads open between 5pm and 6pm for local traffic, so the window to run two races was closing. I looked out of the window of race control and saw all the Supersport riders milling around, waiting to get going. Once again, I turned to John McGuinness, and I make no apology for that. He's an absolute legend at the TT and has so much experience that it would be foolhardy of me not to ask his advice. I also spoke to (leading sidecar racer) Dave Molyneux and came up with the decision to completely switch the race programme around at very short notice. We put the one-lap TT Zero race out first, then held the Sidecar TT, then opened the roads for the local traffic, and then held the Supersport race in the evening. We ended up finishing not that far off when we should have, had all gone to plan. Given the problems we had with all the delays, the low mist, the cloud, the downpour at Quarterbridge and all that stuff, to be able to switch the race programme round at short notice and still fit all the races in in time – and to have the second Supersport race be one of the closest finishes in TT history – was very gratifying. I thought, "Yep, that's been a good day, that has."'

For many, Thompson's job would be a waking nightmare. If he so much as makes a wrong call, riders could die. It's an awesome responsibility, but Thompson thrives on that pressure. 'Oh, I absolutely love it!' he says. 'God knows how the riders must feel though, because when I wake up on race morning I'm totally buzzing! It's just the sheer passion that surrounds the event. The first thing I do is rip open the curtains, praying that it's a bright blue sky, then

I'll speak to the weather guy down at Ronaldsway Airport at 6.30am to get the first weather briefing of the day. Next thing is a meeting at 7am with the Motorsport Operational Group to make an assessment of how the day is going to run – whether there looks like being delays because of the weather and so on. Although everyone has a copy of the race schedule for the day, I always have options B, C and D in my laptop bag, should we need to adjust the schedule. Then it's up to the race control tower at the grandstand for the day and, depending on any delays, I'll get finished anywhere between 8.30pm and 9pm on a race day and maybe 10.30pm or 11pm on practice nights. But if there's any downtime during those hours, then I have to use it to do ACU work, so there's no let-up.'

After two weeks of intense pressure, intense concentration and high-level decision making, Gary Thompson only has one measure of success that he judges himself by. 'If everyone goes away having had a fantastic event – from the riders to the officials and the fans – and they can't wait to come back again the following year, then I've done my job.'

Sadly, not everyone always has a fantastic event, and the clerk of the course also has to deal with the fallout when things go wrong. When Dan Kneen was killed during practice for the 2018 TT, the session was red-flagged, and following riders were stopped by the marshals and instructed to turn around and ride back towards the paddock the wrong way round the course, because there was no safe way through the debris on the track. As he made his way back to the paddock, Steve Mercer had a head-on collision with an official course car travelling at speed in the opposite direction and suffered life-threatening injuries.

The ACU, which runs the TT, admitted responsibility and, in August 2019, issued a statement which included the following words:

'*It should be noted that liability has been admitted and the ACU is eager to bring this matter to a conclusion, but compensation cannot be calculated until Mr Mercer's final condition and future prognosis is known.*'

Four years after the incident, Mercer is still in a wheelchair due to spinal injuries and his rehabilitation is still ongoing, meaning no ruling has yet been made on what level of compensation he will receive. The case could very well drag on for several more years, and it highlights the very serious nature of the clerk of the course's role and the heavy responsibilities that go with it.

At the TT, triumph and tragedy are never very far apart.

CHAPTER 12

The Pits

*'I got fuel splashed all over me bollocks
and the pain was incredible.'*
JOHN McGUINNESS

'I got fuel splashed all over me bollocks and the pain was incredible. It was absolute agony all the way to Ballacraine, and all I was thinking was, "I need to stop. I need to stop to sort me bollocks – or at least make sure they were still there." It was so bad that I thought, by the time I finished the race, my knob would be gone. I made some "adjustments" to the family jewels on one of the straights and eventually the pain disappeared, and I was back in business. But it was pretty uncomfortable for a while, that's for sure.'

As John McGuinness so vividly explained in 2009, even pit stops at the TT can be fraught with danger. They are often a source of great drama too: races can be won or lost during TT pit stops.

In a six-lap Superbike race, riders have to stop twice

to refuel – after the second and fourth laps – and usually change a rear tyre at the same time. In a four-lap race, riders only stop once, after the second lap.

Pit stops have been a feature of the TT since the very beginning, although things were somewhat less hectic in the early years than they are now. The first TT in 1907 featured a compulsory ten-minute lunch break to allow riders time to nibble some bread and cheese, or whatever 'fast food' they could lay their hands on.

Those early racers were not averse to taking on some stronger forms of refreshment to fortify themselves either. It was quite common to see them having an alcoholic drink during a pit stop. In 1925, Howard Davies insisted on the very finest of fuel for his system: a contemporary race report noted that he 'had a hurried drink of champagne and went off again feeling quite refreshed.'

Scotsman Jock West enjoyed a fairly drunken race in the 1935 Junior TT too. In a bid to shake off the flu, he had arranged to have a glass of Scotch prepared for him at his pit stop. He explained the full story in Geoff Davison's 1948 book *Racing Reminiscences*. 'I pulled into the pits for machine and personal refuelling. Everything functioned as arranged and, while attending to the quick filler with my left hand, I found no difficulty in disposing of the contents of the glass that had been thrust into my right. As I knocked the liquid back, I thought that it seemed unusually potent, and by the time I arrived at the top of Bray Hill, a very definite internal glow was becoming apparent, and it dawned on me that my request for a "short" had received such conscientious attention that I had been given a treble brandy! By Quarterbridge I was feeling fine and by Braddan I had a job deciding which road to take. From Union Mills to Ballacraine the road seemed extremely narrow, and I remember hoping against hope that the motor would keep going, as I was certain that I was for the Gaol House if, for any reason at all, I stopped.'

West wobbled home in a respectable fifteenth place, having been sensible enough to refuse the second helping of brandy which was offered up at his next pit stop.

Times have changed, as have regulations. With races now sometimes being won by less than a second (Bruce Anstey beat Cameron Donald by just 0.77 seconds in the first Supersport race in 2012), strict rules are now in place to regulate pit stops. Clerk of the course Gary Thompson explains them: 'The basic rules are that there is a 60kph (37.5mph) speed limit along the whole length of pit lane. This speed limit has to be adhered to once riders cross the white line at the beginning of pit lane, and until they cross the white line denoting the end of the speed limit on the exit, before they rejoin the TT Mountain Course on Glencrutchery Road. When coming into pit lane and heading towards their pit box, riders need to be mindful of other competitors setting off once their pit stop has been completed and, obviously, as they themselves are setting off they need to be mindful of other riders coming down pit lane to their pit box, or to rejoin the course. Pit crews need to wear fire-retardant clothing with appropriate footwear, and any equipment in pit lane needs to be intrinsically safe.'

There are no garages in the pit lane. With space being extremely tight, each rider is allowed a maximum of four helpers and a fuel pump. While their tank is being filled, the rear end of their bike can be lifted up with a paddock stand to allow for a wheel change (which is quicker than changing a tyre). The rider will receive a very quick briefing from a team member, letting him know where he is in the race and whom he's racing against. Some words of advice or encouragement may also be offered but, in general, information is kept to a minimum: the rider already has plenty to think about. Some riders change helmets or visors, due to the build-up of dead bugs which obscure their vision (they also wear about six 'tear-off' visors for this purpose – thin sheets of see-through plastic fitted over the main visor, which they can remove as the bug count builds). Other riders prefer to clean their own visor while their helmet remains in place. This is all down to personal preference.

There are also regulations to govern what technical changes teams are allowed to make during a pit stop. 'They're allowed to change tyres, refuel and make minor repairs or adjustments,' Thompson says. 'They're not allowed to use any kind of ramp – only a paddock stand – or any other equipment that is not deemed to be intrinsically safe. This is a requirement of the Isle of Man's Fire Safety Regulations. "Intrinsically safe" is a protection technique for the safe operation of electrical equipment in hazardous areas by limiting the energy available for ignition.'

The pit lane is policed by technical officials who observe from a safe distance, so as not to impede the teams while they are carrying out their roles. There is also a presence from the Isle of Man fire service. Race scrutineers check over every bike for any obvious signs of damage that may prove dangerous – loose bodywork, a loose exhaust bracket or an oil leak, for example – but they obviously cannot fully inspect every machine close up during a live pit stop.

The pit-lane speed limit referred to by Thompson was introduced in 2010 as things were becoming too dangerous, and a serious accident was only a matter of time. 'Before this, the stop box was in operation at the top of pit lane, where a rider would arrive at the stop box, come to a halt, put his foot down and then speed off to his pit box,' Thompson explains. 'For those riders whose pit box was at the bottom of pit lane, their speeds moving down pit lane were very fast, and the same went for those at the top of pit lane setting off once their pit stop was finished. From a safety point of view, in consideration of those operating in pit lane, it became a no-brainer to restrict the speed limit before someone got seriously hurt.'

Now pit lane is governed by a speed limit which is commensurate with world championship and national road racing. Throughout MotoGP, World Superbikes and British Superbikes, the recognised speed limit throughout pit lanes is 60kph. At the entrance to the TT pits, there's a single white line with a board at each side indicating the speed limit. From this point until the pit lane exit, the speed limit is 60kph, and this is policed by five transponder loops evenly placed throughout pit-lane. The transponder loops are accurate to three decimal points and time penalties are imposed on any competitor breaking the speed limit. These are:

- Over 60kph (37.5mph) but not over 80kph (50mph)
  – time penalty of 30 seconds

- Over 80kph (50mph) but not over 100kph (62.5mph) – time penalty of 60 seconds
- Over 100kph (62.5mph) – disqualification from the race

'In the event of more than one infringement during a single pit stop, the highest penalty will be awarded,' Thompson continues. 'These penalties are considered to be a matter of fact, which means the competitor has no right of protest or appeal. At the entrance to pit lane a display board will indicate the speed of competitors as they approach it.'

To ensure riders stay within these limits, TT race bikes are now fitted with a pit-lane speed limiter, so the rider only has to activate a button on the handlebar to restrict his speed, then de-activate it as he or she rejoins the race.

The new pit-lane speeding penalties have proved to be controversial on occasion, such as in the 2010 Superbike race, when Guy Martin stormed off the podium after being handed a 30-second penalty that dropped him from second place to fourth. His crime was exceeding the pit-lane speed limit by 0.12kph (or 0.7mph). The demotion cost Martin £7,000 in prize money, as well as second place in the race.

Pit lane activity at the TT is frantic, and any time lost or gained by slick teamwork can have a massive impact on the outcome of any particular race. 'The pit stops certainly add to the drama and excitement of the TT,' Thompson says. 'I think pit stops have become part and parcel of the whole race. Yes, the rider has to do the business on the road, but also the team have a part to play in making sure they have a tried and tested operation to refuel and change tyres as fast as they can, so as not to penalise their rider once the pit stop is complete.

It all comes down to practice, and making sure each of the pit crew members know what they have to do when their rider comes in. 'The activity is frantic, and I would imagine blood pressures start to rise,' Thompson says. 'It is a pressured situation: a rider comes in from racing two laps around the longest course in the world, so of course the pit crews want to get it right, and want to get it right first time – any delay just puts the rider under more pressure when he re-enters the race.'

Former Honda Britain boss Neil Tuxworth has overseen more TT wins than any man in history and knows how important pit stops are. 'You don't want to lose time in the pit stop, so you've got to plan it properly,' he says. 'The race starts when the rider leaves the line and finishes when he crosses it again, and everything that happens in between is important, so a pit stop is equally important as being out on the track – and don't forget there are two of them in a Superbike race. The secret is to have practised your pit stop many times, not just to do it in pit lane. We practise in the pits, in the garage, anywhere, for about an hour or so, just to make sure everyone knows exactly what they're doing.'

Tuxworth's strategy, honed over twenty-five years, is simple. 'I can explain it in two words – stay calm,' he says. 'In order to not make any mistakes, you have to make sure that everyone stays nice and calm and sane. The restricting factor in a pit stop at the TT is the time it takes to fill the bike with fuel. It takes us about 32 seconds, because we have to wait for the gravity-fed fuelling system to fill the tank up. That gives us plenty of time to change a rear wheel too.'

In a World Endurance race (where pressurised fast-fillers are permitted), Tuxworth's Honda squad could change both wheels, check the brakes, put oil in, fuel the bike and swap the riders in just 16 seconds, making the TT seem quite leisurely. 'At the TT, you should be ready to go as soon as the fuel is in,' he says. 'Everybody has to have the same fuel filler system, so it's a level playing field, and because it's a relatively slow gravity-fed system, it allows us that bit more time to check everything else is okay.'

Up until the 1980s, teams were permitted to use pressurised quick-filler systems, but they were expensive and only the top teams could afford them. The time they saved gave factory riders a huge advantage over everyone else and could easily make the difference between winning and losing a race. In 1980, with no money, no factory team and no quick-filler system, but no shortage of guile, Joey Dunlop had a bigger fuel tank made for his ratty old Yamaha TZ750 (perfectly within the rules at that time) the night before the Classic race and only had to make one pit stop instead of two. While the big money teams stopped to fill their thirsty machines, Dunlop simply sped on past the pits and won the race, completely outfoxing the mighty Honda team.

Even just filling a bike up with fuel can be hazardous for a rider, as John McGuinness found to his cost when he sloshed fuel all over his nether regions. Eight-time TT winner Jim Moodie had a similar experience during the 1999 Junior TT. 'The very last thing I said to Bill Simpson (former TT winner and father of triple winner Ian Simpson) – who was doing my fuel – was not to get any in my eyes, because he was renowned for getting it into Ian Simpson's eyes. And what did he do? Right in my eyes. And I wear contact lenses too. If I hadn't managed to work the lenses out, I was finished. The petrol helped flush the lenses out, but I couldn't see too great after that – I certainly couldn't read my signal boards. So, I just concentrated on catching Iain Duffus and used him as a bit of a gauge for the next two laps. I was quite glad to finish that race.'

Nerves play a big role during pit stops, and no one is immune; not even former British Supersport champion Stuart Easton, who found out very quickly that working as part of a pit crew wasn't for him. He might have been able to hold his nerve while winning road races at the North West 200 and Macau Grand Prix, but the TT pit lane was a bridge too far for Easton, as Michael Rutter explains. 'Stuart asked to be part of my pit crew one year. He's really laid-back, so we gave him simple jobs like changing my visor, cleaning the screen on the bike and removing the fuel cap. But when I pulled into the pits, Stuart's head just fell off. He hadn't realised how nerve-wracking it was going to be, so he just kind of froze. He forgot to take the fuel cap off and he sprayed about half a gallon of Mr Sheen furniture polish on the screen, then just stood there and looked at me! Anyway, the rest of the lads got me sorted out, so I set off down Bray Hill, but as soon as I lifted my head above the screen, I got a massive face full of Mr Sheen and couldn't see a thing for the next few miles until I got it wiped off.'

In complete contrast, a Honda pit stop, under Neil Tuxworth's steady command, would go something like this. 'One guy changes the back wheel, one guy either changes or cleans the visor, and one guy puts the fuel in,' he explains. 'You're only allowed three people in each pit crew (plus the team boss). Anything to do with the crash helmet or visor is left up to the rider to decide – whether they want to just have their visor cleaned, or whether they want to change visors or even change helmets. The rider also chooses who he wants to do this for him, so it might be a team member or wife or girlfriend. I tend to just watch what's going on and see if I notice anything. I may speak to the rider and tell them what position he's in, or how much of a lead he's got, but I'm not allowed to touch anything on the bike, because I'm not one of the three allocated pit crew. I may catch a back wheel once it's been thrown out, but that's about it.'

Under the extreme pressure of a live pit stop, even apparently simple tasks like changing a helmet can prove tricky and time-consuming. Jenny Tinmouth's pit stop in the 2010 Supersport race didn't quite go to plan. 'I decided to change my helmet in the pits because it was covered in oil,' she says. 'We had borrowed an engine and I don't think it suited the electronics package we had. So, the engine was breathing heavily through the crankcase breather, into the airbox, and oil was coming out of the airbox and getting all over my visor. I'd gone through all my tear-offs, so I decided to change helmets in pit lane, but I'd never practised doing that before with my gloves on. I couldn't get the chinstrap undone, so I had to take my gloves off. Then it took me so long to get my gloves back on because my hands were so sweaty. It felt like I'd lost about half an hour, but it was probably only a couple of minutes.'

Even Neil Tuxworth's vastly experienced Honda team can make mistakes under such a pressure-cooker atmosphere, as he freely admits. 'We had one very bad pit stop in 1990, when we dropped the filler cap down into the fairing of Steve Hislop's 250 Honda in the Junior race,' he says. 'We lost some time, and I'd say it probably lost him the race (Hislop lost out to Ian Lougher by just 1.8 seconds). But that was the sort of mistake that could happen to anyone, and you have to be prepared for the odd thing like that.'

With such a flurry of activity going on around them – activity that is out of their hands and yet could, potentially, affect the outcome of their race – riders also need to learn to keep calm and to let their team members do their job. 'You want a rider who's calm and just sits and waits while everything gets done – not someone who's going to try and close the filler cap before the tank is full, or who is bouncing around, all desperate to get going,' Tuxworth says. 'If the rider is calm, it helps to keep the team calm as well. I remember the biggest problem with Joey Dunlop was that he always wanted to get off the bike and start working on it himself! John McGuinness is very calm to work with, while Phillip McCallen was like a dog on a hot bridge. Opposite ends of the scale.'

While Tuxworth insists that remaining calm is the key to a fast and slick pit stop, Michael Dunlop has a very different approach. 'I have a theory that when you come into the pits you should just roar and shout at everyone to get them all going – get them all wound up!' he says. 'We had a problem with the back wheel one year when they pushed the spindle through, and it pushed off the adjuster. And I had a real butterfingers doing the fuel cap once, who was on his third cap before he got it back on the tank. But I've got a man on the fuel now and it wouldn't matter if you booted him in the stones or told him he'd won the lottery – it wouldn't faze him either way; he wouldn't take his eye off the job. He's so laid-back. He's lucky he has heels or he'd fall over backwards. That's what you need, but you don't get many people like that. But if it's going to go wrong that's where it will happen – in the pits.'

CHAPTER 13

The Man Who Saved the TT

*'He considered it his biggest challenge and his
greatest ever achievement.'*
PAULINE HAILWOOD

With the loss of world championship status in 1977, many predicted the TT would wither and die: a relic of motorsport past, with no place or relevance in the modern world. And it may very well have withered and died, had it not been for a most unlikely hero who would prove to be the saviour of the event.

'He was just bored,' Pauline Hailwood admitted of her husband Mike. 'We were living in New Zealand at the time, and he was just bored. I think in many ways the TT was just a challenge to himself to see if he could still do it.'

When Mike Hailwood announced he was to make a comeback at the infamous Isle of Man TT races after an eleven-year retirement from bike racing, he was middle-aged, partially crippled, overweight and out of shape. He was fabulously wealthy and was happily married with two doting children. What could possibly motivate him to return to the most dangerous race in the world under so much pressure and media attention, and risk his life racing against names he had never even heard of? Even Mike's most ardent admirers – and he could count them in the hundreds of thousands – thought it was an impossible dream and that the best the legend could hope for were a few steady laps to allow spectators a chance to see the man who had once been king. He was, after all, a relic from an entirely different era.

Hailwood had other ideas, as his close friend – and the mastermind behind his outrageous comeback – Ted Macauley noted. 'If nobody else believed it, Mike was set in deadly determination,' he says. 'Not only to do well – but to win. And to win in some considerable style.'

Since Hailwood's last TT (and last world championship campaign) in 1967, the world of motorcycle racing had moved on immeasurably. Power and speeds had increased dramatically, tyre technology allowed riders to achieve seemingly impossible lean angles, their knees scraping along the Tarmac in a style totally alien to Hailwood's classic sit-up-straight poise. Improvements in chassis technology meant bikes could be thrown around in a way Hailwood had never experienced. Even the riding gear was different: riders now wore full-face crash helmets, whereas in Hailwood's era it was all about 'pudding bowl' helmets and goggles. He had nothing going for him in this new world. Nothing, except the fact that he was the greatest motorcycle racer on the planet.

By 1978, the once mighty Isle of Man TT was on its

knees. Having lost its world championship status following the 1976 event, the most famous motorcycle race meeting in the world seemed doomed to become nothing more than a sideshow. Phil Read's return in 1977 had caused more controversy than celebration since he, along with Barry Sheene and Giacomo Agostini, had been amongst the ringleaders calling for the TT to be dropped from the world championship calendar in the early seventies. Without world championship status, and with a growing reputation for being too dangerous for increasingly powerful motorcycles, the TT no longer held the mass appeal it had enjoyed in its heyday in the fifties and sixties. It was clear that the event needed a major boost if it was to survive into the eighties and beyond.

Hailwood's last race on the Isle of Man had been the Senior TT in 1967, when he won the epic duel with Giacomo Agostini, which has widely been cited as the greatest TT race in history. Hailwood hustled his evil-handling Honda-4 round at such a speed, against Ago's MV Agusta, that his lap record of 108.77mph stood for eight years.

When Honda withdrew from racing at the end of the 1967 season, Hailwood also hung up his leathers. He was enjoying a successful car racing career in Formula 1 when a bad accident forced his retirement in 1974. 'He had very little movement in his right foot after that,' explained Hailwood's widow Pauline before she passed away in 2020. 'It was full of staples and pins, and the heel had shattered into so many different pieces it was impossible for the surgeons to do anything with it. He was forced to retire from Formula 1 because of that injury.'

With his badly smashed ankle, Hailwood drifted from country to country in retirement, trying to find something to replace the thrill of racing. He never found it. So, when Phil Read made a successful return to the TT in 1977, it got Hailwood thinking. 'He just said, "Well if old Ready can do it, I can do it,"' Pauline continued. 'There was nothing I could do to stop him, I just had to go along with it.'

And so, at thirty-eight years old, a balding, overweight and semi-crippled Mike Hailwood decided to return to the world's most dangerous race, and the man he enlisted to help him was Ted Macauley. A leading sports journalist, Macauley and Hailwood had become close friends and it was he who was tasked with arranging the greatest comeback in motorcycle racing. 'When Mike phoned me and said he fancied doing the TT again I thought he was pissed – either that or he'd gone mad,' Macauley admits. 'But he said that if I organised it, he would have a go. We originally had an understanding that he would just ride round and enjoy himself, but of course he was lying. I could tell by the effort that he made in the build-up to the race that he was going out to win and when I asked if that was the case he said, "Too right I am." As Mike's manager and best friend, that statement frightened the life out of me – I was scared to death for him.'

In 1978, Mick Grant was one of the TT's fastest men and held the outright lap record at an average speed of 112.77mph. Like every other rider on the grid, he had grown up idolising Mike Hailwood and was honoured to be lining up next to him in a race, so he was shocked when his hero asked for his help. 'Mike was struggling a little in practice and asked me to show him round the course during the Thursday session of practice week,' Grant says. 'I thought, "Fucking hell! That's like God asking me to explain the Bible!"'

Nervous as he was, Grant did his best to impress his hero, but came up short. 'I was good from the start to Ramsey, I was absolutely awful from Ramsey to the Bungalow, and I was exceptionally quick coming back down the Mountain to the start line. So, the only place I didn't want Mike to follow me was up the Mountain. I followed him to Ramsey Hairpin and, sure enough, he waved me past. I made an even bigger balls of going up the Mountain than I usually do – I just completely lost the plot. Afterwards Mike said, "Thank you very much, but how the fuck you get round like you do, I just don't know!"'

Hailwood had arranged to ride a 900SS Ducati in the TT Formula 1 race, which, if he won it, also counted as a world championship. In a bid to help the TT attract spectators, the ruling body of motorcycle sport had granted official status for this somewhat farcical, one-round 'championship'. By contrast, the motorcycle Grand Prix world championships in 1978 took in thirteen races around the globe. But while the world title classification was dubious, the race itself was not: Hailwood would find himself lining up against the best road racers in the world in the F1 event.

His privately funded Sports Motorcycles Ducati, on paper at least, should have been no match for the factory Honda of Phil Read, who had returned to the island despite his unhappy experiences the previous year when he had been pelted with stones while out on track. But while the Honda had all the power, the Ducati handled better, and Mike's later practice times (a best lap of 112.36mph compared to the course record of 112.77mph held by Mick Grant) showed he would be a major threat to Read. There could have been no better sparring partner for Hailwood. Not only was Read one of Hailwood's greatest adversaries from the sixties but, with his current reputation on the Isle of Man, he provided a perfect 'baddie' for Mike, the good guy, to chase. Having both won their first TTs way back in 1961, Hailwood and Read now had 16 world titles and 128 Grand Prix wins between them. The clash of the titans was on.

As race day dawned, Hailwood's entire demeanour seemed to change right before Ted Macauley's eyes. 'When I drove him up to the grandstand on the morning of the race, he was absolutely silent all the way,' he says. 'It was as if someone had let the air out of him; he seemed to have grown smaller and tighter because he was so focused. Then, when I looked into his eyes on the start line, I could see nothing. It was like looking through a porthole on a very clear day. His eyes were absolutely vacant because he was focusing so hard. I told him to enjoy himself and said that there was no pressure, but he didn't even answer me. He just shook my hand and away he went.'

If Hailwood was nervous in the extreme, he did a good job of hiding it once in public, according to Steve Wynne, who supplied the Ducati 900SS for Hailwood to ride. 'Mike didn't say anything to me before he set off for the race because he was too busy leaning on the pit wall talking to a good-looking blonde!' he laughs. 'He had the knack of making all the other riders nervous because he wasn't. To be honest, I don't remember feeling any particular tension on race day. It had been such a roller coaster up to that point that I was just glad to get on with it.'

Fans had been packing every possible vantage point on the 37.73-mile TT course for seven hours before Hailwood's comeback race began. As he lined up alongside his new rivals, they were unaware that Hailwood had needed to be briefed as to who was likely to pose a threat, since he hadn't even heard of most of them. Such was the length of time Hailwood had been out of racing, an entire new generation of riders had replaced those he had raced against in a previous era.

'The pit-lane atmosphere was electric, as it had been all through practice week,' Steve Wynne remembers. 'In my forty-odd years of going to the TT, it's the only time I have seen the stands packed to overflowing, even during every practice session. During practice, the riders left the bikes at the end of the pit lane and had to walk back past the packed stands. As Mike passed, a great cheer went up, but when Phil Read walked past everyone booed and hissed. Phil didn't help himself much by walking the length of the pit lane giving the crowd the V sign! Nobody seemed to be supporting Phil so I decided I would, and during the whole race, even in the pits, I wore a Phil Read shirt!'

When the flag finally dropped for the 1978 TT F1 race, Hailwood, riding number 12, set off 50 seconds behind Read, who carried the number 1 plate. Mike's plan was to catch Read on the road. Tom Herron led the race for a brief period on lap one but, after that, it was Hailwood all the way. After setting a new lap record at 110.62mph, by the third lap, to the utter joy of the record crowds, he had caught Read on the road and the two old rivals wound the clock back more than a decade as they fought it out neck and neck, wheel to wheel, giving a masterclass in TT riding.

Even Read was caught up in the excitement of seeing Hailwood back on a bike. 'For Mike to come back to the TT was brilliant,' he says. 'It was great. He rode really well and it was a fantastic race. For three and a half laps we were together, swapping places; we pitted together, we came out together, and it was just so inspiring to watch him through some of the corners. He was riding like he'd never been away. When he caught me up on the road, I knew there was no way I could beat him unless his bike blew up or he fell off. But he didn't.'

Hailwood and his team had thought of any and every way to gain an advantage over their competitors, including devising the first organised communications system that allowed the team to know exactly where Hailwood was during each race, and how much of an advantage he had. 'Mike's friend, Ron Winder, had organised four signalling stations with radios at key points and these were relayed back to the pits,' Steve Wynne explains. 'We were probably the only team doing this back then. He only pitted for fuel once in six laps so there was a fair wait, but keeping track of the race, and watching the riders go through, always makes the time pass in a flash. My only admission to nerves was checking the fuel rig worked several times. The pit stop went like clockwork, except the bike would not restart until halfway down the pit lane. But then it did, so that was okay.'

Macauley was a bundle of nerves as he watched the race unfold under clear blue skies. 'I sat in the press box for most of the race because that's where most of the information was coming through,' he says. 'The atmosphere in there was like a football match. I'd never seen such excitement. The thrill in the grandstand when he came past for the first time – well, I go cold even now thinking about it. He didn't even glance at his pit; he was just head down, tucked in and rocketing straight towards Bray Hill. It was remarkable.'

Read was forced to ride his Honda to destruction in a bid to better Hailwood. On the fifth lap, while ahead on the road but well behind on corrected time, his engine started smoking, and by the 11th Milestone it was all over. Covered in oil and having suffered several dangerous slides, Read pulled in and became just another spectator of the fairy tale. Hailwood had only one more lap of the 226-mile race to go.

Steve Wynne was convinced his rider had things covered as Hailwood hammered his Ducati round on the sixth and final lap. 'I was confident for the race because I had the world's greatest rider on board,' he says.' We had been testing at Oulton Park and had practice week behind us and he was just cruising. Even though he broke the lap and race records, he could have gone much faster.'

At Hailwood's insistence, his wife Pauline was not present in person for the race. 'Mike didn't want me to go over for the actual race,' she said. 'I stayed with my parents and the children in England. He wanted to give the races his full attention and didn't want to worry about me getting bored or waiting around for him. He knew what it would be like with all the attention he would get. There were no arguments – he said what was happening and that was me told.' Pauline was, however, there in spirit, receiving a running commentary from Ted Macauley in the press office. 'When it came to the last lap he was screaming: "He's gonna do it! He's gonna do it!"' Pauline recalled. 'There was so much excitement – everyone was going crazy during those final few miles.'

Crazy, indeed. The biggest crowd in TT history responded as one when Hailwood passed, roaring its approval and flapping tens of thousands of rolled-up programmes. The commentary team was beside itself with excitement, the media was preparing to file fairy tales back to editors the world over (light aircraft stood by to rush photographers' films back to Fleet Street) and, from Bray Hill to Governor's Bridge, grown men wept. Every father who had told his son that Mike the Bike was the greatest motorcycle racer who ever lived watched through welled-up eyes as the man himself proved it in front of a whole new generation of doubters who considered him some kind of racing relic.

As Hailwood crossed the line to take victory it was, without doubt, the greatest moment in the TT's long history. It was also one of the finest moments in twentieth-century sport and has more than once been called the greatest sporting comeback of all time. Hailwood himself wept tears of joy as he took the chequered flag marking his thirteenth, and greatest, TT victory. Yet they could so easily have been tears of another sort. No one knew it at the time but, as Mike crossed the line, his Ducati's engine expired. It would not have gone another hundred yards.

Steve Wynne explains, 'As Mike got to Signpost corner on the last lap, miles in the lead, I decided to take off the Phil Read shirt and promote my own company, Sports Motorcycles. But when I pulled off the shirt one of my crew said, "Don't take it off – it may be bad luck." Just as Mike crossed the line the engine blew up and, although I'm not superstitious, I've often wondered if I had taken the Phil Read shirt off, would the Ducati have broken down before the finish line?'

It was not until Wynne took the Ducati apart that he discovered it had stripped the main bottom bevel gear which drove its camshafts and, in the process, bent the con rods and valves. Phil Read still ponders how different things might have been. 'If I'd kept running for an extra half a lap and been pushing him, then maybe his Ducati might have blown up a mile from the finish line, instead of 500 yards from it, and he wouldn't have won the race. But then I'd have been the most unpopular winner on the island!'

It was the strangest sight to see so many older spectators in floods of tears at Hailwood's achievements. None had expected to ever see their idol race again, let alone win, and emotions ran high all over the Isle of Man. Mike Hailwood had been a riding god, but his time had long since passed. He was a legend of the 1950s and 1960s, yet here he was, in 1978, showing the next generation of much younger riders he was still the boss. The pride that brought out in his older supporters was extreme. 'There were many grown men crying when he crossed the line to win, and I was one of them,' Ted Macauley admits. 'I remember jumping up and down on the track and I was actually embarrassed at my own reaction. But I was overjoyed, first because my best pal was home safe and sound, and secondly because he'd done it – he'd won the TT after an eleven-year retirement. I didn't come down for a long time after that. As Mike and I walked up through the avenue of people leading to the winner's enclosure, we both had tears streaming down our faces. Everybody was jostling to pat him on the back, and it was just remarkable. I was very proud to have organised something which gave so much joy to so many people. It was an amazing sensation.'

According to his wife, Hailwood himself could scarcely believe he had won. 'When Mike called me after the race, and it was as if he was saying he'd won, but it was difficult for him to believe that he had actually done it,' Pauline explained. 'All the adulation he received was completely overpowering for him. It was something that surpassed anything that had gone before. That win meant an awful lot to Mike. His father Stan had died just a few months before and he dedicated the win to him. I would say it meant more than any other race he'd ever ridden in. I saw film of it, and I'd never seen him cry like that after a win before. He considered it his biggest challenge and his greatest ever achievement.'

But it could all have turned out very differently, had one particular race steward not been sympathetic to Hailwood, as Steve Wynne explains. 'After the race I was in deep discussion with one of the stewards who had a noise meter to test the winning bike and I can tell you now, it would NOT have passed. He was saying to me, "It won't start, will it?" Not knowing it had blown the engine, I was saying, "Of course it will." It was only when he repeated, "It WON'T start, will it?" that it dawned on me he didn't wish to be lynched for disqualifying Mike Hailwood from this historic victory.'

The celebrations lasted long into the night as Hailwood and his crew painted the town of Douglas red. 'We had a great celebration that night at a restaurant down near the harbour,' Wynne says. 'It ended by us dismantling the décor, which was rope and nets, and going out into the street for a tug of war to see who was going to pick up the extensive bill – including damages. The sides were split into the Ted Macauley team and the Sports Motorcycles team. We won, but we're still waiting for Macauley to pay the bill!'

More than forty years after the event, Ted Macauley still seems to be in a state of disbelief over Hailwood's achievement. 'I still go cold when I think about it,' he says. 'The honour that I still feel at having been involved in that is extraordinary. To sit in that grandstand while he went out to do what he did, at the speed he was doing it, and knowing the dangers of it – as I did – was the most scary and thrilling experience of my entire life. It was just remarkable, and just a total privilege to have been with him and to have organised that whole thing, and to be with him out on the town later that night. Boy, did we get drunk!'

Mike Hailwood had single-handedly revived interest in the TT and had attracted the greatest crowd the event had ever seen. He had proved that a loss of world championship Grand Prix status didn't matter – the TT could offer its own dramas and its own tales of triumph over adversity as a stand-alone event. It had hosted one of the greatest comebacks in sporting history and proved that it could survive without Grand Prix stars or Grand Prix status. The organisers must have breathed a deep sigh of relief. Hailwood's extraordinary triumph had saved their event, given it a new lease of life and set it on a course for the future.

Three years after that epic comeback, Mike Hailwood was taking his seven-year-old son David and nine-year-old daughter Michelle for fish and chips near Portway in Warwickshire when a truck driver performed an illegal U-turn in front of Mike's Rover SD1. Hailwood had no chance to react. His daughter Michelle was killed instantly and Mike himself died two days later in hospital, aged just forty. The truck driver was fined £100.

CHAPTER 14

A New Beginning

'Foggy and I both knew we'd have to ride round the most dangerous circuit in the world faster than anyone else had ever done before.'
STEVE HISLOP

After Mike Hailwood's miraculous comeback in 1978, and his final appearance at the event in 1979 (when he won the Senior race), the TT needed a new star to take it into the eighties and, by good fortune, Joey Dunlop took his first major win in the first year of the new decade.

He had already won the Jubilee TT in 1977, but none of the biggest stars had entered that event. But in the 1980 Classic, Dunlop really hit his stride by beating the mighty factory Honda team on a very scruffy and privately owned Rea Racing Yamaha TZ750. Joey looked every bit as scruffy as his bike, spoke quietly and seldom, loved a vodka, loved his cigarettes, loved working on his own bikes, and would soon win the hearts of countless millions of race fans all over the world with his humble attitude and shy demeanour. To many of them, he would become synonymous with the TT, and he would, in an extraordinary career that lasted for over thirty years, win more TT races than anyone else in history.

Dunlop was born dirt poor, into a house with no electricity or running water, several miles outside the town of Ballymoney in Northern Ireland. He had taken part in his first race as far back as 1969, but limited funds meant limited racing in the early years, and it wasn't until the 1980 TT that he really made everyone sit up and take notice.

Not being able to afford one of the expensive 'quick-filler' refuelling systems employed by the big teams like Honda, Dunlop knew he would lose the race in the pits while he waited for his gravity-fed fuel system to fill his tank. In the absence of cash, he resorted to cunning, and had an oversized fuel tank made up the night before the race. It was completely within the rules at the time, and it would mean Dunlop would only need to stop for fuel once, not twice, like the other riders, thus negating the advantage they enjoyed with their quick-filler systems (Dunlop's pit stops were taking 53 seconds while the official Honda riders were in and out in 12 seconds).

On a bike that most other riders didn't think would finish one lap, never mind six, Dunlop smoked the big-money factory teams, set a new outright lap record at 115.22mph, and suddenly found himself in great demand. After a few outings on a factory Suzuki, he opted to sign for Honda and would remain loyal to the firm for the next twenty years. He would also prove to be the biggest crowd-puller at the TT over that same time period and would become the greatest TT rider of all time.

Even being shipwrecked didn't deter Dunlop from winning TT races. Always unconventional and never one for being flash, despite being a factory Honda rider, Dunlop's custom was to travel to the TT in a converted fishing trawler. In 1985, it struck rocks in Strangford Lough and sank with Dunlop, his brother Robert and ten others on board. Dunlop helped rescue those who couldn't swim by tying jerry cans round them and cutting a dinghy free with a knife to get them to safety, never losing his cool at any moment. Several men on board credited Dunlop with saving their lives. Seven bikes also went down in the sinking, as well as racing helmets, boots, gloves, leathers and spares. Most were recovered and, thankfully, Dunlop's precious race bikes were taken to the Isle of Man by Honda, rather than on the fishing trawler.

Practice had already begun when Dunlop flew to the island the day after being shipwrecked but, completely unperturbed, he proceeded to become the first man since Mike Hailwood in 1961 to win three TT races in a week. If he had been loved before, Dunlop was adored now. Here was no ordinary Joe.

As always, the death toll continued to rise throughout the 1980s; the worst years being 1986, when four riders lost their lives, and 1989, when the death toll rose to five. The Production 1300 race that year was a particularly grim affair, claiming the lives of two of Britain's most popular riders – Phil Mellor and Steve Henshaw.

Mellor had been fighting for the lead in the race when he

crashed at Doran's Bend and sustained fatal head injuries. His team-mate and close friend, Jamie Whitham, rode through the wreckage of Mellor's crash and was seriously upset by what he saw. So upset that, just a few miles up the road, he too crashed at Quarry Bends but was fortunately uninjured. Steve Henshaw was not so fortunate. In trying to avoid Whitham's wreckage, he and Mike Seward touched and, while Seward suffered critical injuries – from which he later recovered – Henshaw lost his life in the crash.

On hearing of the double tragedy, several teams and riders packed up and went home, Jamie Whitham among them. He never raced in the TT again.

One rider who wasn't put off was a young Scot called Steve Hislop. He had first won a TT in 1987 but, by 1989, was a factory Honda rider and the new man to beat in the absence of Joey Dunlop, who had suffered serious injuries in a crash at Brands Hatch and had to sit out the TT that year. Dunlop's road back to fitness and winning ways would be a long, drawn-out struggle, but would eventually provide the TT with one of its finest moments.

In Dunlop's absence, Hislop won three races in a week and became the first man to lap the course at an average speed of 120mph. He had set the bar so high that it seemed no one else could follow him, but one man who was convinced he could was Carl Fogarty.

Now a household name, 'Foggy' became famous not only for winning four World Superbike titles in the 1990s, at the height of the Cool Britannia movement, but also for winning the reality TV show *I'm A Celebrity . . . Get Me Out of Here!* in 2014. But in 1989, Fogarty was just an up-and-coming young road racer, as well as a great short circuit rider, just like Hislop.

Fogarty would win the Formula 1 and Senior races in 1990, while Hislop had a dire year, but the classic encounter between the two came in 1991, when Honda shipped over two priceless, full-factory RVF750 machines for the team-mates to ride. 'There was a lot of pressure on Carl and me that year because Honda had shipped in some really exotic, one-off bikes for us to make sure they won the Formula 1 TT, as that would give them ten F1 wins in a row,' Hislop explained. 'They didn't care which one of us won it, but one of us *had* to.'

The intense rivalry between the two started getting dangerous during practice week, as Hislop admitted. 'We were busting each other's guts during practice week, as I would put in a 121mph lap, then Carl would go out and do a 122mph lap. Then I'd go out and lap at 123mph, and it went on like that all week. These were speeds that no one had ever seen round the TT course before, and we were breaking records almost every time we went out for a lap.'

Hizzy and Foggy's riding even scared the boss of Honda's racing division. 'Mr Oguma, the chief of HRC (Honda Racing Corporation), had come over to the island from Japan, and he was going mental at our antics, terrified that we were going to crash and kill ourselves,' Hislop explained. 'He called a meeting and sat Foggy and me down at a table like naughty little schoolchildren. We got a right bollocking for going so fast. Apparently, we'd scared Oguma-san shitless when he watched us at the bottom of Bray Hill! He was a fierce-looking man, and he pointed this big, stubby finger at both of us in turn and shouted, "You and you, not enemies. Honda and Yamaha are enemies. Honda and Suzuki are enemies. Honda and Kawasaki are enemies. You two not enemies. Must decide now which one will win big race."'

Team orders are, thankfully, very rare in motorcycle racing and this wasn't a team order in the conventional sense (instructing one rider to help another rider achieve a win), it was about ensuring both men stayed alive. Naturally, both chose to ignore the order. 'So, there we were, both completely determined to win the Formula 1 race and we were being told to draw lots over it,' Hislop said. 'No way. As we left that office I said to Carl, "I had a shit TT last year, and there's no way I'm going to lose this." Carl was equally determined to win, so we agreed between us that the first man to reach the finish line would be the victor; there was just no way either of us were going to concede that race without a fight.'

The atmosphere on race day was electric, the grid even more jittery than usual. 'The morning of that 1991 Formula 1 TT was the most tense experience I've ever had in racing,' Hislop admitted. 'Michaela Fogarty (Carl's wife) came over to me on the start line and said, "Steve, you're a bit more sensible than that idiot (meaning Carl). You'll back off if it gets scary, won't you?" I was thinking, "No bloody way will I," but I just nodded sweetly to reassure her.'

It was tense, because both men knew *exactly* what they were about to do, and it involved riding into the unknown. 'There was so much adrenaline pumping as Foggy and me both knew we'd have to ride round the most dangerous circuit in the world faster than anyone else had ever done before if we wanted to win. And boy, did we both want to win.'

In the end, Hislop won the race by over 40 seconds as Fogarty's bike was intermittently cutting out at high speed. He also set a new outright lap record of 123.48mph.

The 1992 Senior vies with the 1967 Senior (which saw Mike Hailwood and Giacomo Agostini going head-to-head) as the greatest TT of all time. Once again it was a straight fight between Fogarty and Hislop, but there were no exotic factory machines this time around. Fogarty accepted a ride on an ageing Yamaha OW01 and Hislop, with no other options, finally accepted a ride on a British-built Norton, after having initially laughed when he was asked to race it. Norton team boss Barry Symmons described the bike (not inaccurately) as 'a bike built in a shed in Lichfield'. Nobody thought the Norton could win a TT. It wasn't even an option.

As Hislop lined up on the grid with his home-made machine and his seriously underfunded team, he was aware that the last time a Norton had won the Senior TT was in 1961 when Mike Hailwood rode one to victory. But Carl Fogarty wasn't in a sentimental mood and set a blistering pace to lead by the end of the first lap. Hislop chased hard on the viciously fast Norton but was struggling to control it. 'I was hitting bumps and getting lifted up out of my seat,' he said afterwards, 'and the wind at those speeds was really wrenching my neck and shoulders, threatening to blow me off the back of the bike.'

By the pit stops at the end of the second lap, Hislop was

2.8 seconds ahead, but lost the lead by taking on a fresh rear tyre while Fogarty only stopped for fuel. He had all the work to do again. At half race distance, Hislop had closed to within a second of his rival, who was trying everything he knew to stay ahead. 'I was riding so hard that the bike was falling apart around me,' Fogarty said. 'None of the clocks were working, the front fork seal had gone, the rear brake was bent up, the rear shock was broken – the bike was an absolute mess.'

The lead continued to see-saw back and forth but, as the pair entered the final lap, Hislop held the advantage. Fogarty said, 'I was nine seconds behind at the start of the final lap, which was a lot to make up. To make matters worse, the exhaust blew coming over the Mountain as I made that final push.'

Hislop knew his rival would pull out all the stops in a final bid for glory. 'There was no doubt in my mind that he'd try everything that he knew on that final circuit.'

Hislop was right. Fogarty's last lap was astonishing: his speed of 123.61mph was faster than either rider had managed on infinitely superior factory machinery one year before (and it stood as the outright lap record for seven years). Yet it wasn't enough. After Fogarty flashed across the line there was an agonising three-minute wait before Hislop was due. 'On the last few miles, I started talking to the bike,' Hislop admitted. 'I was urging it home, nursing it every inch and mile of the way.'

The commentator's countdown ensured everyone knew the result as Hislop flashed across the line, 4.4 seconds to the good. He had won the Senior TT on a British-built

Norton: the impossible dream had come true. 'I'd never seen anything like it on my final circuit,' Hislop said. 'It must have been incredible for all those fans to see a British bike threatening to win the Senior TT after more than thirty years, and it was very hard not to be distracted by them. Every vantage point was packed with fans hanging out on to the road, waving their programmes, cheering and taking photographs – it was a spectacular sight.'

After one of the greatest races of modern times, both Hislop and Fogarty announced they would not be returning to the TT. Fogarty stayed true to his word, Hislop was forced to break his.

The 1992 TT provided another extraordinary moment when Joey Dunlop brought the house down at the Villa Marina prize-giving ceremony. After suffering serious injuries at Brands Hatch in 1989, he had struggled enormously to get back to fitness and back up to speed as a racer. In 1990, he had struggled not to be lapped at the Ulster Grand Prix – a race he had previously made his own. He even admitted to feeling that people were laughing at him. They weren't. And they certainly weren't after he equalled Mike Hailwood's all-time record of fourteen TT wins by winning the 125cc Lightweight TT. It had been three years since Dunlop's last TT win and, because of his injuries, he was more comfortable on smaller bikes, so the small, less powerful 125cc machines offered the best opportunity. That win made him the most successful *living* TT racer but, when he repeated the feat in 1993, he became the most successful of all time, and remains so to this day.

In 1994, Steve Hislop returned to the TT, largely against

his will. 'It's not that I wanted to race there,' he admitted, 'but Honda was very keen to promote the (new) RC45, so it was written into my contract that I had to race at the TT.'

Hislop's first lap on Honda's new bike reminded him of why he no longer wanted to race on the Isle of Man. 'If I had ever needed convincing that the TT was too dangerous, riding the RC45 round there was proof enough – it was absolutely lethal at the beginning of practice week,' he said. 'On my first lap I clipped a kerb at 150mph on Bray Hill, then smacked my leg on a wall at Ginger Hall and ripped my leathers and my knee open. The bike had a mind of its own and just went wherever the hell it wanted. It was so out of control that, for the first time in my life, I considered withdrawing my entry and going home – and so did Joey Dunlop. He came into the garage on the first night of practice, threw the bike into his van and said, "That fucking thing's not going to kill me."'

After managing to set the bike up slightly better, Hislop won both the Formula 1 and Senior races, before turning his back on the TT for good.

The 1994 Formula 1 race was marred by a horrendous accident involving Joey Dunlop's younger brother Robert, and it proved yet again just how many things can go wrong in a TT race. As he landed from the famous jump over Ballaugh Bridge and accelerated away, Dunlop's rear wheel completely disintegrated, and he was thrown into a stone wall at 130mph. It was a special aftermarket racing wheel but was designed for short circuit racing on smooth Tarmac, not the excessive rigours of the TT course. Dunlop was rushed to intensive care with life-threatening injuries. The nerves in his right arm and leg had been completely severed, and both limbs were badly broken and fast turning black. A double amputation looked the most likely outcome.

A six-hour operation helped to stabilise Dunlop, but he spent the next 48 hours fighting for his life and, when he regained consciousness, his struggle was not with pain, but with the hellish hallucinations caused by the amount of morphine that was being administered to him. 'They kept me on morphine, which is a horrible drug – a *horrible* drug,' Robert later explained. 'I had hallucinations and it was terrible. I was moving about the bed quite a lot and they (the nurses and Dunlop's friend and mentor Liam Beckett) more than likely thought it was pain, but it was these hallucinations that I was getting – trying to fight off people with razor blades. It was horrible. Really horrible.'

Eight years and twelve operations later, Dunlop accepted an out-of-court settlement of £700,000 by means of compensation, as the accident clearly hadn't been his fault. He would never be able to ride a Superbike again, but he did return to racing smaller, lighter bikes and, in 1998, he pulled off one of the most determined and gutsy TT wins of all time.

Although his right arm and leg were practically useless appendages after his TT crash, Robert Dunlop set to work converting his 125cc Honda – and his race gloves – to enable him to ride. His father cobbled together an ingenious right-hand glove that had springs on the backs of each finger. Since Robert was unable to grip the handlebar tightly enough – and was completely unable to use the front brake lever – the springs on the glove would assist him by offering mechanical support: as Robert tightened his grip, the springs would compress and, as he loosened it, they would recoil, allowing him to hold on to the bike's handlebars more securely.

To address the front brake problem, Robert switched the traditional brake lever for a thumb-operated brake paddle, mounted on the left side of the handlebars. Another problem solved. Changing gears was no problem, as Robert's left leg was working normally, but he couldn't use the rear brake because of the nerve damage to his right leg. Simple, Robert thought – I won't use the rear brake.

But the modifications didn't end there. He was also forced to turn the handlebars upside down to allow him to hold on more comfortably. Each of these modifications were serious compromises and many felt Robert would be a liability to both himself and others if he returned to racing. The point seemed to be proven when, attempting to ride the bike on an airfield for the first time, Robert crashed heavily and badly broke his arm, the bone actually protruding through his jacket this time.

He had attempted to race at the North West 200 in 1996 but had been refused permission by race organiser Billy Nutt. Worse was to come when the Motorcycle Union of Ireland (MCUI) revoked Robert's racing licence altogether, claiming his injuries were too serious to allow him to control a racing motorcycle, and also claiming that his heavily modified machine was not race-worthy.

Undeterred, Dunlop launched a legal action and eventually won his licence back, but Nutt continued to refuse him an entry to the two races he controlled – the North West 200 and the Ulster Grand Prix. The organisers of the TT *did* allow Robert to race, and he returned there in 1997, astonishing everyone by taking a podium. He could be seen on the longer straights putting his overworked left arm behind his back to give it a break and ease himself into a more comfortable position, while hanging on only with his disabled right hand. Most spectators could only shake their heads in disbelief at the levels of drive, determination and sheer guts on display. Others saw only madness.

Three weeks before the 1998 TT, Dunlop had finally been allowed to compete at the North West 200 again, but probably wished he hadn't bothered. He was knocked off his bike by another rider and suffered yet another break to his right leg and another broken right collarbone. Broken, but not in the least bowed, Dunlop turned up in the Isle of Man on crutches, fully intending to race. Having somehow been passed fit by the medics, he then went on to achieve one of the grittiest victories in TT history by winning the Ultra-Lightweight race.

Had it happened in a Hollywood movie, it would have been laughable, so far-fetched did the end result seem. But it happened for real, and the crowds at the prize-giving ceremony were sent into raptures when Dunlop took to the stage on crutches before throwing them into the crowd and standing on his own two feet. It was the stuff of legend, and in that one race Robert Dunlop proved himself the equal of his more famous brother, once and for all. No one in racing could remember seeing such a display of bravery, grit and sheer bloody-mindedness. 'I lost count of the number of times I questioned if I could run at the front again,' Dunlop admitted after his emotional win. 'I guess this is two fingers up to those who said I couldn't do it.'

It seems there's no end to the list of bizarre things that can go wrong during a TT race and, in the 1994 Supersport 600 race, Ian Simpson discovered a new hazard to add to the list. 'I lost both my contact lenses and one of them got stuck to my lips, and I got so annoyed with it I bit it and swallowed it,' he explains. 'I couldn't see a fucking thing, so I just followed Iain Duffus for a lap and a half. It's a good job he never went into a hedge, because I'd have gone straight in behind him.' Half blind, Simpson followed the blurry shape of a rider and bike in front of him and came home in second place.

One year later, in the Formula 1 race, Phillip McCallen added to the list again. 'I didn't know what was wrong; I was in such a state of nervous tension it's difficult to describe,' he explained after the drama. 'The only similar situation I can think of is if you can imagine you're the pilot of an aircraft. Now imagine it's got a terrible problem, you're hurtling towards the ground fighting the controls all the way, knowing any second now you're going to crash.'

McCallen was racing round the TT course at 190mph with a loose rear wheel, which threatened to fall off at any moment. It was no one's fault; the new wheel simply didn't fit his Honda RC45 as well as it should have done, and the extra movement this caused had resulted in the wheel nut chewing right into the hub of the wheel. According to McCallen, 'The whole thing was only being held on by the remains of the nut, tight up against the fragile little sprung "R" clip, which is only designed to stop the nut coming off, not to hold a whole wheel on.'

Naturally, McCallen did not back off and went on to win the race.

Clearly not wishing to be left out, Scotland's Iain Duffus added a new entry to the list of hazards TT riders must contend with. He had to withdraw from the event in 1998 thanks to an incident involving his young son. 'There was about ten minutes to go before the practice session and I was just getting my helmet on,' Duffus explained. 'My wee boy decided to go for a walk on his own, and I got into a bit of a panic looking for him. I saw him in the distance and just went to run to catch him and I heard my leg snap, and I tumbled over and that was it – a broken leg.'

Before he even got on his bike.

While Duffus sat on the sidelines throughout the 1998 TT, Joey Dunlop proved in the Lightweight 250 race that cunning and experience are just as important as a fast bike. Riding in great pain (after losing the top half of his ring finger in a crash in Ireland, the half-empty finger of Dunlop's glove had been flapping maddeningly against the still-raw stump of his amputated finger during TT fortnight), he employed brilliant tactics in the weather-hit event. The race was cut from four laps down to three just before the start, and most riders planned to pit after one lap for fuel. Showing years of TT experience, Dunlop defied his Honda team and gambled on doing two straight laps, believing the weather would worsen and the race would be stopped after two laps. That was exactly what happened, and Joey Dunlop won his twenty-third TT in the most atrocious weather conditions and still in great pain.

David Jefferies changed the TT in more ways than he could have imagined when he beat the might of Honda on a private, production-based Yamaha R1 to lift the Formula 1 Trophy in 1999. Honda had won the F1 race every year since 1982 and, over the years, had shipped in some of the most exotic – and expensive – four-stroke motorcycles on the planet to guarantee victory. Cost was not an issue for the world's biggest motorcycle manufacturer, and it was no different in 1999 when Honda supplied Joey Dunlop and Jim Moodie with World Superbike-spec RC45s. *Motor Cycle News* estimated the cost of each bike to be around £500,000 and calculated the team spent another £1 million on back-up.

In contrast, David Jefferies was mounted on a bike which started life as a bog standard £8,299 Yamaha R1 road bike. By the time it had been readied for racing by the V&M team, its total value was estimated at around £20,000. It seemed impudent to even think about challenging the might of Honda on such a budget, but Jefferies and his V&M team were up for the challenge.

The Formula 1 race was red-flagged following a (non-fatal) crash at Bray Hill and, in the four-lap restart, Joey Dunlop quickly took the lead from Iain Duffus and David Jefferies and held it until the pit stops at the end of lap two. When Dunlop lost 20 seconds in the pits, he rode harder than ever to claw it back, and set his fastest ever lap of the course at 123.06mph. But it wasn't enough: Jefferies responded with a lap at 123.36mph – just 3.1 seconds off

Carl Fogarty's outright lap record. It was enough to give him his first TT win. 'I can't believe this,' he said. 'I never thought I'd win. I just didn't think I had the experience to do it. I can barely tell you how good it feels to take a win on a bike that costs about £20,000 in front of these massively expensive Hondas.'

Jefferies' win (and his subsequent win in the Senior on the same bike) changed everyone's perception of the TT. If glorified street bikes could win, what was the point in building multi-million-pound factory specials? Suddenly, even the most prestigious TT races were within the reach of modest teams. The TT had come full circle and returned to its 1907 roots as the ultimate test for production-based motorcycles.

CHAPTER 15

Ordinary People

*'Sometimes people are surprised to find a
TT racer working in a shop.'*
CAMERON DONALD

They're not superheroes. To millions of fans around the
word, they might appear to be, but TT racers, for the
most part, are just ordinary people doing extraordinary
things. Plumbers, bricklayers, construction workers,
mechanics, plasterers . . . When they're not racing the
Mountain Course at superhuman speeds, TT riders are a
pretty ordinary bunch, which can come as quite a surprise
to fans.

Australian Cameron Donald won two TT races in
2008 and was one of the event's biggest stars at the time,
but during the off-season he would work as a plumber
or help out in his friend's bike shop. 'Sometimes people
are surprised to find a TT racer working in a shop, but
most people who come in know me and they just have
a good laugh when they see me on the front cover of

the TT DVD or something like that,' he says. 'The other day a guy came in and wanted a copy of the 2008 TT on DVD (which features Donald on the front cover) for his uncle's birthday. He said he'd seen some copies signed by Cameron Donald for sale and was really disappointed that we didn't have any left. I said, "That's no problem, I'll sign one for you now." It was so funny seeing the look on his face and his wife's face. They couldn't believe it. He said, "I've been watching you racing on TV but had never seen you with your helmet off!" It's really nice when things like that happen.'

For Donald, working in a shop was a luxurious break from his usual off-season jobs. 'Usually, I work as a plumber during the off-season, but I only did a handful of days this year because of my shoulder,' he said in 2010 while recovering from injury. 'I've been doing proper rehab work on it, and lugging plumbing tools around wasn't going to be the best way to fix it. So, I've been working in my mate's bike shop, just doing over-the-counter stuff. I've worked there for years, usually just on the weekends or when someone wants a couple of days off during the week. But I have done a few days on the tools (plumbing) and digging holes with the excavator. I do a lot of driving diggers and drainage stuff for the family company. Normally, I come back home after the racing season and try to work really hard on the tools up until Christmas, and then only work a couple of days a week to give myself a good break before I get back to racing.'

John McGuinness has won more TT races than any man alive and has an MBE and comfortable lifestyle to show for his efforts, but it wasn't always so. 'I was brought up on a council estate and used to go club racing on Giros, so the TT was completely out of my reach in my early days of racing,' he admits. 'I even picked mussels in Morecambe Bay for a while to make ends meet. You need a good team and a good bike for the TT, and I just didn't have the money.'

When he did finally make his TT debut in 1996, McGuinness still had less money than most spectators. 'I never had a budget!' he laughs. 'I had a couple of hundred quid in my pocket and that was it. No credit cards, no plastic. The plan was just to sleep in the truck and go to the supermarket and live off beans on toast. It was a total wing and a prayer job – I didn't have a clue what I was doing. I didn't sign many autographs that year.'

Before becoming a TT legend, McGuinness had an altogether more normal job. 'I was still a full-time bricklayer at that time,' he says of his debut year on the island. 'The first proper job I got was as an apprentice and I got about £50 a week. Once I had served my time, I worked for a firm called The Kitchen Building Company and I got paid £6 an hour. So, I took home about £250 after my first week and I didn't know what to do with it. I showed it to Becky (then girlfriend, now wife) and said, "Jesus, look at this!" We'd been living on about £30 a week and saving £20 a week. I ended up buying a truck with it for my racing.'

Despite their hard-as-nails image and their unquestionable toughness, some TT riders have backgrounds in more gentle arts. Lee Johnston had intended to study engineering but ended up studying to be a hairdresser – although his motives were not altogether pure. 'All my mates and me were queuing up to do mechanical engineering at Enniskillen College, and I noticed that there were about twenty gorgeous girls in the queue to do hairdressing, so I thought that looked like better craic and changed queues!' he says. 'I did it for about a year, and even worked in a hairdressers' for a while. My mates used to take the piss, until they saw me out at lunch every day with all those women and they wanted to come with me. I told them to sod off and go for their hairy welders' lunch!'

While Peter Hickman is now a professional motorcycle racer (few TT riders can lay claim to such a luxury), he was still working when he made his TT debut in 2014 and continued to do so until 2015. 'I was working a normal job right up until the start of this year,' he said at the time. 'I was a plasterer originally, but I've done all sorts – sheet metal engineering, powder-coating, vinyl stickering, general building work, you name it. As long as it pays at the end of the day, who cares?'

Coming from all sorts of backgrounds as they do, some TT racers have impressive qualifications. Australia's David Johnson is now, like Hickman, a professional rider, but that wasn't always the case. 'I'm a qualified CNC machine programmer,' he says. 'I did my apprenticeship in that before I came over to the UK in 2002 and have dabbled with it a bit since then.'

Davey Todd was still working when he made his debut at the TT in 2018, and he also has impressive qualifications, but was forced to abandon his well-paid job. 'I'm actually qualified as an electrical engineer and used to design and build prototype wiring harnesses for high-end car companies like Bentley and Aston Martin,' he says. 'But that job came to a close two years ago as I couldn't get enough time off to go racing. Ever since, I've just picked up any jobs I can – working for mates and whatever comes along.'

Naturally, given their connections and passion for the subject, some racers work within the motorcycle industry itself. The TT's fastest female, Jenny Tinmouth, is now retired from racing and runs her own motorcycle workshop, as well as doing an increasing amount of stunt riding for major Hollywood movies like Tom Cruise's *Mission: Impossible* films.

But when she first went to the TT in 2009, the sacrifices she made in order to compete were typical of many TT racers. Working as a self-employed bike mechanic at the time, Tinmouth invested everything she earned into racing, but it was still nowhere near enough. 'When people say they have no money, I don't think they know what that means,' she said back in 2010. 'I have absolutely no savings, no house – I live at home with my parents – and I don't even have a car now because I sold it to pay for the TT. In 2005 I sold my 600cc race bike to get the money to start the Two Wheel Workshop in Ellesmere Port. Everyone thinks I must be loaded because Brad (business partner, mechanic and close friend Steve 'Brad' Bradley) and I have our own business, but it's a proper struggle. We don't draw any wages – we just pay the bills, and the rest goes into racing. When you consider it cost me £8,000 just to do the TT and that it costs more than £1,000 for tyres every race weekend (in the British championships), you can appreciate just how expensive it is to go racing. Every now and then I think about the expense, and it freaks me out a bit, but then I think, "Sod it – I've got to go for it."'

There are, of course, always exceptions, and not all TT racers have working-class backgrounds. At the opposite end of the scale are two of the greatest TT riders of all time – Giacomo Agostini and Mike Hailwood – who were both sons of multi-millionaires and enjoyed playboy lifestyles. It might be seen as even more remarkable that such men would risk their lives racing motorcycles on the world's most dangerous course when they could have simply enjoyed their inherited wealth in great comfort and safety.

In complete contrast to Agostini and Hailwood was Joey Dunlop. The most successful TT racer of them all was born extremely poor in rural Ireland, into a house with no running water or electricity.

There is no stereotype for a TT racer; they come from every kind of background imaginable, united only in their desire to win, and their willingness to take immense risks to achieve that goal.

Budgets obviously play a huge part in the TT. It's a hugely expensive event to take part in, and those with limited funding are clearly at a great disadvantage. To compare the budget of a privateer rider with that of a major team is to reveal the great divide between the two.

When Jenny Tinmouth first contested the TT in 2009, she was already racing in the British championships, so she already had the basics like a race bike (she paid £13,000 for her Honda CBR600) and a truck (which cost £10,000). Without the budget to rebuild the engine in her bike ahead of the TT, it dropped a valve during the race, leaving Tinmouth with just her (borrowed) Superstock bike.

The bill for mechanic's wages was zero, as Tinmouth and her business partner Steve Bradley did all the work themselves. They already had spare parts from British championship racing, and the TT organisers covered the cost of race entries and the return ferry trip to the Isle of Man. Tyres and oil were covered by sponsors, but fuel for the truck and the races bikes came to around £500. The food bill for Tinmouth and Bradley was around £600 for the two weeks but accommodation cost nothing as the pair slept in their race truck in the paddock.

Team clothing was not an additional expense as it had already been bought for the British championships, although £100 was needed to buy new regulation fire-retardant overalls for Bradley to wear in pit lane. Tinmouth did spend an additional £600 on riding gear for the event but says the greatest expense of the TT came from two weeks without earning: the Two Wheel Workshop had to be closed for the duration of the event.

In contrast, a bigger team like Michael Rutter's Bathams outfit spent almost £200,000 in contesting the TT in 2017. The bikes cost £95,000, with a further £20,000 spent on spare parts, mechanic's wages came to £7,500, getting an articulated race truck (worth £50,000), a motorhome and a support van to the event cost £2,500, tyres cost £7,500 (although this was covered by a sponsorship deal), fuel costs were £1,500, the food and drink tab for the team came in at £2,500, a further £4,000 was spent on consumables like oil, chains and sprockets (again, largely offset by sponsorship), and £2,500 was spent on team clothing.

All in, it cost the Bathams team £196,000 to contest three races at the 2017 TT, which equates to £65,166 per race. The team's rewards were a sixth place in the Superbike TT, a fifth place in the Senior, and a fourth in the Superstock race. Top ten placings do not come cheap at the TT.

Having a factory bike can make a huge difference at the TT, as elsewhere, and can mean the difference between winning races and losing them. In 1998, Ian Simpson was given a factory Honda RC45 to try to help Honda celebrate its fiftieth birthday in style. Simpson had already proved he didn't need a factory bike to win a TT, but he was amazed at just how good the real deal was. 'The full factory RC45 was incredible compared to the bike I usually rode – unbelievably better,' he says. 'The brakes were better, the clutch was better, the gearbox; it felt smaller to sit on, it was more comfortable. The throttle was lighter, the clutch was lighter, it was more stable – just everything you could imagine a bike doing, it did it better. It was a real sickener when I had to get back on my own bike after the TT, because then I realised what a heap of shit it really was!'

Simpson used his factory RC45 to good effect, winning both the Formula 1 and Senior races for his grateful employers.

Official teams like Honda Racing do not reveal their TT budgets but, in 1990, the carburettors alone for Joey Dunlop's Honda RC30 were worth around £20,000. Not that Dunlop cared. Even when he was Honda's most important factory rider, he preferred to go about his racing like a true privateer. His team boss at the time, Neil Tuxworth, takes up the story. 'Honda Japan had sent over some very special flat slide carburettors for Joey's RC30,' he explains. 'There were only two sets in existence, and they were worth around £20,000 each, which was an awful lot of money at the time, and I was told we had to take very good care of them. It was my first year as team boss for Honda Britain, and a man called Michihiko Aika came over from Honda Japan that year. He used to be Mike Hailwood's mechanic and was, by 1990, head of Honda Motorsports. I was told to collect him at the airport and to really look after him because he was senior Honda management. I was quite nervous about meeting him, but I picked him up and asked if he wanted me to take him to the hotel or to the paddock. He said, "No, I want to go to Joey Dunlop's garage," and I just thought, "Oh, no."'

Instead of operating out of the impressive Honda team camp in the TT paddock, Dunlop preferred to use a shabby little garage away from the crowds, down by the harbour quay in Douglas. Tuxworth still cringes when he recalls what happened next. 'When we got to Joey's garage there was nobody there, but the RC30 was sitting outside in the pissing rain. The cylinder head had been taken off the bike and there must have been an inch of rainwater in the top of each piston. The garage was next to a little river, and Mr Aika looked over the wall and saw a twig sticking out of the wall with those £20,000 carburettors hanging off it, dangling over the river. Mr Aika looked at me, and I was shaking, and must have had the fear of God in my eyes – I was certain that I had just lost my job. But he just looked at me and said, "Neil-san, please do not be concerned – we all know about Joey Dunlop!"'

Whatever their backgrounds and financial positions, TT racers cannot expect to become rich, even if they're multiple winners. If a rider leads all six laps of a Superbike or Senior TT, they stand to win £18,000 (this figure will be less if they do not lead every lap, as cash prizes are awarded for positions at the end of each lap), but this drops to £8,000 for winning the Superstock race and just £5,000 for a Lightweight TT win. The total prize fund for a Superbike race at the TT is £587,400. By contrast, the winning team in the Formula 1 World Championship is awarded an (estimated) £75 million, and the total prize money for one season in the UEFA Champions League is £1.1 billion. It is perhaps just as well that TT riders race purely for the love of it.

CHAPTER 16

Chariots of Fire

*'I know drivers who have pissed blood and not been able
to walk for a week after the TT.'*
Tim Reeves

While they may look fearless as they skim stone walls at 180mph, there is one position that most TT racers would be too afraid to fill: that of being a sidecar passenger.

Sidecars originated as a cheap and practical means of transport, allowing a motorcycle rider to take a passenger along in relative comfort. Most road-going motorcycles could be fitted with one; they consisted of an extra wheel and a covered space for a passenger, bolted on to the side of a bike. But racing sidecars – also known as 'chairs', 'outfits' or 'chariots' – are more akin to Formula 1 cars than motorcycles. They are purpose-built three-wheelers, have an ultra-low profile, and a very small platform for the passenger to 'sit' in, although they spend very little of their time sitting. They use motorcycle engines and have a set of handlebars, but bear practically no further resemblance to

motorcycles. The rider, or 'driver', doesn't even sit on the
machine, instead lying on his chest with his feet out behind
him. The right foot changes gears (the gear lever is on the
opposite side from a normal motorcycle) while the left foot
operates the single brake pedal that controls the front and
rear brakes.

But it's the passengers who are considered the crazy
ones, even by solo TT riders. They are not at the controls
of the outfit and are at the absolute mercy of the driver: if
he makes a mistake, both parties suffer the consequences.
The passenger must, quite literally, trust the driver with
his life.

Because they're so low to the ground, sidecar outfits
have very little in the way of suspension, meaning a lap
of the hideously bumpy TT course is a truly brutal affair.
Dan Sayle has won eight TT races as passenger for three
different riders. 'You have practically no suspension on a
sidecar – just a couple of inches of travel,' he says. 'But as
soon as you hit the Ginger Hall to Ramsey section, you're
not steering the thing, you've just got the throttle back to
the stop, and it's just bouncing from one side of the road
to the other. It just goes where it wants to. You bounce
off one bump, turn the bars a little bit, bounce off another
bump, and it just goes on and on like that all the way
to Ramsey. The drivers are getting battered around and
I'm trying to lock myself into position in the chair, trying
to push myself in as tight as I can. On the first night of
practice, you get covered in bruises, by the second night
you're adding to them, and by the end of race week you're
just black and blue all over.'

There are stories about some drivers whose kidneys take such a battering at the TT they urinate blood for days afterwards. 'The TT gives you a real battering,' former winner Tim Reeves agrees. 'The run from Ginger Hall to Ramsey is particularly bad. By the time you get to Ramsey you can't actually breathe properly because of the battering your chest and stomach has taken on the bike. It's not happened to me yet, but I do know drivers who have pissed blood and not been able to walk for a week after the TT.'

A passenger's job is not simply to hang on for dear life; the way he moves his body around the machine is absolutely critical. On right-hand corners, he will hang off the side of the outfit using handholds. On left-hand corners, he hangs his backside out, so close to the road that many passengers wear sliders on the seats of their leathers, like solo riders have on their knees to skim along the Tarmac.

This movement of the passenger not only prevents the outfit from tipping over, but also forces the fat rear tyre into the road to generate more grip, thereby allowing the driver to get on the power faster and harder. There are no seatbelts or harnesses of any kind. Sidecar passengers climb all over the outfit at speeds of up to 150mph, just millimetres from the unforgiving Tarmac beneath them.

On straights, passengers can't even see where they're going. 'There are lots of parts of the course that I simply don't get to see, because I'm tucked into the chair with my head down,' Sayle reveals. 'Places like the bottom of Bray Hill, or anywhere that's really fast, I never actually see. Places like the top and bottom of Barregarrow are taken absolutely flat out on a sidecar, but I get to see them because they're corners too, so my head is out of the chair. You really feel the speed through there. Heading for that gap at the bottom of the hill without shutting off takes some balls. That's when you think, "Jesus, we're moving now." But it's crucial to keep your head tucked down. If you stick your head up on the fast straights, you can actually hear the revs go down on the engine. Even if your leathers are a bit loose and flapping at the shoulder, you can hear the engine note go down and the bike losing revs.'

One of the most successful sidecar crews of all time are brothers Ben and Tom Birchall. They've won twelve TT races as well as four world championships, yet even world championship racing isn't as tough as racing a sidecar around the TT course, as passenger Tom admits. 'It's such a stress and strain on your body. No amount of short circuit riding can prepare you for that. The sheer speed, the fact that your body is taking such a beating, the concentration levels required – it's all through the roof compared to world championship level.'

Ben Birchall agrees. 'Yeah, to be successful at the TT means you lose some of the enjoyment. I used to love going to the TT. I mean, I still do, but to do 119mph laps you've got to put everything on the line, it's as simple as that. It's not easy, either mentally or physically. To do those kinds of speeds you also really need to ask yourself, "Is this what I want to be doing?" Because if you're not completely committed, you couldn't do them.'

Sidecars don't enjoy the same level of media attention or the big money backing that Superbikes do and, while there is still a world championship held for them, most competitors see the TT as the biggest race of the year in the sidecar calendar, and rate a TT win as something above and even beyond winning a world title. 'It's weird,' Tim Reeves says. 'In motorcycle sport in general, a world championship is viewed as higher than a TT win. But in sidecar racing, a TT win is seen as being more special. You get better recognition for it too.'

The first TT race for sidecars was held in 1923, but after two years it was abandoned due to a lack of interest. It wasn't reinstated until 1954 but has been a staple of the programme ever since. The chariots get two races of three laps (113.19 miles) each, with no need for a pit stop. Despite the fact they are now limited to using 600cc engines (Superbikes are 1000cc) at the TT, and that these smaller engines have to carry the weight of two people as well as propelling the 200kg mass of the outfit along, sidecars have a top speed of around 150mph and the lap record is just short of 120mph. The reason they can achieve such incredible average lap speeds is because drivers hold the throttle fully open for around 60 per cent of the lap.

Because there's not as much money in sidecar racing as there is in solo motorcycle racing, riders and passengers often have to go to extraordinary lengths to fund their addiction. With seventeen wins to his credit, Dave Molyneux is the most successful TT sidecar racer of all time, but even he has struggled to make ends meet over the years. 'Racing is a hobby,' he said in 2010. 'Neither myself nor any of the other sidecar racers are professionals – there's not enough money in the sport. My effort this year has cost around £35,000 to put together, which is more than my year's salary, so you've got to duck and dive and do some pretty hard deals here, there and everywhere, to try and put that kind of thing together. Last year I wasn't in that position, so I had to go to the bank for it. By the start of practice week last year, I was £20,000 overdrawn and my bank manager gave me a right bollocking.'

Due to this perennial lack of funding, many sidecar racers, Molyneux included, build their own machines from scratch. 'Every part has to be hand-made – you can't buy these things in shops,' he says. 'And we can't afford to pay for full-time mechanics either, so we have to do it all ourselves. Every sidecar team can say that, with no exceptions. But that's what makes the sidecar paddock so good – it's proper old-school racing and everybody helps each other.'

In taking up sidecar racing, Dave Molyneux was following in his father's footsteps. The fact that John Molyneux was killed in a racing accident when Dave was just fourteen years old didn't deter him in the slightest.

In sidecar racing, father and son, father and daughter, brother and brother, and even husband and wife teams are relatively commonplace. There have also been all-female crews at the TT. Those close relationships can make fatalities seem even more tragic when things go terribly wrong.

In 2004, Ian Bell made a vow to God never to race at the TT again. At the time, he was being dragged along the TT course, trapped upside down by his sidecar outfit, and losing flesh from his right arm at an alarming rate as it ground away on the Tarmac. 'It did scare me quite a bit,' Bell was unafraid to admit. 'I was upside down for so long and I said to Him upstairs, "Let me away with this one and I promise not to do the TT again!" I must have said that about half a dozen times and when I finally came to a stop, I thought He must be looking after me, so I sold my outfit and all my racing stuff to keep my end of the bargain.'

Ten years later, however, Bell reneged on his vow and made a racing comeback at the very event he had vowed never to contest again. Two years after that, with his son Carl as his passenger, Bell lost control of his outfit on the final lap of the second Sidecar TT in 2016 and was killed instantly. His son was uninjured.

It was the grimmest of ironies. Speaking in 2014, Ian Bell revealed that it was his son's dream to become a sidecar passenger that had persuaded him out of retirement. 'He'd never said anything to me about it, but he told my brother Geoff (himself a double sidecar winner at the 1992 TT) that he'd like to try his hand at being a passenger. That was in 2006, and I had an old chassis lying around that I'd picked up from Dave Molyneux, so we decided to build it up and have a go with me driving and Carl in the chair. If he hadn't taken an interest, then I would probably never have raced again.'

The 2022 TT saw more than its fair share of tragedies, including the deaths of the father-and-son pairing of Roger and Bradley Stockton. Roger Stockton was making his twentieth appearance at the TT while his son was making his debut as a passenger. They had finished a highly respectable eighth in the first sidecar race of the week before losing their lives in the second race.

In that first race, tragedy was heaped upon tragedy when

race organisers announced that French sidecar passenger Olivier Lavorel had died following a crash at Ago's Leap, while his driver, César Chanal, had sustained critical injuries. It would be five days before a second statement was released clarifying a case of mistaken identity. It was Chanal who had lost his life and Lavorel who had sustained life-threatening injuries. The reason for the confusion had been down to the two men inexplicably swapping the dog tags that all TT racers are forced to wear to confirm their identity in just such a situation. Such was the nature of the injuries sustained by both riders, their correct identities were only established following DNA and blood group tests. One can only imagine the heartache and stress such a tragic situation must have caused for both riders' families. Lavorel had been flown to a hospital in Liverpool, but Chantal's mother believed it was her son who had survived the crash and been transferred to a mainland hospital. It was only upon arrival that she discovered it was not her son, and that he, not Lavorel, had in fact been killed. Lavorel would cling to life for four months before succumbing to his injuries in October 2022.

All in all, the 2022 TT claimed the lives of six riders, making it as bad a meeting as there had ever been. It was not unprecedented – five riders had been killed in 1989 – but, after a two-year lay-off due to the Covid-19 pandemic, hopes had been high for a safe and exciting return. It was enough to make many people question the continued existence of the TT, and to reignite the debate about whether it should be stopped. But, as usual, the calls for it to be banned came from outside the motorcycling world, not from within. Mainstream news coverage of the TT rarely occurs unless there are tragedies to report.

In 2014, Conrad Harrison and his son Dean became the first father and son to both win TT races in the same week – Conrad won the opening sidecar race of the week, while Dean won the Lightweight solo race. Despite having little concern for their own safety during their respective races, both father and son admit to feeling nervous during the other's race. 'It was definitely more nerve-wracking than winning my own race!' Dean said after watching his father win his first TT in 2014 after twenty years of trying. 'When you're in your own race you don't really think about it – you just get your head down and away you go.'

For a father, watching his son race round the Isle of Man TT course is no easy task either. 'I was sitting in the awning listening to the radio,' Conrad says of the 2014 Lightweight race, which gave Dean his first win. 'I didn't watch Dean going past on the start line – I can feel where he is when he's racing. I can hear him through every commentary point on the radio, and then I can visualise it and feel exactly where he is on the course. Every commentary point he passed through, it made me a bit happier. When it's your child out there, it's a lot, lot, lot, lot more nerve-wracking than when you're racing. It's a totally different ball game. I mean, I've done the TT for twenty years and I didn't realise how selfish I was to put my loved ones through that kind of worry.'

Before making his fateful return to the TT in 2014, Ian Bell summed up a TT racer's mentality better than most; how they rationalise the dangers and compartmentalise them, to be able to get on with the job in hand. 'The TT is a worrying place, don't get me wrong, and I had a bad accident there, even though I didn't break a bone,' he explained. 'But you have to think that what's going to happen is going to happen. Your life is all mapped out, and if somebody upstairs had wanted me, then they could have had me quite a few times before now. If I'm not happy in practice then I won't race, simple as that. Thinking about it now is a bit of a worry, but once you actually get there and get on the bike, there's nothing like it in the world. You can't explain it to people – it's such a one-off place. It's like you're getting away with doing something really naughty and you know you're not going to get nicked for it!'

Sidecar racers are as deeply committed to the TT as the solo racers. They all face the same risks, the same challenges, and they also have to overcome a serious lack of funding. But it's the passengers in particular who are viewed as the men, and women, living closest to the edge. 'I think we get branded as the maddest men in the paddock,' Dan Sayle admits. He's probably right.

CHAPTER 17

Heaven Can Wait

*'I was told there were risks of blindness, paralysis and
even death.'*
Conor Cummins

Once the TT bug has bitten deep, it seems no punishment
short of death itself will turn the bitten shy. Many
riders have returned from horrendous, life-threatening
injuries, and made superhuman efforts to push through
pain barriers most people could not even imagine, to get
back on a bike and return to the TT.

Lee Johnston is just one example. He crashed during
practice for the 2017 TT and was lucky to escape with his
life. 'I broke my back in three places, broke my coccyx,
broke my hands, cut my face open and needed a lot of
stitches, and I had bleeding on the brain too,' he says. 'The
doctors were worried about the bleeding for the first couple
of days, but then it just stopped.'

On top of the extreme pain he suffered, Johnston also
found himself experiencing hallucinations. 'The bang on

the head definitely affected me,' he explains. 'About a week later I was lying in bed with my partner Christy, and her phone flashes when she gets a text message. I saw the flashing and started going mad because I thought I'd been caught by a speed camera! We had a proper, full-on argument about it. She was trying to tell me it was only her phone but, apparently, I wasn't having it. I was hard work at that stage – all my anger was coming out and I was feeling really anxious, but I didn't know all this until I went to see a specialist.'

Mercifully, the severity of his injuries meant Johnston was spared the memory of the accident itself. 'I don't remember anything about the crash,' he says. 'I don't remember getting out of the hospital or getting the ferry home – I don't even know how I got home!'

Johnston's memory blackout also helped him when he returned to racing just two months later. 'My first race back after the TT was the Ulster Grand Prix, and I got on the podium in my first race. Everybody was saying, "That's amazing – how did you put the TT crash out of your mind?" But I didn't have to because I didn't remember it! If someone told me the reason why I felt so beaten up was because I got a kicking outside Tesco, I'd have believed them, because I just didn't know any better. It would be great if that happened with every accident – a dream scenario!'

Phillip McCallen also found himself hallucinating after a crash in the 1990 Senior race. He was convinced he was dead. Remembering the crash, he said, 'There was an almighty bang on impact, total blackness, and then I was just floating, higher and higher. The little white houses got smaller and smaller, and I was thinking to myself, "This is definitely it – I'm on my way to Heaven." The feeling wasn't bad at all, my mind was quite peaceful, except for the terrible noise which wouldn't stop. A girl's face floated into my vision and spoke to me. "Everything's fine, don't worry, Phillip, you're okay now with us. You're in the helicopter and we're taking you to the hospital – you've only been out a few minutes." Heaven will have to wait a bit longer for me then, I thought – and that was the end of my TT for that year.'

Rather than an imaginary trip to Heaven, John McGuinness found himself in a very real hell after being thrown from his Honda Fireblade at the 2017 North West 200. He suffered compound fractures (where the bone breaks through the skin and is exposed) of his right tibia and fibula, four broken vertebrae, three broken ribs and two broken thumbs. Such was the extent of the damage to McGuinness' right leg that it had to be fitted with an external fixator cage for nine months.

The crash almost cost McGuinness his career, his sanity and his marriage. He was forty-five years old at the time. Most felt McGuinness would retire; it was the most sensible thing to do. 'I was going to retire when I couldn't walk, couldn't do anything, lying smashed to bits at home,' he admits. 'I was like, "That's me done." My wife was ready for a divorce, but I was in denial.'

It wasn't so much the injuries that McGuinness struggled to deal with but, rather, the effects of the heavy medication he was prescribed. 'Drugs are horrible things,' he says.

'I never thought I'd be sitting here as a bike racer talking about drug addiction, but they do put you in a state of denial and make you think everything's all right when it's clearly not. Becky gave me an ultimatum. She said, "You're not the John I know, so it's either the Tramadol or me." I was like, "Fuck this – I can't afford a divorce!" It was a big deal to sort that out, but Becky was so strong, and it was her that got me off the drugs by hiding them away or throwing them out.'

Plagued by mood swings and depression, there seemed to be no light at the end of the tunnel for the most successful living TT racer. He even lost his self-respect. 'I couldn't get jeans on over the cage, so I wore tracksuit bottoms for nine months. It's funny, but I lost all interest in what I looked like after a few weeks. I just didn't give a shit.'

Lugging around such an awkward cage on his leg also took its toll on the McGuinness household. 'The coffee table at home is knackered with scratches and dents from my cage,' he says. 'The sofa's knackered, the bed sheets are all ripped, my wife's shins are knackered – that bloody cage destroyed everything.'

With the help of his long-suffering wife Becky, McGuinness eventually weaned himself off the morphine and turned a corner. 'It was coming off the drugs that was the big step forward for me,' he says. 'Once I came off the drugs and painkillers, I started thinking about racing again. And once the public started asking me what I was planning and saying how much they'd like to see me back on a bike again, I got all fired up.'

Ordinarily, John McGuinness is a laid-back, rational

man who calls a spade a spade and rarely makes a fuss, but the heavily medicated McGuinness was a very different beast. 'Coming off the morphine was the hardest part,' he admits. 'I was shouting at people who were helping me – my wife, my close friends. I mean, my wife was even having to wipe my arse for me, and that's a real test of a marriage, believe me! But I was doing book signings and public appearances because I still had to put bread on the table for my family. I really wasn't well, and probably shouldn't have been doing that.'

Ultimately, it was an ultimatum from his wife that helped McGuinness to pull through. 'I was a real arsehole at that time, and at one point Becky said, "You'd better get off these drugs or I'm gone." So, she made me stop the Tramadol and I went through four days of hell like that scene in *Trainspotting* when he goes cold turkey. I had ants walking across my shoulders, down my back, up my back and across my shoulders again. Marching ants. In my head, at least. It was hideous. I didn't get out of bed for a day and a half – never moved. Then I was scratching, itching, getting out of bed, into bed, lying awake at four in the morning. It was the weirdest thing in the world. And yet it went from being like that to, within minutes, being absolutely fine. It was mid-morning one day and I just experienced instant relief. Just gone. All the itching stopped, my temperature came back down to normal and the imaginary ants were gone.'

With the phantom ants gone, McGuinness set about planning a return to the TT. The following year he won the Senior Classic TT (held on the TT course as part of the Manx Grand Prix meeting in August) then, in 2019, he returned to the TT proper and finished second in the TT Zero race for electric bikes.

During his recovery, McGuinness had a close ally in Ian Hutchinson. After becoming the first man in history to win five TT races in a week in 2010, Hutchy then, somewhat ironically, suffered career-threatening injuries in a crash at Silverstone – supposedly one of Britain's safest circuits.

Hutchinson's left leg was so badly shattered (having been run over by another bike after he crashed) that, for a time, amputation seemed the only possible outcome. But he didn't give up. 'I just continued to believe that it would be all right,' he said. 'I fought through thick and thin, and totally refused to accept any suggestion that I might have to lose the leg. It took a lot to convince other people and get them to work hard with me, but I was really lucky in finding two amazing surgeons who helped me. One was Matija Krkovic (consultant orthopaedic and trauma surgeon) at Coventry, who was so dedicated to getting me back to racing it was unreal. There are quite a few people in the NHS who are against motorcycle racing, and who would have just put a cage on my leg and said, "Go away – in three months, you should be able to walk again." But Mr Krkovic was superb.'

Hutchinson found another ally in David Watt, a plastic surgeon at Bradford Royal Infirmary. 'He did all the skin graft stuff for me. He was in a difficult position because we got to the point where, if he couldn't make the skin graft work, I would have lost the leg, but he went through two massive operations to make sure that didn't happen.

The first was 13 hours, and many of the surgeons thought it would never work, and it didn't. But he took me back down again for 15 hours and it worked. With so many people doubting him after the first operation, it would have been quite easy for him to just accept that it wasn't going to work and, at that point, I would have had to just take it on the chin and get on with life some other way. But he put everything into it and worked from 12 noon until 4am the following morning, and made it happen. He not only cared for me but was fully behind me and my racing as well.'

Like McGuinness, Hutchinson also suffered much mental anguish during his long rehabilitation. 'In my darkest moments I wasn't even thinking about racing – I was thinking about saving my leg,' he says. 'Other than that, when it looked like I would keep the leg, I was just thinking about coming back racing again.'

It took five years of pain, rehabilitation and further operations but, in 2015, Ian Hutchinson won three more TT races on bikes that had been heavily modified to account for his mangled left leg.

Two years later, Hutchinson suffered another horrendous crash during the Senior TT and smashed his left leg all over again. But he was back on the start line for the 2018 TT, unperturbed. 'The first time, in 2010, all the damage was from the knee down, and you don't use much on a bike from the knee down,' he explained in 2018. 'But this time it was my ankle, and it's now fused, so that's a bit of a different feeling on the footrest. Luckily, I had already changed over to the right-hand gearshift after 2010, so that was one less thing to learn. I also smashed my femur to bits, and that's been the really hard bit, because of all the muscle wastage on my upper leg. That's the third time it's had muscle wastage. After the first injury I had some muscle removed from my upper leg to help fix my lower leg, so it's been really tough trying to get my upper leg strong again.'

Speaking in 2019 – some nine years after first shattering his left leg – Hutchinson admitted he had forgotten what it was like to be without pain. 'People always ask me if my leg's hurting and I say no, but I'm sitting here right now and it's absolutely throbbing,' he explained. 'It's just constant now. I don't remember what it feels like not to be in pain.'

For many competitors, the urge to compete in the TT is overwhelming and, no matter how badly injured they are, all they can focus on is getting back to racing there. In Bruce Anstey's case, even cancer didn't get in the way of his most urgently held desire. Anstey was often teased about his love of sleeping – he would often sleep in his race truck right up until the start of a race and almost missed a race once because he was still in bed – but his ability to go from fast asleep to flat out down Bray Hill in a matter of minutes puzzled even John McGuinness.

In 2010, Anstey revealed the real reason for his apparent laziness. 'It really comes from the testicular cancer that I had in 1994/95, and the chemotherapy I went through to treat it,' Anstey explained. 'That sort of made me tired. Since I had cancer, I can get tired easily and can feel weak and run-down. Everyone reacts differently to chemotherapy. The cyclist, Lance Armstrong, was the other way round –

it boosted him. It all depends on what sort of treatment you get. That's why I missed the TT in 1997, because I was still going through treatment. And then I came back in 1998.'

Having cancer didn't change Anstey's approach to racing. 'It didn't slow me down much at all; I just carried on with what I was doing,' he says. 'People ask me, "Oh, what did you do? How did you cope?" But I just carried on. I had my treatment during the week and then, on a Saturday morning, I'd get the lads to pick me up and I'd be straight off to the racetrack and out on the bike. Racing gave me something to look forward to – some sort of focus during that period.

'I would have chemotherapy treatment for a week, then have two weeks off, and that cycle continued for about six months. But after 1996 the cancer came back and I had to go through it all again, and I had to have a stem cell transplant as well. I lost all my hair and stuff, but no one in the racing world really knew about it because I didn't tell anybody. I talked about it in 1998 or 1999 but then it got lost a bit and forgotten about.'

Anstey was forced to endure another two-year absence from the sport between 2018 and 2019 due to his cancer returning but, in late August 2019, at the age of fifty, he returned to the Classic TT and won the Lightweight race. It was one of the bravest and most emotional wins ever witnessed on the Mountain Course, and Anstey was cheered every mile of the way, by spectators who knew how hard he had battled just to still be alive. He led the race from start to finish.

In the same year that Ian Hutchinson broke all records

with his five wins in a week, Manxman Conor Cummins was not so fortunate. On the second lap of the 2010 Senior TT, he suffered one of the most horrific crashes ever caught on film at the TT. Over the following year, Cummins redefined the meaning of courage. Battling depression and facing blindness, paralysis and even death, the young Manxman utterly refused to give up on his dream of winning a TT. His body may have been shattered, but his spirit proved much harder to defeat.

The fightback began at precisely 15.33 hours and 32 seconds on Friday, 11 June 2010. That's when Conor Cummins was launched off the side of the Verandah (a fast section of the TT course that winds its way around the shoulder of Snaefell mountain) when he lost the front end of his Kawasaki ZX-10R during the second lap of the Senior TT. And that's when the fastest Manxman in the history of the TT began his epic struggle back to fitness. From the moment he came to rest, after tumbling some 200 yards down the side of Snaefell mountain, he had just one goal in mind: to get back on a motorcycle and win a TT race. But he would have to endure an astonishing amount of physical and mental pain before that could happen.

Travelling at around 150mph, Cummins had tipped into the third of four consecutive right-hand corners that lead on to the Verandah and, in an instant, his entire world changed. 'I remember flying through the air as if I was in one of those bad dreams – like falling off a cliff and never landing,' he says, his voice distant as he tries, and fails, to summon a more accurate memory of the crash. 'That's all I can remember, and even that took a while to come back to me. Reports state that I was chatting away when the doctors arrived, but I can't remember a thing about that. I don't remember losing the front and falling off the bike. I just remember the feeling of falling through the air.'

The accident was caught by a helicopter camera but was deemed too horrific to be shown as part of ITV's race coverage (although it was later included, with Cummins' blessing, in the 2011 documentary film *TT: Closer to the Edge*). Yet the footage perhaps offered some sort of closure for Cummins; if he could watch it, and come to terms with what happened that day, maybe he could put it behind him and move on. But it took the twenty-five-year-old Manxman a full five months to pluck up the courage to view the footage. 'I didn't watch it until November,' he says. 'To be brutally honest, it was horrible leading up towards it. I had arranged to watch it with my friend, Chris Palmer, who's a very experienced road racer (and former 125cc TT winner) so I knew I could talk to him openly and honestly about the accident. I knew that by watching the footage with someone like Chris then I'd be able to get closure on it. But I'll be honest, I was crapping myself at the thought of watching it. The waiting was the worst part – knowing that I was going to see it. But when I finally watched it, it was as if it wasn't me that it was happening to. I couldn't believe it was me. But as I watched it, over and over, I became less and less bothered about it. Then I found it really interesting, to be honest. After I'd watched it, I thought, "Right, that's that done then."'

What actually caused the crash is still anyone's guess.

Cummins' last memory before the incident was of getting a signalling board from his uncle at the Gooseneck, several miles before the Verandah. Whether a gust of wind took out his front wheel while the bike was banked hard over, or whether a slight bump in the road proved enough to destabilise his Kawasaki ZX-10R at such high speed, may never be known – a fact that Cummins has come to accept. 'There's a whole list of possibilities but there's no definite answer as to what set the bike off,' he says. 'But once the bike was unsettled, with the speed I was doing, it was in the hands of the gods after that. I suppose I'll never know for sure what caused it. It seemed like a front-end crash but, let's be honest, at those sorts of speeds, anything can happen. You could hit a slight ripple in the road or anything small like that, and the speed just accentuates it.'

The Verandah is a stretch of road that cuts into the side of the mighty Snaefell mountain, which gives the Mountain Course its name. The drop off the edge of the road at that point is severe, as Cummins unwittingly discovered. 'I went straight over the side,' he explains. 'There's a wall in the field that runs straight down the hill, and I was a on a collision course with it but, thankfully, I bounced just before it and went right over it. When you look at the point where I'd left the road to where that wall is, it's well over 200 yards.'

The injuries Cummins received as he was thrown down the mountainside were horrendous. 'I broke my back in five places,' he says. 'There were four stable fractures of the vertebrae and one unstable fracture, which they called a burst fracture, which meant it had completely come away.

I also dislocated my leg and utterly destroyed my knee, including all the ligaments and tendons (he now has donor tendons in his reconstructed knee). I broke my upper arm in four places and suffered nerve palsy in it too, so I lost the use of my left hand. I fractured my pelvis and my left shoulder blade, as well as suffered bruising to my lungs. So, it was my back, my leg, my arm, my pelvis, my shoulder blade and my lungs.'

The emergency medical response teams at the TT are highly experienced and Cummins was, mercifully, receiving expert treatment within minutes. Not surprisingly, his memory of the hours and days that followed are vague and disjointed. 'I vaguely remember being in A&E at Noble's Hospital,' he says. 'I was heavily sedated, so wasn't really sure what was going on, but I remember lying flat on my back getting my leathers cut off, and I remember my arm was crunching a lot because it was so badly broken. But I don't have much recollection of that whole first week in Noble's.'

In July, when he was stable enough to be moved, Cummins was taken to the Royal Liverpool University Hospital for the first of four major operations to try to mend his battered body. It was the beginning of a process that brought the young Manxman to the depths of despair, as he lost all personal dignity and started to sink into depression. 'It was never actually diagnosed, but I knew I was lower than a slug's balls,' he says. 'I was really, properly down. I tried to stay as mentally positive as I could throughout the whole thing, but it was so, so hard. My dignity went out of the window big time and being away from home – even though

Liverpool was only about 50 miles away, it felt more like a million – it really got to me, especially the last week or two. That was mentally challenging. I was drained. I couldn't go to the toilet on my own, I had to stay in my bed all the time – God, it was just ridiculous. But having said that, the care that I got was absolutely second to none.'

It was during this period that Cummins faced the horrifying prospect of being left blind, paralysed or even dead, if the operation on his back was not successful. 'It was because of that burst vertebrae,' he explains. 'I've since seen the X-rays and it was dangerously close to my spinal cord. I had two options: one was to put me in a body cast for six weeks and hope it would heal, the other was to operate and get it fixed there and then, which was the option I chose. That was all well and good, but the big eye-opener, the big wake-up call, was when it came to signing the consent form. There are no guarantees with that sort of operation, so I was warned of the risks, and they were incredible. I was told there were risks of blindness, paralysis and even death. As soon as the surgeon mentioned a risk of mortality I thought, "Holy shit! This is a big deal." I didn't need a reality check, but that gave me one anyway.'

The operation was successful, and Cummins received a major boost when he was told he could return home for the remainder of his treatment. 'I got a big perk-up when they said I could go back home to the Isle of Man. It proved to me what a proper home boy I really am. I was in Liverpool for the best part of a month, so I got back to the Isle of Man in late July, just in time for the Southern 100, where my dad was racing. I was really keen on seeing that, even though I was totally knackered. I turned up with a pair of tracksuit bottoms over the cage on my leg, and I had my slippers on and an old coat. It was crap, just horrible. It was a real struggle but seeing the boys out having fun on the track gave me a real kick, and that was when the light came on and I realised I had to get back to racing again. It was far from certain at that point that I'd ever be able to but, looking back, that's the moment when I realised that I wanted to.'

Despite being so badly bitten, Conor Cummins had clearly not turned shy, though a desire to return to racing would not be enough in itself – he would also need to be physically fit enough to race and, at that point, Cummins had no way of knowing if he would ever fully recover from his injuries. The realisation of this, and acceptance of it, led him to explore a Plan B. 'I made enquiries about getting on a carpentry and joinery course at the local college, but I was too late with my entry,' he says. 'And to be fair, I wasn't in any fit state to be going in and sawing up great lumps of wood. I'd have been a bit of a health and safety hazard, knocking around on crutches and without the full use of my left hand. That was back in November, when I still didn't know if I was going to make a full recovery. It was touch-and-go from day one, so I had to be realistic and have a Plan B if things didn't work out.'

Fortunately, things did work out and, by mid-December 2010, Cummins turned a major corner, both mentally and physically. 'Just before Christmas everything started to kick in,' he says. 'I was walking a lot better, albeit with a crutch, then in January I got off my crutch and that's when I got a real kick-start and I thought, "Right, I'm going to have a real good stab at this."'

Over the following months, Cummins pushed himself harder every day, teasing a tiny bit more movement out of his nerve-damaged hand, gaining a little more strength in his mangled knee, working through the pain barrier and pushing his body, little by little, back to the supreme level of fitness it was in before the crash. 'The surgeons said that my level of fitness had carried me through a lot of the trauma, and that I must have been really fit prior to my accident,' he says.

No one could accuse Cummins of not trying, but he admits he only made it through his agonising ordeal thanks to the incredible support he received from family, friends and TT fans from all over the world. 'I've got great sponsors who backed me from day one, my family are always there for me, and my girlfriend has been fantastic too,' he says. 'But then, you sort of half expect that from the people closest to you. What I didn't realise was just how many people loved bike racing and really cared about me and followed me. It's only when something like this happens that you realise that. I got so many cards and well wishes – it was absolutely mind-blowing. It's thanks to all those people that I got through this thing. They carried me through.'

Unsurprisingly, the accident, and what he has had to endure since, has changed Cummins' outlook on life. 'You do realise how petty some of the things are that we worry about,' he says in his quiet Manx tones. 'At the end of the day, there was a big chance that I might not have been here to do this interview, and that makes you realise that it could all be over tomorrow, so you've got to live life to the full. I mean, don't take the piss, but just be grateful for everything you get in life and get on with it as best you can. I always had that sort of philosophy anyway, but having the accident has really set it in stone.'

Conor Cummins returned to race again at the event that so nearly killed him. In 2022, he recorded his fastest ever lap of the TT course on his way to second place in the Superstock race. His average speed was 133mph. He remains undaunted and is as determined as ever to take his first TT win.

CHAPTER 18

Red Flag

'That one, quick moment changed my life forever.'
LEANNE HARPER

When a race is red flagged at the TT, it is always a desperately worrying time. The flags inform riders that the race, or practice session, has been stopped, usually due to a serious incident out on the course. It does not always signify a fatality – sometimes debris has blocked the course or heavy rain has made it too dangerous – but it very often does.

Because the course is so long, few people have any idea what has happened, or which rider or riders have been involved. All that teams, family, friends, loved ones and supporters can do is wait. It can be hours before any announcement is made. Manx Radio's live coverage of the races switches back to the studio and music is played to fill the time while everyone waits, hoping for the best, but fearing the worst. For those with partners out on the course, it is a nerve-shredding experience.

Leanne Harper had been Dan Kneen's girlfriend for eight years at the time of the 2018 TT and was, as always, helping his team in pit lane during the Wednesday practice session on 30 May.

Kneen, a local boy whose dreams had come true when he signed for one of the biggest teams in the paddock ahead of the 2018 season, had been competing at the TT since 2009 and had made history the year before that by becoming the first man to win three Manx Grand Prix races in a week. Racing was in his blood; his father, his brother and four of his fraternal uncles had all raced in either the TT or the Manx Grand Prix.

After signing for Tyco BMW, Kneen was determined to become just the fourth Manx rider to win a TT, and no one doubted his ability to do it. 'He was like a dog with two dicks when he signed with Tyco,' Leanne Harper laughs. 'It was his ultimate dream. He was absolutely buzzing.'

Kneen had come close to winning a TT before, finishing third in the 2017 Superstock race, but now he had the team and the resources behind him to seriously challenge for a victory. He was thirty years old and in his prime: 2018 was going to be his year.

Harper, another local resident, had grown up with the TT and watched it with interest, though not fanatically. 'I met Dan in December 2010, so the TT wasn't mentioned much because it was a long way off,' she says. 'I rode horses, he rode bikes; it was no big deal. I certainly didn't feel afraid for him or get put off seeing him because he was a TT racer.'

Over the next eight years, the pair travelled all over the

UK, Ireland and farther afield, taking part in races and living life to the full. It was a high-adrenaline, nomadic lifestyle that they both embraced wholeheartedly.

Practice week had gone well for Kneen in 2018. He was on the pace, feeling comfortable, and was just working at fine-tuning his settings ahead of race week. Everything was going to plan. Kneen readied himself for the session in his usual way. 'He'd had a little power nap in the caravan before the practice session got under way,' Leanne explains, 'so I made sure to wake him up in plenty of time and got all his things ready.'

Leanne's job was to take care of all Kneen's visors and helmets, and to make sure he had his electrolyte energy drinks and anything else he needed to hand. With everything in order, Kneen set off down Glencrutchery Road on his Tyco BMW S1000RR, business as usual.

Then, around ten minutes into the session, as the leaders on the road approached Ramsey on their first lap, the red flags came out, and silence descended around the TT Mountain Course.

'I was in pit lane, as usual, during the session, keeping an eye on the live timing on my phone, so I always knew roughly where Dan was on the course,' Harper says. 'I was checking his sector times and noting places where he needed to make up time. I was 110 per cent behind him and wanted him to succeed as much as he did. I'm not really a worrier, but I always got butterflies every time he set off from the start line at the TT. I would always have a lump in my throat too because I was so proud of him. Keeping an eye on the sector times, and making sure I had all his things ready, helped keep me involved and stopped me from worrying too much. But, as soon as the red flag goes out, that's when you start to really worry.'

She didn't know it at the time, but those red flags would change Leanne Harper's life forever. 'I had nipped back to the caravan on the scooter during the session because I had forgotten one of Dan's visors,' she explains. 'When I got back to pit lane, one of the team said the red flags had come out. I didn't panic straight away, but me and Denver Stewart (Kneen's Tyco BMW mechanic) looked at the timing screens and he said that Dan would have been in the vicinity of where the accident was. He said we should probably go to the race office to see if there was any more information. We stood outside there for a while, and more information started to filter through from other teams. Some riders had made it through to Ramsey, so they were obviously okay, but Dan hadn't. That was the first time when I thought, "Fuck. It could be Dan." We found out the accident had happened at Churchtown, and I know how fast that section of the course is. That's when I felt my gut wrenching. But you still hope for the best and think it will all be okay.'

It wasn't okay.

Harper found herself standing outside the race office with other wives and partners, all desperate to learn that their rider was safe, and that no one was badly hurt, waiting for the lottery of grief to be called. 'We were basically waiting, hoping not to be the one that got picked out of the line to be told devastating news,' Harper says. 'You're praying that it's not going to be you, but you don't want it to be the other girls either – even though every one of us would probably have thought, "Thank God," had one of the others been called forward. It's just human nature.'

Harper drew the short straw.

'Finally, a liaison officer came down and told me to follow her up into the office. I had been around racing with Dan long enough to know how paddock procedure works, and that I was either going to be told he was in an absolute mess and that I'd have to get up to the hospital, or that he was simply not here any more. I started pulling at her, almost dragging her back down the stairs, thinking, "No, no, no, don't take me up here. Don't take me.'

The world seemed to slow for Harper as the nightmare played out and the dread grew stronger. 'Two members of the Tyco team were with me and we had to wait in a room while things were confirmed,' she recalls. 'Then a doctor came in and told me Dan was gone. He was dead. I immediately started thinking, "Right, where's Dan's dad? Where's his mum?" And then I realised Dan's younger brother Ryan was out on track. He had been taking part in the same practice session, so I told the organisers they needed to get Ryan back, but not to tell him yet, as he still had to ride his bike back to the paddock. He had been pulled over and was stopped at Sulby Bridge.'

Harper's concern for others was a natural reaction; she had yet to absorb what she had just been told. 'I was completely in shock. Just a feeling of utter disbelief. I only partly remember what happened – it was almost as if my brain just shut down. I don't think I burst into tears; it was more a complete numbness.'

Dan Kneen had been travelling between 180 and 190mph when the front wheel of his motorcycle 'tucked' and slid away from him, causing him to crash. The bike smashed into a tree, bursting into flames, while Kneen slid along the track. He was killed instantly. No mechanical defects were found with his bike and the coroner would later record a verdict of misadventure.

'That one, quick moment changed my life forever,' Harper admits. 'With the click of a finger, your whole life is changed. One day you're just doing normal, everyday things, and the next day, that world is completely gone. Me and Dan didn't go back to the caravan on the scooter that night, we didn't go home together, we didn't have dinner together . . . You have to learn to live a different life from that point forwards – from the moment you step outside the race office, and you know that everyone else knows.'

Just two days later, Harper surprised even herself by turning up in the paddock. Rather than being embittered by the sport that had so cruelly changed her life, she found herself drawn back into it. 'I had seen many girls in the paddock over the years who had lost their husbands or boyfriends to racing accidents, and always wondered how on earth they could return to a racing paddock after suffering such a loss,' she says. 'I couldn't comprehend it. But then, two days after Dan's death, I did exactly the same thing. It's all we know, and it's where we feel comfortable. Paddock people understand what you're going through: they *get* it. I'd been part of racing paddocks for years by then, and it's the same, familiar, friendly faces in all of them. It really is like an extended family, so they're the best people to support you when something bad happens. I got a lot of support from racing widows, too – people who had been through exactly the same thing, and they've been a great source of comfort.'

Seeking support amongst the paddock family is not unusual for those who have lost a loved one. It's almost unheard of for a racing family who has lost one of its own to turn against the sport or to blame it in any way. This is the very glue that holds events like the TT together. 'I can't think of a single racing widow who has turned against racing,' Harper says. 'I think it's because they all know the risks and they know the riders do too. Dan obviously didn't want to die, but had he known the fate that awaited him, he would still have raced at the TT. He lived for it. I have no regrets. Obviously, I regret that Dan died, but I don't regret that he lived the way he lived.'

It's also true that only those close to the competitors get to see the sheer joy and sense of fulfilment the sport gives them when things are going well. 'Most people don't see the sheer euphoria that the riders get out of the TT – only their families get to see that,' Harper points out. 'Dan lived the equivalent of three lifetimes in the short time he was here.'

The day after Dan Kneen's funeral, over 1,000 bikes and riders turned out to take part in a lap of the TT course in his honour. Despite dire weather conditions, the course was also lined by thousands of people, clapping respectfully as the Kneen family was driven round in a bus at the head of the convoy. Leanne drove the white BMW that had been given to Dan as part of his deal with

Tyco BMW, a thousand motorcycles following her and the family at a respectful pace, all mourning the loss of one of their own. 'It was a massive, massive turnout,' Harper says. 'I've never seen anything like it. I don't even know how many miles of bikes there was in one long line. I was driving Dan's car and there was also a bus with his family and close friends in it. Thousands of people lined the course and were throwing flowers at the car. It was surreal. We all stopped by Dan's crash site and the lads on bikes were all doing burnouts for him. It was so emotional, and the turnout was just amazing.'

It's this kind of support that provides racing families with the strength to carry on and to rebuild their lives after such a tragedy. It's a therapy like no other but, in quieter moments, the desperate grief still has to be dealt with. 'I believe you have to sit in your grief for a while – that's the only way to deal with it,' Harper says. 'You can't sweep it under the carpet, but you also have to learn not to dwell on it *all* the time. You have to just live through it, because it's real – it's your new reality. Each day I would make myself do things, just little things, like making sure I would open the curtains, because that's a positive, and you can build on that.'

Despite her terrible loss, Harper has discovered new-found strength in dealing with her grief, and in realising what's actually important in life. 'Dan's death has made me a stronger person,' she says. 'I'm quite a positive person, in general. I mean, don't get me wrong – it was devastating, and it still *is* devastating, but I do find myself being so strong, and that's the positive that I take from Dan's death.

It threw me into my cycling and my yoga, and that really helps with my mental health, and it made me more aware of myself. Before, I was just bumbling along but, when that happened, it somehow cleared all the noise; it cleared all the bullshit away for me at a young age, which I will always be thankful for.'

Ryan Kneen raced at the TT the year after losing his big brother and Leanne Harper continues to work in the TT paddock, amongst the extended family who helped put her back together again.

* * *

A red-flag incident also saw Mike Booth's life change in an instant during the 2022 TT. He was riding his Triumph 675 on the final day of practice week when he lost control at the 26th Milestone and was thrown feet-first into a stone wall or grass banking (he's not sure which) at 120mph. 'I broke the tibia and fibula in both my legs, both femurs were badly smashed – all segmental fractures, so they were all in pieces,' Booth explains. 'My right femur had come out; it had burst through my skin and my leathers with the impact of the crash. A big piece of it was missing, as if it had been ground away on the Tarmac. There was a lot of blood. I also broke two ribs, punctured a lung and broke my back in four places.'

Booth was a hugely experienced racer, having ridden in support classes in the British Superbike Championship for nine years. He first raced at the TT in 2016 and was completely blown away by the experience. He was helplessly addicted from the outset. 'I thought that racing in the British championship was the best thing in the world, and that things simply couldn't get any better than that,' he says. 'And then I went to the TT and, suddenly, short circuit racing wasn't enough any more. The British championship was like a gateway drug, whereas the TT was like the hardest smack you could ever have!

'Because you're out on your own, you're just focused on riding the bike and riding the circuit, and on no other circuit can you hold the throttle wide open in top gear, on a 200bhp Superbike, for mile after mile after mile. It's just nuts. It took the fun out of BSB for me, really. It's the coolest, and most exciting, thing in the world.'

A motorcycle journalist by profession, Booth approached the TT cautiously, and felt he could enjoy the event without taking too many risks. 'To be honest, I thought I could do the TT safely,' he confesses. 'I thought I could ride in a way that almost negated many of the risks. For a long time, riders were racing the TT course at about 90 per cent of their abilities, and I thought that those riders who were having big crashes were maybe just pushing too hard. So, my attitude towards risk was like, yes, anything can happen, but I don't want it to happen to me, so I'm going to ride it in a way that I think is safe. Obviously, I got that completely wrong.'

Booth has no memory of the crash that changed his life and has had to rely on others to discover what actually happened. 'I can't remember where my memory fades before the crash, but I remember being put into the helicopter, and I remember being in a triage room at Noble's Hospital with catheters and cannulas and all sorts of shit hanging out of me,' he says. 'So, I remember flashes, and bits and pieces, but nothing of the crash itself. One of the marshals told me I just lost the front of the bike, but (TT winner) Gary Johnson told me that, from the marks on the road, it looked like I had lost the front really early in the corner, and that caused me to smash into either a wall or a grass banking feet-first at around 120mph.'

When he did regain consciousness enough to be made aware of the extent of his injuries, Booth's attitude was typical of a bike racer: he simply accepted the situation. 'To be honest, it wasn't that difficult to accept my injuries, because I've spent my life crashing bikes and breaking bones,' he says. 'It wasn't my first rodeo. I had already been in hospital for broken legs and broken pelvises and broken spines and broken wrists. I knew it was probably the worst set of injuries I'd had in one go, but my attitude was more like, "Here we fucking go again," rather than being like, "Oh my God, I've broken my legs." I knew my head was all right and my brain was okay, so I figured broken legs could be fixed.'

In his first two weeks in hospital, Booth visited the operating theatre ten times. 'That was really fucking exhausting,' he says. 'And when I wasn't in theatre, I was either in too much pain, or on too many drugs to keep my eyes open.'

One of those operations was to amputate Booth's right leg beneath the knee. The damage to the limb was simply too great to fix. 'The reason they had to take my leg off was because I got compartment syndrome in my calf,' Booth says. 'I did quite a bit of shouting and yelling from the pain of that, and the drugs they were giving me hardly helped at all. My calf was so swollen, it was restricting blood to my foot, so the foot was pretty much dead. I actually told them to take my leg off because I couldn't bear the pain any longer. No one had even mentioned amputation at that point, and my doctor, Simon Scott, said, "We don't use the 'A' word in this ward – we're going to try to fix it." He performed another two operations, but it was no use, and he finally agreed to amputate. I had the option of keeping the leg, but it was no good to me with a dead, useless foot on the end of it, so I said, "Fuck it – just take it off." We've all seen what can be achieved with prosthetics nowadays, so it didn't feel like the end of the world.'

In total, Booth would spend two months in hospital, dealing with the pain and mentally coming to terms with losing a limb. Yet he feels his fiancée, Kaye Lyon, had a much worse time of it than he did. The couple had started the process of buying a house in Scotland before the TT, and the plan was to move in immediately after the event. Unable to halt the process, Lyon had to go through with everything on her own. 'Kaye had to do all the moving herself, while I lay in a hospital bed,' Booth says. 'She had to move everything from my house in Hull, and everything from her house, and move it all up to the new house in Scotland. She drove up and down the road from Hull to Scotland, then back down to Liverpool to the hospital to see me, so many times – she was just incredible. They say that moving house is one of the most stressful things you can do in life, but I think it was another level of stress in Kaye's case. I just wanted her beside me in hospital to hold my hand, but she had everything else to deal with so, in a lot of respects, my crash ended up being more difficult for Kaye than for me.'

The support Booth received while in hospital overwhelmed him. Not just from family and friends, but from complete strangers who were TT fans. Thousands of them. 'It was beyond anything I could ever have imagined,' he says. 'I'm still replying to messages I received on social media, and we're five months down the line now. Complete strangers, offering to help me, to give me lifts around town, or just to talk if I felt the need to talk . . . just offering to help in any way they can. It's been overwhelming. And Alastair Fagan from 44teeth.com – the biking website I work for – set up a crowdfunding page for me, and that raised over £90,000 to help me through my rehabilitation.'

That rehabilitation is now well under way, and Booth's positive mental attitude is clearly going to play a huge part in his recovery. He fully intends to get back to doing everything he did before, with the exception of returning to the TT. 'I see no reason why this should stop me from riding motorbikes,' he says. 'I might even race again, although I think this crash has changed the way I look at racing. I don't want to do the TT again, because I've discovered I can't do it safely, and I really don't want to put Kaye through that again. She didn't want me to do the TT in the first place, because she knew there was a good chance that something bad could happen. But I went anyway, so I feel quite a bit of guilt on that front. But, even taking my relationship out of the equation, I don't think I would go back anyway. I genuinely thought that, if

I just rode well within my limits, then I could do it without anything going wrong, but that's obviously not the case.'

Yet, like everyone else who has been adversely affected by the TT, Booth holds no grudges and points no fingers of blame. 'Everybody who races at the TT understands the risks involved, and it's everyone's own decision to race there,' he says. 'But it's one of the most selfish sports you can do, because you're massively putting yourself in harm's way. The fact that I've had a big crash and lost a leg, well, I knew that could happen – I knew that *worse* could happen. But I still think the TT is the most incredible race, the most incredible event, held on the most incredible circuit – it's the best thing you can ever do on a motorbike. Lots of people would give an arm and a leg to race there, and I only had to give a leg so, the way I see it, I'm still quids in.'

CHAPTER 19

The Modern Era

'You can't really see much at 206mph.
I just keep it pinned.'
BRUCE ANSTEY

Joey Dunlop had been the TT's biggest star for decades by the time he lined up for the Formula 1 race in 2000. It was a race he hadn't won for twelve years and, at the age of forty-eight, with his hair fully grey and a pair of reading glasses propped on his nose while he worked on his bikes, he was determined to win an F1 race one last time before hanging his leathers up.

Dunlop had realised in a pre-season test that the Honda Fireblade he was supposed to ride at the TT was not competitive. And when Honda then agreed to supply him with one of its new SP-1 V-twins (a type of bike Joey had never ridden before), things didn't get much better. He could only finish fifth in the Superbike race at the NW200 against the Yamaha R1s of David Jefferies and Michael

Rutter and declared that the SP-1 'doesn't stand a chance against the R1s on the island'.

Joey knew that he needed something special for the TT. With the help of Bob McMillan from Honda UK – who pleaded with his Japanese bosses for a better machine – Joey managed to secure the use of Aaron Slight's factory SP-1 World Superbike engine along with other special factory parts and three Japanese engineers for the TT, which many thought would be Joey's last. Yet still he had trouble. Throughout practice he suffered severe handling problems, and it wasn't until some 1999-spec tyres were shipped in for him that Joey finally thought he had a set-up capable of challenging for F1 honours.

It was still the longest of long shots. Dunlop was almost fifty years old and had suffered many serious injuries in more than three decades of racing. His opposition consisted of young, aggressive riders who were all experienced in the cut-and-thrust world of international short circuit racing. Men like David Jefferies, Michael Rutter and John McGuinness should all, on paper at least, have had the beating of a man old enough to be their father.

But by the time Dunlop reached the bottom of Bray Hill on the opening lap of the 2000 Formula 1 race, it was obvious to all that he had his 'race face' on and meant business. Jefferies, Rutter and McGuinness chased hard but, in the patchy conditions, Dunlop led the way and completed lap one with an advantage of 0.2 seconds over Rutter. But after Rutter suffered several dangerous slides on damp patches, he lost his confidence and the race became a straight fight between Jefferies and Dunlop.

On laps two and three, Dunlop held the advantage but, after posting the fastest lap of the race on lap four, Jefferies briefly snatched the lead, only for Dunlop to regain it with a quicker pit stop. The duo were neck and neck in the early part of the fifth lap with both men clearly giving it everything they had when suddenly the race was over: Jefferies' R1 had destroyed its clutch basket and he was forced to retire.

Although their hero still had more than a lap and a half to go, Dunlop's fans – which meant practically everyone watching the race – sensed a fairy-tale victory was within reach. The reception he received all the way home was spectacular. Programmes were waved frantically as, on every corner and down every straight, fans and marshals alike strained their necks to catch a glimpse of the famed yellow helmet flashing past them faster than it had ever done before.

As he had roared away from his last pit stop, even rival teams had cheered Dunlop on, all thoughts of their own riders' progress temporarily forgotten. Like Mike Hailwood's comeback in 1978, no one was immune to the emotions of witnessing one of the TT's greatest moments.

As Dunlop flashed across the finish line, the crowds around the grandstand area rose as one to cheer home the most unlikely hero any sport had ever produced. The shy, humble folk hero of Ballymoney had achieved his last great ambition – to win back the Formula 1 crown that he had made his own in the 1980s, when he had been a much younger man. Joey Dunlop was back where he belonged.

The tributes were universal. Four-time World Superbike

champion Carl Fogarty said, 'To still be winning races at forty-eight on the hardest and most dangerous circuit in the world . . . well, he's got all my respect.' Steve Hislop added, 'What he's done is a great achievement. He seems to be more up for it now than ever.' And Phillip McCallen admitted that 'When everything goes right for Joey, on his bike and in his mind, he's virtually unbeatable. There will never be another TT rider like him.'

Joey himself seemed relieved at the end of the race and admitted that 'The pressure was really on me because of having Slight's engine, and because there were a lot of top men from Japan here. I'm just glad I could repay them for the faith they've shown.'

He went on to win two more races that week (the Lightweight 250 and Ultra-Lightweight 125) to complete a third treble at the TT. He had never ridden better. Three weeks later, he lost his life in an obscure race in Estonia and the world of motorcycling in general, and the TT in particular, went into mourning. The sport of road racing had lost its greatest star, and the most popular road racer of all time. Eight years later, his brother Robert Dunlop was killed during practice at the North West 200 and, in 2018, Robert's son William was also killed in a racing incident at the Skerries in the Republic of Ireland. William's brother Michael races on and is now the third most successful TT racer in history.

And still the speeds kept rising. In 2000, David Jefferies became the first man to lap the TT course at an average speed of 125mph. He also took his second consecutive triple, winning the Junior, Production 1000 and Senior races, to establish himself as the new king of the mountain, and the fastest road racer on the planet.

Few could imagine a TT without Joey Dunlop, so it almost seemed right that the 2001 races were cancelled. With foot-and-mouth disease causing havoc on the UK mainland, the Manx authorities decided it posed too great a risk to have thousands of people tramping through fields to watch the TT and, quite possibly, spreading the disease amongst the local livestock. It was the first time since the Second World War that the races had been cancelled.

When racing resumed in 2002, David Jefferies took yet another triple, making it three in a row – something no one had ever done before. Sadly, it would be his last TT. DJ would lose his life during practice for the 2003 event, when he crashed out at the 160mph Crosby Corner.

Despite the world of motorcycling being sent into deep shock once again by the news of Jefferies' death, his family insisted that the TT should go ahead as planned. David's father Tony, himself a three-time TT winner, said, 'It doesn't really change our attitude to the TT. We knew the risks and it's voluntary. But if there's anything that can be learned from this to make the place safer in future, let's do that.'

Tony Jefferies had been paralysed from the chest down in a crash at Mallory Park in 1973 and had been confined to a wheelchair ever since. He then lost his son to the same sport that had already taken so much from him, but never once blamed that sport, never regretted participating in it himself, and never blamed it for the loss of his only son. Instead, he took strength from the people in the paddock;

the people who understood; the people who shared in his grief and were united by their love of the sport, no matter how cruel it could be. He knew the risks. David knew the risks. Every TT racer knows the risks. The only difference is the gulf between their ideas of acceptable risk, and those of the average person in the street.

There were to be further tears when David Jefferies' team-mate, Adrian Archibald, offered up the best tribute possible for his late friend. The TAS team had been ready to abandon the meeting out of respect for its fallen rider, but the Jefferies family had insisted on business as usual. Team manager Philip Neill said, 'The final decision to carry on was left to the Jefferies family. Tony Jefferies said DJ would have gone berserk if he had any idea the team was going to pull out.'

Carrying a 'DJ 1' sticker on his GSX-R1000 Suzuki, Adrian Archibald rode his heart out to claim his first ever TT win in honour of Jefferies. He repeated the feat in the Senior race and brought the 2003 TT to a typically bittersweet end. TAS team owner Hector Neill was bursting with sadness and pride at the end of a roller-coaster fortnight. He explained, 'Mrs Jefferies had said, "You can't pull out – David would go mad if you did that. You must stay and give Adrian the chance. Tell him to have a nice, safe week's racing and, if he can win one, win it for our David." Well, we didn't win one, we won two – and the two main ones. It's recorded for evermore that TAS – a wee team from Ireland – won the Formula 1 and won the Senior.'

It was somehow fitting that, in David Jefferies' absence,

his best friend John McGuinness took over as the man to beat at the TT. He won his first big bike race (the Formula 1) in 2004 then added wins in the Lightweight 400 and Junior to take his first treble.

By 2006, onboard telemetry was becoming commonplace on TT bikes, meaning every aspect of a machine's performance was digitally recorded and that information could be downloaded on to laptops. The speed reached by Bruce Anstey's Suzuki GSX-R1000 that year shocked even hardened TT campaigners. The telemetry showed that Anstey was travelling at 206mph down Sulby Straight; houses, walls, trees, a pub and a shop on either side of him. It was simply mind-blowing. 'You can't really see much at 206mph,' he admitted. 'I just keep it pinned.'

You can't really see much at 206mph.

As the TT celebrated its 100th anniversary in 2007, another huge barrier was reached and breached, when John McGuinness became the first man to lap at an average speed of 130mph. Charlie Collier and Rem Fowler, who had ridden their hearts out in 1907 to set average lap times of just over 40mph, would never have believed such speeds were possible. So much had changed in the century since those two pioneers became the first winners of an Isle of Man Tourist Trophy race; the motorcycles had gone from making 2 horsepower to over 200bhp, and top speeds had risen from 56mph to 206mph. Riding gear had changed from flat caps and tweed jackets to one-piece leathers and full-face crash helmets, medical back-up had moved on from boy scouts to emergency helicopters, and the paddock had changed from being a field full of beer crates to a multi-million pound gathering of articulated trucks and hospitality units.

The TT had moved on in so many ways, yet one constant remained: the challenge itself, and the dangers that accompany that challenge. As the TT celebrated its centenary with firework displays, parade laps by past masters, free-flowing champagne, and even a re-enactment of the original 1907 TT on the original St John's Course, yet another tragedy played out on the notorious Mountain Course.

When newcomer Marc Ramsbotham suffered a fatal crash at the 26th Milestone during the Senior TT, his cartwheeling motorcycle also killed two spectators. As incredible as it may seem, it was the first time in 100 years of TT racing that spectators had been killed, and it marked a turning point for the TT and road racing in general. It was one thing for riders to willingly take risks with their own lives, but another thing altogether for spectators to be killed while simply watching a sporting event.

Public liability insurance costs were increased to such an extent that some smaller road races folded as the organisers could no longer afford to pay the premiums. And that's not to mention the considerable compensation payments that have to be made under such circumstances. Fatalities are costly affairs.

The TT underwent a thorough overhaul after the Centennial tragedy, with many areas adjacent to the course being declared 'restricted areas' where fans were no longer allowed to spectate. While everyone recognised the need to improve safety, there was still a feeling amongst many TT spectators that they had lost a certain amount of freedom:

some had been watching at the same spot for decades, and now no longer could. It may seem trivial, but TT traditions run deep.

In 2009, the TT enjoyed some positive PR when the world's most famous motorcycle racer accepted an offer to visit – not to race, but to bear witness. Valentino Rossi watched some racing and also completed a lap of the course behind the safety car, though still travelling at a swift pace. 'The lap is great and impressed me a lot, because I know that it's dangerous and also fast,' he said of his experience. 'I don't expect a road like this to be a track, and it is unbelievable to be going flat out around it on a Superbike. You need to have two great balls! It is very dangerous and is not possible to make a mistake. It's impressive.'

Rossi even stated that he wanted to come back in the future to do more laps of the Mountain Course in order to 'understand it better'.

The following year saw another MotoGP legend, this time Jorge Lorenzo, visit the TT. He, too, was impressed by what he saw. 'What an amazing experience,' he said after completing a speed-controlled lap. 'Now I understand why people enjoy the experience of riding at the TT. I only did one lap and I would definitely like some more practice. I was able to make a few wheelies and wave a lot to the crowd – there seem to be so many people here. It was a very, very good experience. I have read all about the TT in magazines and have seen TV programmes, but nothing can prepare you for the real experience.'

That same year, Suzuki brought its MotoGP bike to do a lap of the course. Current Grand Prix bikes hadn't competed at the TT since the 1970s, so it offered a rare chance for fans to see one of the fastest bikes in the world in action on the world's most demanding racecourse.

Since Suzuki's MotoGP rider, Loris Capirossi, had never been round the course before, Cameron Donald was chosen as the rider of the MotoGP bike, since he would be able to unleash more of the bike's potential and allow crowds (and Suzuki engineers) to get a more realistic idea of what it was capable of.

Capirossi did at least enjoy a lap on a road-going Suzuki GSX-R1000 and was amazed by his experience. 'This place is incredible,' he beamed afterwards. 'I've seen the TV footage before, but nothing prepares you for the TT course. The surface is much bumpier than I imagined, and when you see the speeds that these guys run at, it is simply amazing. It's a fantastic event that you could never replicate anywhere else in the world.'

Cameron Donald was every bit as thrilled by the performance of the MotoGP missile, which was clocked at over 200mph down the Sulby Straight. 'Man, that was just amazing,' he said when he returned to the paddock. 'I thought the bike would be really difficult and twitchy to ride, but it was great. I was expecting to ride a steady lap, but it was so good that I was able to get a great rhythm going and pick up a fast pace. In fact, it was so good, I reckon we need to get some regulation changes for next year as this thing with a few more laps on it would really fly here!'

In the same year that Valentino Rossi attended the TT, the race organisers started looking towards the future and announced a new race – the TTXGP. Anticipating a future without combustion engines, the race was for zero emissions, battery-powered motorcycles, but the limitations of these fledgling new machines meant it had to be a one-lap race, as they were simply incapable of covering a greater distance. Traditionalists scoffed at the very idea of a rider being able to claim a TT win after one (relatively slow) lap of the TT course, and even more questioned the validity of a race for just fourteen motorcycles over a single 37.73-mile lap. That meant spectators spent a lot of time staring at an empty road. Others bemoaned the lack of noise, arguing that sound makes up a crucial element in all forms of motorsport.

The speeds were spectacularly unimpressive too. Spectators, accustomed to seeing riders lapping at 130mph, now watched the winner of the TTXGP Open Class lapping at just 66mph – a similar speed to that set by Jimmy Simpson way back in 1925. The winner of the Pro Class fared better, but still only lapped at 87.43mph. Freddie Frith had lapped at 90mph on a combustion-engine motorcycle as far back as 1937. Adding to the overall feeling of disappointment was the fact that there were only six finishers in the Pro class and just three in the Open class. There was clearly a lot of work to do if the future of the TT was going to rely on batteries.

A decade later, the renamed TT Zero race was still being run over just one lap, and it still attracted just nine entries, of which only six managed to finish the lap. Speeds, at least, had improved, with Michael Rutter and John McGuinness eventually lapping at over 120mph. A staunch defender of the class, McGuinness had a perfect answer for those who mocked the speed of the electric bikes and the one-lap format. 'If you don't think it should be classed as a TT win, grab a seat on the back and I'll take you for a lap.'

But, while the race limped along for a decade, the experiment clearly hadn't worked, and the TT Zero event was abandoned after the 2019 TT. The future had lasted for ten years and had proved to be a major disappointment.

By 2010, Guy Martin had become one of the TT's most popular stars: outspoken, oddball and frighteningly fast, he openly admitted that the biggest draw of the event for him was the dangers. 'If you get it wrong, you're fucked. And I like that.' In his seventh year of trying, Martin still hadn't managed to win a TT as he lined up for the 2010 Senior, and he was in determined mood. His charge lasted three laps. As he rounded the fearsome 160mph Ballagarey Corner (where Australian rider Paul Dobbs had been killed the day before), he lost control of his machine, which then exploded into a fireball as it smashed into a stone wall. Spectacular photographs showed the billowing flames from the wreckage and smoke engulfing the entire width of the road, with Martin's Honda Fireblade emerging from the inferno without its rider. Martin, still conscious, lay in the middle of the course with a broken back. He was astonishingly lucky. The race was stopped while Martin was airlifted to hospital. Typically, he played down the incident, and his injuries. 'It did look right spectacular,' he admitted. 'There was a load of flames, and I was in hospital for a bit. I broke my back. It does sound spectacular, but it wasn't really.'

That Martin was one of the riders being followed by a film crew that year for the feature-length documentary *TT: Closer to the Edge* didn't hurt his profile, and his cheery eccentricity, engineering skills and willingness to have a go at anything dangerous would soon make him a TV star. It was a future he was very lucky to have. Few people survive a crash at Ballagarey.

When the race was restarted, there was another horrific crash. This time it was Conor Cummins who got thrown down the side of the Mountain when he lost control of his machine on the Verandah section. His injuries were hideous and included fractures to his back, leg, arm, pelvis, shoulder blade and a bruised lung.

Cummins returned to the TT the following year and finished sixth in the second Supersport race, his enthusiasm for the event entirely undiminished.

The eventual winner of that unlucky Senior race, Ian Hutchinson, pulled off the seemingly impossible by winning all five solo races (excluding the TT Zero race, which he did not enter) in 2010. With so much potential for things to go wrong – mechanical breakdowns, messy pit stops, other riders holding him up, changing weather conditions, rider error – it should have been impossible, and must be considered one of the greatest feats ever achieved at the TT.

Hutchinson was aware of just how much the odds were stacked against any rider pulling off such a feat. 'It should have been absolutely ridiculous odds,' he admits, 'but I had this guy come up to me at a bike show, who gave me a huge hug and thanked me, because he'd put £50 on me winning all five races and he won £2,500. So that's just 50/1 odds. I think it should have been much higher than that.'

Hutchinson's team boss that year was Clive Padgett. He was in charge of making sure the bikes were completely reliable and he too was astounded at what his team and rider achieved. 'If you'd asked me before 2010 if I thought that was even possible, I'd have said no,' Padgett readily admits. 'I don't think anyone thought it was possible. There had been over 100 years of TT racing at that point, and no one had ever achieved that. I still get speechless now when I think about it! It was just one of those incredible things.'

In the second Supersport race of the 2011 TT, John McGuinness discovered yet another hazard facing competitors at the TT course and wasn't shy of discussing it. 'When I hit the bottom of Bray Hill, my foreskin came back, and I had a bit of chaffage for an hour and a quarter,' he happily confessed. 'I'll maybe get (wife) Becky to check it out later.'

McGuinness' confession had the assembled members of the media at the post-race press conference in tears of laughter and served to highlight just how different TT competitors are when compared to robotic, sponsor-friendly, corporate Formula 1 drivers who seem preprogrammed in their interviews. The contrast is absolute.

Just six years after two spectators had been killed at the Centennial TT, another ten were injured when newcomer Jonathan Howarth crashed at the bottom of Bray Hill in the 2013 Senior race. Manx Radio reporter David Harrison witnessed the crash and later described the chaos. 'The wheel and the petrol tank of the bike flew straight across the road,' he said. 'It actually came over my head, only yards away from us. Everyone ducked and screamed and ran away in the panic.'

Although, thankfully, there were no fatalities this time around (and Howarth himself only suffered slight injuries), it was a worrying scenario nonetheless: after 100 years of spectators watching the TT in safety, there had now been two serious incidents in the space of six years. If anything was going to put an end to the TT, it was spectators being killed. The event looked to be on very thin ice, with fresh calls for it to be banned in the mainstream media.

But the danger of the event also clearly held an appeal and, by 2014, North One's television coverage of the TT was reaching 26 million people in 130 countries, and the figures were growing, year on year. In a world becoming suffocated by health and safety restrictions, the TT stood out as a relic of a more dangerous past, and it obviously fascinated audiences who weren't even motorcycle fans.

With MotoGP riders attending the TT now being somewhat routine, Scott Redding had been due to make a visit in 2014 but changed his mind after two close friends of his, Bob Price (a family friend who helped Redding extensively in his early career) and Karl Harris, were killed in the event. 'This is not racing any more,' Redding posted on social media. 'It's like a death race. Lost too many friends. All the riders that finish are relieved to finish in one piece and see their loved ones. The bikes are far too advanced for road racing nowadays. Would you drive your car at 132mph through a village?'

In fact 206mph would be more accurate, but he had made his point. The grieving Redding's comments caused a vicious backlash on social media. For some diehard fans, the TT is beyond criticism.

As always, there were heart-warming stories to counter the tragedies and, in 2014, Conrad and Dean Harrison became the first father and son to win TT races in the same week; Conrad taking the opening sidecar race win and his son Dean taking his maiden win in the Lightweight race.

Conrad Harrison had been trying to win a TT for twenty-one years and his debut win was, somewhat ironically, down to his being knocked off his motorcycle by a car driver. 'I got knocked off a road bike a few years ago and received £16,000 in compensation, and I spent the lot on a sidecar!' he explained after finally taking an emotional debut win. 'I was about forty-seven or forty-eight, and I said to the wife, "The house is sorted, the kids are grown up; I wonder if I'm just shit at the TT, or whether a good outfit is all that I need?" So, I went out and bought everything I could – I spent £22,000 in all – but it was worth every penny, because I eventually won a TT. I talk a lot me, but when I won the TT, I just couldn't talk. I just couldn't believe I'd finally won.'

There was another hugely emotional win in the first Supersport race at the 2015 TT, when Ian Hutchinson returned to the top step of the podium for the first time since winning all five solo TT races in 2010. In that time, he had endured no fewer than thirty operations and more than fifty hours on an operating table to fix his mangled left leg. As part of his recovery, Hutchinson's leg had to grow eight inches of new bone, with the help of an external cage. It had been an agonising five years of unimaginable pain, but Hutchinson had never given up on his dream of winning another TT. 'When I was coming up over the Mountain, knowing that I was going to win a TT, I was thinking back to lying in a hospital bed in tatters, drugged out of my mind on morphine,' he said. 'All the work I'd gone through for those five years. I just thought, "I can't actually believe I'm going to win again." It was really, really weird. The most emotional race ever.'

For good measure, Hutchinson won the second Supersport race and the Superstock race too. Few could appreciate just what he had gone through to achieve those wins, but they must surely rank amongst the hardest victories ever achieved in any sport.

Hutchinson would take another treble in 2016 and would finally win a Superbike race in 2017 – the first time he had done so since 2010. But then, incredibly, it all went wrong again. He crashed out of the 2017 Senior race and fractured the same left femur and ankle that had taken thirty operations and all those years to heal.

Hutchinson turned up at the press conference ahead of the 2018 TT with his leg still in an external fixator cage (which holds the bones in place as they grow back). It was removed before the actual racing got under way, but Hutchinson still needed a walking stick on the grid, just to get to his bike, and his plan was to just have a steady week to build towards the following year. He had a best finish of eleventh place in the second Supersport race.

John McGuinness was on a parallel injury path. He too

had a cage fitted to his leg after a crash at the 2017 North West 200, and he too had it removed ahead of the 2018 TT, fully intending to race. But he also broke it again during a family holiday and was forced to sit out his beloved TT, unable to add to his tally of twenty-three wins.

With McGuinness absent, Hutchinson far from fit and Bruce Anstey having to withdraw at the eleventh hour as his cancer returned, Michael Dunlop went into the 2018 TT as the man to beat. His team-mate in the Tyco BMW squad was young Manxman Dan Kneen, who finally had a big-money team worthy of his talent. He was thrilled at the prospect of having the weapon he needed to become just the fourth Manxman to win a TT. His dream, and his life, ended on the Wednesday night of practice week, when he crashed at the fast, tree-lined Churchtown section and succumbed to his injuries at the scene.

To heap tragedy upon tragedy, another serious accident occurred as an indirect result of Kneen's crash. Since the course was strewn with so much debris, riders were stopped by race marshals and instructed to return to the pits by riding the wrong way round the course. Unbeknown to them, an official course car was speeding towards the crash site in the normal direction of the course. Four riders suffered head-on collisions with the car, with Steve Mercer left fighting for his life. He remains in a wheelchair four years later and is still fighting to receive compensation.

As usual, the racing went ahead regardless, and it was faster than ever. Peter Hickman had been struggling to land a decent ride in British Superbikes in 2014 and had decided that a good showing at the TT might boost his chances of one. He became the fastest newcomer in history that year and, by 2018, was ready to start winning.

While Dean Harrison had won a Lightweight TT back in 2014, he too had now come of age and was ready to push to the limits on a Superbike. Together, Hickman and Harrison would raise the bar at the TT and lap at speeds never seen before.

After a full two weeks of blazing sunshine, the Mountain Course was in perfect condition, and the speeds throughout race week reflected this. But it was in the Senior race at the end of the festival that a new barrier was broken, when Peter Hickman became the first man to lap the course at 135mph. 'I had a feeling that, if that's what was needed to win the race, then the 135mph lap would come,' he explains. 'If you've got a 20-second lead in a race then you're going to just make sure you get the bike home without pushing it too hard, but when there's only seconds between you and your rivals then that's when you see really fast lap times posted. Basically, I needed to lap at that pace to win the race.'

To break through the 135mph barrier, Hickman gave it absolutely everything he had on that final lap of the Senior race. He had nothing left in the tank. 'You build up speed over the full two weeks and, by the end of the last lap of the last race, you just need to put everything together that you've learned over the fortnight,' he says. 'Dean (Harrison) was really fast out of the blocks but then didn't seem to go any faster, whereas I like to build up to a faster pace over time. But I'd say on the last lap of the Senior, I gave it everything I had – there certainly wasn't much left in reserve.'

There was no chance of upping the lap record in 2019, as bad weather affected the meeting to such an extent that five races had to be held on one day – another first for the event.

And then the pandemic hit.

Until 2020, the only things that had caused the cancellation of the TT had been two world wars and an outbreak of foot-and-mouth disease. But the Covid-19 pandemic ensured there would be no TT racing for two years. The event organisers used the enforced break to overhaul the TT, in a bid to improve safety and streamline the racing schedule.

A reduction in race starters was announced, to ensure all competitors were fast enough and did not pose a danger to other riders. A maximum of fifty starters was announced for the Superbike races, and sixty for the other events. Since riders start alone during races, it was also decided this system should be employed during practice week, rather than riders setting off in pairs like they traditionally did. For the first time, a race day warm-up lap was added, to give riders a final chance to ensure their bikes were set up properly, and to have a look at course conditions on race day morning. A new, bespoke GPS system was set up to track riders and official vehicles, and an electronic red-flag system was set up at thirty locations around the course, in addition to the usual red flags displayed by marshals, should a race need to be stopped. A new medical centre was introduced in the paddock, and more advanced training was to be provided for all marshals.

In short, the race organisers tried everything they could to make the event safer, but the 2022 event sadly proved that road racing can never be truly safe. After a two-year break, there was much excitement ahead of the 2022 TT, but it turned out to be one of the darkest years in the event's long history, with five riders losing their lives over the fortnight, and a sixth succumbing to his injuries four months later.

Despite all the improvements, trees, walls and houses remain very solid objects to hit at 150mph and, when travelling at that kind of speed, things can still go wrong in the blink of an eye: there is rarely time for a rider to react.

Now, 115 years down the line, the challenges of the TT remain the same, as does the appeal of it. The sustained high speeds, the difficulties and the dangers are what attracted riders in 1907, and they still attract them today. Whether a sporting event that claims the lives of so many competitors can continue into a future that's becoming more obsessed with health and safety is anyone's guess. But, for now at least, the greatest challenge in road racing continues.

CHAPTER 20

What It Means

'Winning a TT almost meant more than being world champion.'
GEOFF DUKE

'When I was young, most budding racers felt the TT was the be-all and end-all of racing and I, for one, never lost that feeling,' Geoff Duke said before he passed away peacefully in 2015 at the age of 92. He was not alone in revering the TT. If MotoGP is the most elite circuit-based motorcycling world championship – the two-wheeled equivalent of Formula 1 – the TT is the pinnacle of road racing; the event that every road racer wants to win. And, despite being both a multiple Grand Prix world champion and TT winner, Geoff Duke rated the TT above all other events. 'Winning a TT almost meant more than being world champion,' he continued. 'It's so different; it's a very demanding race, which required the utmost concentration from a rider and, the bigger the challenge, the better I preferred it.'

Duke won the last of his six world titles (and took his sixth and final TT win) in 1955 and was superseded by the equally mercurial John Surtees. Despite winning world championships on both two and four wheels, for Surtees too, the TT was the greatest challenge of all. 'I think in Grand Prix racing in the 1950s and 1960s, the TT was the optimum challenge, which was there to be, if possible, conquered,' he said. 'If you succeeded there it gave you immense satisfaction, because you were on the world stage competing against the world's best riders. The future of the TT, of course, does not hold that, nor does the present. What the present riders do around the Isle of Man is quite fantastic, but it has developed into a specialist, one-off, type of event.'

By the time Surtees had switched to racing cars in the 1960s, Phil Read was doing a lot of the winning on two wheels; again, both in Grands Prix and at the TT. He also rated the Mountain Course as the ultimate test. 'The TT course is the greatest challenge of man and machine – ever,' he said. 'So, to conquer that course, and lap at reasonable speeds for six laps, gives great satisfaction. There's fantastic camaraderie and spirit amongst riders at the TT. It's almost like flying in a Spitfire squadron in wartime – you all make the most of the moment because you know you might be dead the next day.'

For Read, success on the Mountain Course depended on several crucial elements. 'The difference between a good TT rider and a great TT rider is in his determination to win, his focus and his ability to set up a bike,' he said. 'You also need to learn the course well and be able to drum up enough courage to go through corners at higher speeds than you know is sensible. And you can only pray that you don't have any mechanical problems; that your gearbox doesn't seize, or the frame doesn't break, or whatever.'

When Charlie Williams started winning TT races in the 1970s, the same challenges, and the same satisfaction in rising to them, remained. For him, it was the very technical nature of the Mountain Course that provided the ultimate challenge and, therefore, the ultimate satisfaction when all went well. 'I may have got great pleasure from winning other big races, but for actual riding satisfaction nothing came close to the TT,' he says. 'One of the most satisfying things in racing was to do a near-perfect lap of the TT course. And, while I enjoyed racing on other road circuits, nowhere else was as technical as the Isle of Man. You can make a mistake on the TT course and still be paying for it two miles farther down the road.'

Ireland, and Northern Ireland in particular, has always been a hotbed of road racing. Although many events have now folded due to the increasing speed of the bikes, or because of a lack of finance, or the increased costs of public liability insurance, there are still many road races held in the Emerald Isle, but even the Irish consider the Isle of Man to be the Mecca of motorcycling. 'On the world calendar, the TT was *the* race,' says eleven-time winner Phillip McCallen. 'Coming from Ireland, if you wanted to be a proper road racer and really earn the name, you had to conquer the TT. Our races at home were really just junior races compared to the TT – it's the toughest, meanest road race in the world. It was hours of flat-out riding, as fast as you wanted to go, not just a 20-minute jaunt.'

For some riders, just lining up on the famous Glencrutchery Road start line was the culmination of a lifelong ambition. 'When I was a kid, even going to the TT to watch the races seemed unachievable,' says Scotsman Jim Moodie. 'For me, to compete there would have been a dream, but I could never even have dared to dream that I would one day win a TT – it would have been beyond my wildest expectations.' Moodie far exceeded his wildest expectations, eventually taking eight TT wins between 1993 and 2002.

Many TT riders are also avid historians of the event, with a deep knowledge and respect for its history. John McGuinness is one such rider. Speaking ahead of the Centennial TT in 2007, he said, 'The TT is 100 years old because it's special – it's not just another piece of road. It's like the holy grail of motorcycle racing – it's part of history and, for me, it's great to be part of that.'

While riders want to win TT races so badly they're quite literally prepared to risk their lives to do so, many team bosses are equally determined to win, although they do not have to risk their own necks in the process. 'Because of the global audience, and the fact that the TT is an event that only happens once a year, the hype that's built up around it is massive,' says TAS team manager Philip Neill. 'The Senior TT only happens on one day every year, and if a team can win that one, it's probably enough to justify a full year's racing, in terms of achievement. That's how big the TT is – that's how significant it is.'

The event means every bit as much to Padgett's team

owner, Clive Padgett. 'It's everything to us; it's what we strive for all year – the whole team,' he says. 'It's the absolute pinnacle of our entire racing effort, and I think most of the TT team managers would agree on that one. With the TV coverage now, the TT is so prominent. People in Japan know about it, people in Italy know about it – it's truly global now. If you're into motorcycling, you know about the TT.'

For both historical and personal reasons, the TT has always been of great importance to Honda, the world's biggest motorcycle manufacturer. In 1954, the company's founder, Soichiro Honda, issued a press release that included these words:

'I here avow my intention that I will participate in the TT race, and I proclaim, with my fellow employees, that I will pour all my energy and creative powers into winning.'

There was much laughter amongst the British and European motorcycle manufacturers upon reading this bold statement of intent. No Japanese manufacturer had ever raced at the TT before, and Japanese motorcycles were considered inferior in every way to their European counterparts. By 1961, however, all the sniggering had stopped. After debuting at the TT in 1959, the Honda team took its first win in 1961, thanks to the magnificent Mike Hailwood, who not only won the Lightweight 125 race, but then went out and won the Lightweight 250 race for the Japanese firm later the same day. Since then, Honda has won more TT races than any other manufacturer (191) and has always maintained a strong presence at the event in honour of its founder. 'The TT is where Honda enjoyed its first international success in racing, so it still means a lot to Honda,' says former Honda team boss Neil Tuxworth. 'We're the most successful manufacturer in TT history, so obviously every win is a bit special because you're adding to that incredible record. It's such a hard event to win because it doesn't happen over a short period – these are two-hour races and there's so much work and preparation that goes into it that a TT win is just very, very special.'

According to seven-time winner Mick Grant, the will to win a TT – the desperate desire to do absolutely anything to make sure it will happen – is the key factor in ultimately making it happen. 'When I was running race teams and was looking for staff, I never looked for riders or mechanics with the most experience, I always looked for the ones that wanted it most,' he says. 'You can have a clever rider, a rider who may be incredibly gifted with lots of natural riding ability, but if he doesn't want it badly enough, then he's just going to be pissing into the wind.'

While every TT win is important, some have added significance and emotional involvement. The Singles race (for single-cylinder machines, now discontinued) produced one of the most emotional victories ever witnessed at the TT. Dave Morris had won the race for three years in succession before losing his life in a crash at Croft in England in 1999. His sons, Neil and Lee, then went through the unimaginable grief of losing their mother, Alison, to a heart attack just one week later. Focusing their energies over the following nine months, the brothers vowed to honour their father's success at the TT. Using money left to them in their parents' wills, the brothers finished building the two machines their father had been working on for the TT in 2000 and named them AMDMs – the initials of their parents. John McGuinness and Jason Griffiths were approached to ride the bikes and, after receiving special permission from their respective teams, both agreed. The result was a real tear-jerker. McGuinness and Griffiths brought the bikes home in first and second place, and as the sound of Dave Morris' engine roared across the line to victory, Neil and Lee wept openly as the whole paddock applauded their efforts. Of the brothers' awesome achievement, Neil Morris simply said, 'We've been through a lot, but this was the best way to pay tribute to our parents and take a step into the future.'

No amount of prize money could have meant more.

There is something much deeper than the pursuit of money or fame or status that drives TT racers. They are prepared to take extraordinary risks, to fight back from hideous injuries, and even to continue racing when they have witnessed friends being killed in front of their very eyes, just to win a TT race. They are driven, by an all-encompassing desire that outsiders simply cannot comprehend, to win one of the hardest-earned trophies the sporting world has to offer. They do it because they love it. They do it because no other experience in their lives comes remotely close to giving them the same thrill and rush and sense of achievement. And no punishment, short of death itself, will stop them. That's how much it means. That's why, in the face of overwhelming odds, they continue to do it. That's what makes them some of the most extreme sportsmen on earth. That's what makes them TT racers.

CHAPTER 21

An Uncertain Future

*'I think the future of the TT must be to
build a short circuit.'*
GIACOMO AGOSTINI

Almost since its inception in 1907, the TT has attracted controversy and struggled against calls for it to be banned. That controversy has never gone away, and only becomes more inflamed during years like 2022 when six riders lost their lives.

A huge part of the TT's attraction lies in the very fact that it is at odds with an increasingly risk-averse society: people with very little interest in motorcycles tune in around the world to watch it because it seems completely surreal that an event like the TT is even allowed to happen. It is the very fact that it is dangerous that gives it mass-market appeal. But can it really survive into the future? Can such a death rate continue to be acceptable, as increased legislation and an obsession with health and safety conspire to deny individuals the right to free choice?

And it's not just about the dangers. The Isle of Man is an offshore financial centre and, while the TT brings in a much-needed £30 million boost to the economy each year, it's also a massive inconvenience for many businesses, for locals who have no interest in the races, and for the many people who have made the island their retirement home and just want a quiet life.

On top of all this, the infrastructure of the Isle of Man itself has changed over the decades, meaning accommodation for visitors is now much diminished. While it was once awash with hotels and guest houses, as befitted its role as a popular holiday destination, most of those establishments have long since been converted into luxury apartments and business premises in the wake of cheap foreign holidays. If you don't book accommodation for the TT a year in advance, the chances of finding any become exceedingly remote.

The riders themselves seem uncertain of the future of the TT and can't agree on what form it may have to take in order to survive. 'I wouldn't like to say what will happen to the TT in the future – circumstances may cause it to be stopped,' Phil Read said. 'It affects businesses, which in turn affects the Isle of Man's economy, and now all the boarding houses are closed, and the camping sites are not particularly good, so they don't get the crowds over and the money being spent on the island like before.'

John Surtees shared similar concerns. 'I wonder – with the way the Isle of Man is developing – whether the TT has a future,' he said. 'The important thing is to remember what has passed, and particularly the good parts. It would be sad to see the opportunities that still arise from the Isle of Man authorities' willingness to work and co-operate with the world of motorsport, lost to us. I would think that there's more potential in turning the TT into more of a festival, not only of yesteryear, but also of motorcycle racing today – rather like Goodwood, where the latest F1 cars and Grand Prix bikes mix with machines from bygone years. Perhaps there could be one feature race at the TT, with the rest of the fortnight being centred around the past, and maybe not just for two wheels either. It may be that there could be a hill climb and a race on a shorter circuit, perhaps on the Clypse Course (a shorter version of the TT course that was used for smaller capacity and sidecar races in the 1950s), and possibly a historic race on the main course. If you bring that festival factor in, you could widen the interest and make it more commercially viable. But, of course, against that is probably the fact that if you did create a big commercial interest, there probably isn't the hotel capacity to take advantage of it.'

There are other riders, Giacomo Agostini among them, who believe the TT needs to be run on a much shorter circuit, either purpose-built or incorporating existing roads over a safer route. 'I think the future of the TT must be to build a short circuit,' he says. 'I suggested this to the Isle of Man government – to keep the traditional grandstand and the traditional paddock, but to build a safe circuit. There is a lot of space on the Isle of Man to make a circuit of maybe 9–10 kilometres, and I'm sure everybody would be happy to come back to the Isle of Man – even MotoGP riders. But we need to make a safe track. I don't understand why it's not been done, because I think it's possible.'

Jim Moodie agrees. 'I think the way forward for the TT is to build a Spa-Francorchamps-type short circuit (the legendary Belgian track was once 8.76 miles long but was reduced to run over a safer 4.35-mile route in 1979), incorporating part of the TT course – maybe from Kate's Cottage down towards Creg-ny-Baa, and then back on to a short circuit. It could be used for the Manx Grand Prix, the Manx Rally and the TT, as well as hosting corporate events and track days. The Isle of Man is a very nice place, and it's not the most difficult place in the world to get to, so if a short circuit was marketed properly, I don't see why it wouldn't work.'

The arguments for a short circuit *not* working are numerous too. Not only would a purpose-built track cost tens of millions of pounds to create, it also wouldn't have the same appeal for riders and fans. There are already many such circuits on the UK mainland which don't require expensive travels plans to reach, either by sea or air. The main appeal of the TT lies in its uniqueness; change that, and it really might spell the end of the event.

Yet, despite all the problems, optimism remains. After all, the TT has been through many traumas in the past and has weathered them all, as Geoff Duke pointed out. 'There have been times, like when the TT lost its world championship status in 1976, that I thought it was the beginning of the end, but it didn't happen,' he says. 'The TT kept going because of the enthusiasm of the young people who wanted to ride in it, and because of the spectators who came over on a regular basis to watch. This is what has kept the event going over the years. There is always the danger that, if the TT has a really bad year in the way of fatalities, then that could have serious consequences for its future. But, otherwise, it seems to go from strength to strength – and long may it continue to do so.'

Charlie Williams puts forward a similar argument. 'I wouldn't begin to try to predict the future of the event, because I did that in the 1970s and was completely wrong!' he laughs. 'But all we can hope for is that it carries on and doesn't claim too many more lives, because that is the big issue. I've lost a lot of friends and colleagues at the TT, but I would never dream of suggesting that it should be stopped on those grounds. It's always been a trade-off: you get such a fantastic buzz from the place, but you also know that you might not come home. Maybe for some people, that's what the attraction is.'

For every person who wants to see the TT continue, however, there's another (usually with no intrinsic interest in the event) who insists it's barbaric and should be banned. Reacting to the six fatalities at the 2022 TT, motorsport journalist Danny Herbert wrote an article on hotcars.com claiming that 'The Isle of Man TT is easily the most absurd, nonsensical and ridiculous race of the modern age of motorsport – a far cry from any other motorsport or sporting event.'

Displaying his lack of knowledge of the event, however, Herbert went on to (wrongly) state that 'Once a year, twenty riders take to the mountainous, kerb- and building-strewn mountain roads of the small Irish Sea island.'

Given that the Supersport race alone had 68 starters in 2019, and there were eight races held that week, it's easy to see that the actual number of riders who compete each year is in the hundreds, not just twenty. But facts are not usually high on the agenda of sensationalists.

While not condemning the event, Neil Clark writing in *The Spectator*, stated that 'No other sporting event has casualty figures anything like the TT. Nothing comes close.'

It's a truth that's impossible to escape. The TT *is* dangerous, and it *can* be deadly, but no one is forced to compete in it, and no one is forced to watch it. So, the arguments both for and against hinge on an individual's attitude towards acceptable risk, and how much other fully grown adults need to be protected from themselves. The riders are fully aware of the dangers, yet they return year after year to take part in what is, for most of them, the greatest event in their lives. Surely, therefore, the decision as to whether or not the TT should continue must be left to them. They are the ones who have weighed up the odds and accepted them. They are the ones willing to put their lives on the line to test their skills against the most demanding racecourse in the world. They are the ones who sacrifice so much. They are the ones who stand to lose everything. The choice must surely be theirs.

Former TT winner Tony Jefferies was paralysed from the chest down in a motorcycle racing accident at Mallory Park in 1973 and was confined to a wheelchair for the rest of his life. He lost his son, David Jefferies, at the TT in 2003, but never turned against the sport that had taken so much from him. Before his death in 2021, Tony Jefferies wrote the following words as part of a foreword for a biography of his late son:

I was recently asked by someone who does not avidly follow motorcycle racing how I could justify following a sport, which they perceived as so full of tragedy. I thought for a moment before answering, because it is so easy to say, 'Do you realise how many people are killed each year rock climbing? Hundreds. How many are seriously injured each year through horse riding accidents? Hundreds.' When I was in hospital with a broken back, the single most common cause of paraplegia and quadriplegia was through diving accidents in shallow water. I did not mention any of those facts. I simply said, 'You have to have a passion for it. Without the passion you will never understand.'

It's a passion that is difficult for many to understand. Most people attempt to navigate their way through their lives avoiding dangerous situations, so cannot comprehend those who seek out risk; those who embrace it, who accept it. Yet the TT is oversubscribed every year: more riders wish to compete than are actually permitted to. The will to race on the world's most dangerous course is undiminished, and it's this abundance of willing competitors that provides some optimism for the future of the event.

John McGuinness is at the forefront of the optimists when it comes to the future of the TT. 'I think the TT has a safe future because there will always be people who want to do it,' he says. 'It's always been a magnet for bike racers, and I'm sure it will carry on, but I don't know if it'll be around in another hundred years.'

* * *

By Sunday night, two days after the Senior TT, the race paddock is once more an empty field and the TT course is just an ordinary stretch of road, playing host to ordinary, everyday vehicles travelling at pedestrian speeds. The advertising hoardings have mostly been taken down, the temporary grandstands are being dissembled, and there are 40,000 fewer people on the Isle of Man. There are no lights on in the TT grandstand; it's locked up and now merely stands sentinel over the start line and the cemetery on the other side of it. The small island in the middle of the Irish Sea returns to its usual, sleepy pace; the last ferries and flights laden with race trucks, transporters, bikes, teams and riders have left, and a sharp sea wind whips through what was the TT paddock, scattering the litter that has been missed by the clean-up teams. The PA systems stand silent, the sound of 10,000 visiting motorcycles now nothing but a memory.

The TT is over for another year. The sense of urgency is gone. The noise, the crowds, the speed, the danger and the excitement with it. The winner's rostrum remains in place, just a bare metal framework now that the sponsors' banners have been removed. As it begins to rain, a small boy pulls up his hood and climbs on to the top step to take a selfie on his smartphone and immediately posts it on social media. He has no idea what it truly means to stand there; no concept of the levels of determination it takes to earn the right to stand there for real. No awareness of the pain, the heartbreak, the financial sacrifices, the injuries, the risks, the dangers, the courage, the bravery and the sacrifices that have been made by the riders who have stood there before him, celebrating the greatest moment of their lives; the cumulation of everything they have striven for over so many years. Nor has he any idea how many riders have sacrificed their lives in trying to reach that very step, and how many families have grieved over their loss.

The boy loses his footing on the wet top step. 'Come down off there!' his father shouts up at him. 'It's dangerous.'

The boy grins back at him. 'Everything's dangerous, according to you.' He holds his fists high in the air and mimics the sound of cheering; imagines the adulation of the crowd as he turns to face the grandstand, feels goosebumps tingling his arms. 'I'm going to win a TT one day,' he says to his father.

And so it begins.

Acknowledgements

My most sincere thanks to all the riders, team bosses, officials and riders' friends, family and loved ones who have been kind enough to grant me interviews over the last twenty-five years, excerpts of which have been used in this book. In no particular order, they include:

Glenn Irwin, Ian Simpson, John McGuinness, Keith Amor, Ryan Farquhar, Roger Marshall, Conor Cummins, James Hillier, Mick Grant, Steve Hislop, Chip Hennen, Ron Haslam, Dean Harrison, Michael Rutter, Dan Kneen, Peter Hickman, David Johnson, Josh Brookes, Neil Tuxworth, Philip Neill, Clive Padgett, Pete Extance, Ian Lougher, John Surtees, Jim Moodie, Rob McElnea, Guy Martin, Johnny Rea, Hector Neill, Davey Todd, Michael Dunlop, Steve Plater, Charlie Williams, Barry Symmons, Phil Read, Geoff Duke, Phillip McCallen, Lee Johnston, Cameron Donald, Gary Johnson, William Dunlop, Paul Owen, Jenny Tinmouth, Ian Hutchinson, Bruce Anstey, Giacomo Agostini, Chas Mortimer, Gary Thompson, Pauline

Hailwood, Dan Sayle, Tim Reeves, Tom Birchall, Ben Birchall, Dave Molyneux, Ian Bell, and Conrad Harrison.

Huge thanks must also go to Leanne Harper and Mike Booth for telling me of their own harrowing experiences in such painful detail.

I would also like to thank my agent, David Luxton of David Luxton Associates, as well as James Hodgkinson and everyone at Bonnier Books/John Blake for all their help and support with this project.

A special mention goes to my youngest reader, Gary Costello, for choosing one of my books for his school project. Thanks, buddy!

And, finally, a massive thanks to Steve Mort – without whose help you might not be reading this book.